S0-BEV-382

AMERICAN CHESS ART

PITMAN CHESS SERIES

Walter Korn, General Editor

C. H. O'D. Alexander: *Alexander on Chess*
Leslie H. Ault: *Elements of Combinations* (*The Chess Tutor*)
Walter Korn: *Modern Chess Openings, 11th edition*
Harold M. Lommer: 1357 *End-game Studies*
Luděk Pachman: *Pachman's Decisive Games*
Translated by A. S. Russell
Samuel Reshevsky: *How Chess Games Are Won*
A. P. Sokolsky: *The Modern Openings in Theory and Practice*
Translated and Edited by H. Golombek and E. Strauss

For more information about chess titles, contact Sir Isaac Pitman
and Sons, Ltd., London, or Pitman Publishing Corporation, New York.

WALTER KORN

AMERICAN
CHESS
ART

250 PORTRAITS OF ENDGAME STUDY

PITMAN PUBLISHING

SIR ISAAC PITMAN AND SONS LTD.
Pitman House, Parker Street, Kingsway, London, WC2B 5PB
P.O. Box 46038, Banda Street, Nairobi, Kenya

SIR ISAAC PITMAN (AUST.) PTY. LTD.
Pitman House, 158 Bouverie Street, Carlton, Victoria 3053, Australia

PITMAN PUBLISHING CORPORATION
6 East 43rd Street, New York, N.Y. 10017, U.S.A.

SIR ISAAC PITMAN (CANADA) LTD.
495 Wellington Street West, Toronto, 135, Canada

THE COPP CLARK PUBLISHING COMPANY
517 Wellington Street West, Toronto, 135, Canada

Library of Congress Cataloging in Publication Data

Korn, Walter.
   American chess art.

   Bibliography: p.
   1. Chess—Endgames. I. Title.
GV1450.7.K62   794.1'24   74-18409

UK ISBN 0-273-00222-8
US ISBN 0-273-07215-3

Manufactured in the United States of America

1.9 8 7 6 5 4 3 2 1

Table of Contents

Outline and Scope

American Chess Art considers an aspect of Chess—artistic composition—which has immense meaning for practical play, and also for understanding the total depth of the game.

Chess compositions, generally, are abstractions based on a planned idea, or a combination of such ideas, often called "themes", involving elements of strategy, difficulty, beauty, or surprise in achieving the desired result. Composers create artificial positions that bring such elements into focus, using only as much material as is essential for the execution of a particular idea.

Compositions are of two types: problems (including fairy chess), and endgame studies. This book is about the Endgame.

Generally, the distinction is not difficult. The orthodox chess problem requires a mate to be achieved within a definite number of moves; its construction and material need bear no relation to the actual game. The endgame study stipulates a given outcome (to win or draw), without a stated limit to the number of moves. The composed ending often demands a profound knowledge not only of basic, but also of complex, endgame theory, thus providing a close link with practical chess play.

In this book, the basic ingredients of a compostiion will be explained gradually and leisurely and the reader will thus absorb and learn to appreciate the aesthetics of chess artistry. The interlocking panorama of 250 portraits illustrates the diversity and depth of stratagems inherent even in seemingly simple settings, not just in a few masterly conceived constructions of incredibly complex nature.

Yet, American endgame art has basically remained rooted in sound pragmatical common sense. It has shown itself able to handle even excessively abstract experimentation but has always rested, thematically and technically, on a natural and logical base, maintaining a bridge between chess art and chess play.

I an truly indebted to Professor Wm. M. Spackman, former editor of *The Chess Correspondent*, for providing the final polish to much of the phrasing; and to Professor Orrin Frink—himself a noted composer—for methodically combing the descriptive notation and thus being able to make some very valuable contributions to the analyses in my manuscript.

In a footnote to each completed page, the main line of each solution is given also in figurine algebraic notation, designed to transform this volume into an internationally acceptable presentation.

A special vote of thanks is due to the Editorial Board and managerial staff of Pitman Publishing for their wholehearted support of a chess topic of documentary value.

Explanatory Notes

The solutions are given in full descriptive notation. In a foot-note to each diagram the main lines are repeated in abbreviated figurative algebraic notation, in a version blending West- and East-European usage.

The generally accepted symbols in both notations are:

+ win—next to the diagram: White to move and win.

in the notes: After White's (Black's) move: White (Black) wins.

= draw—next to the diagram: White to move and draw.

in the notes: After White's (Black's) move: White (Black) draws.

‡	mate
⊖	stalemate
∞	any move (White's or Black's)
†	check, in algebraic notation
ch	check, in descriptive notation
dis.	discovered, in front of check sign
!	good move—*or* best choice among several alternatives
?	a questionable move
×	"takes" in descriptive notation
:	"takes" in algebraic notation
§	after the composer's name denotes a non-American author, otherwise the by-line assumes that the composition is by a composer claiming American nationality over a meaningful period

Comparative Chart of Chess Notations

For the benefit of those not familiar with the English (descriptive) notation, we give a diagram of the board with a comparison of the English and algebraic definition of the squares, and a table of international equivalents for the English symbols for the chessmen.

In the English notation, the symbol before the hyphen indicates which piece is being moved, the symbol following the hyphen the square to which it is moved. On the board below, the notation in brackets indicates Black's moves, with the board seen from Black's point of view.

	a	b	c	d	e	f	g	h	
8	(QR1) QR8	(QN1) QN8	(QB1) QB8	(Q1) Q8	(K 1) K 8	(KB1) KB8	(KN1) KN8	(KR1) KR8	**8**
7	(QR2) QR7	(QN2) QN7	(QB2) QB7	(Q2) Q7	(K 2) K 7	(KB2) KB7	(KN2) KN7	(KR2) KR7	**7**
6	(QR3) QR6	(QN3) QN6	(QB3) QB6	(Q3) Q6	(K 3) K 6	(KB3) KB6	(KN3) KN6	(KR3) KR6	**6**
5	(QR4) QR5	(QN4) QN5	(QB4) QB5	(Q4) Q5	(K 4) K 5	(KB4) KB5	(KN4) KN5	(KR4) KR5	**5**
4	(QR5) QR4	(QN5) QN4	(QB5) QB4	(Q5) Q4	(K 5) K 4	(KB5) KB4	(KN5) KN4	(KR5) KR4	**4**
3	(QR6) QR3	(QN6) QN3	(QB6) QB3	(Q6) Q3	(K 6) K 3	(KB6) KB3	(KN6) KN3	(KR6) KR3	**3**
2	(QR7) QR2	(QN7) QN2	(QB7) QB2	(Q7) Q2	(K 7) K 2	(KB7) KB2	(KN7) KN2	(KR7) KR2	**2**
1	(QR8) QR1	(QN8) QN1	(QB8) QB1	(Q8) Q1	(K 8) K 1	(KB8) KB1	(KN8) KN1	(KR8) KR1	**1**
	a	b	c	d	e	f	g	h	

Comparative Tabulation of Symbols

Fig.	Eng.	Czech	Dut.	Fr.	Hung.	Ger.[1]	It.[2]	Pol.	Roum.	Russ.	FIDE
♔	K	K	K	R	K	K	R	K	R	Кр	K
♕	Q	D	D	D	V	D	D	H	D	Ф	D
♖	R	V	T	T	B	T	T	W	T	Л	T
♗	B	S	L	F	F	L	A	G	N	C	S
♘	N[3]	J	P	C	H	S	C	S	C	К	N
♙	P	(P)	(P)	(P)	(g)	(B)	(P)	(P)	(−)	(Д)	−

[1] These are also used in the Scandinavian and Yugoslav notations.
[2] These are also used in the Portuguese and Spanish notations.
[3] N for Knight in modern usage, replacing the archaic symbol Kt. Problemists sometimes use S, taken from the German "Springer".

Early Beginnings

Systematic development of modern endgame study composition began in the 19th century and in Europe was pioneered by the German–British pair of Bernard Horwitz and Joseph Kling. The style of their very sound productions may be described as analytical and positional, although they were somewhat dogmatic in their conception.

In the United States, the endgame composition was slower in maturing. North America was a stronghold of problem chess of two-, three-, and multi-movers. Studies were occasionally lumped together in this category; often called "endings", they merely resembled crowded game endings, culminating in a "brilliant" combination, but lacking the technical polish, economy, discipline, and didactic values of the accomplished composition.

But American composers soon became conscious of the special attraction of the composed ending and of the selective quality required. Thus, the latter part of the 19th century witnessed a burst of rather imaginative ideas, originating in the United States, but unnoticed elsewhere, because of the "oceanic" distance which separated America from Europe.

These pages will tell much of that heritage and continued activity.

The Exploring Pioneers

The Nestor of American problem and endgame study alike was *Eugene Beauharnais Cook* (1830–1915). He also had an outstanding reputation as solver, and was feared and respected for his ability to detect any flaw in a composition. It has even been suggested that Cook's remarkable aptitude as an analyst was the origin of the term "cook"—meaning the presence of a second solution, or a study which is found to have no solution and is therefore defective, i.e. "cooked". Another version has it, however, that the term may be attributed to Kling and Horwitz's notice in *The Chess Player*, in 1851, that they were going to "cook", i.e. to comment on, endgame studies as time went by.*

One of the truly massive monuments to Cook's place in the chess arena is his anthology *American Chess-Nuts* (Kingston, New York, 1868, now out of print) which consolidates all the best compositions of its time in the northwestern hemisphere. Diagrams 11, 30, 33, 51, 59 and 60 are taken from that representative compilation.

Our first four diagrams show Cook's earlier attempts at endgame study composition. In fact, they were posthumously published by H. Keidanz. Cook himself might have considered them mere sketches waiting in his portfolio for the opportunity to be worked into a more ambitious spectrum; they disclose the making of an artist.

E. B. Cook, known as the "Sage of Hoboken", quickly realized the difference between the realms of the problem and of endgame study. In this field he did some fine work and several of his endgames are of permanent merit. They are interesting and instructive, especially for the practical player, and a few have been included among these selections.

Samuel Loyd (1841–1911), born in Philadelphia, was one of the world's most versatile and imaginative chess artists. He composed the bulk of his chess output before the age of twenty and then made still wider use of his phenomenal ability in the sphere of other, most intricate formal exercises which earned him the epithet of "Puzzle King". His chess style was characterized by the humorous, the spectacular, and the deceitfully unexpected. Like many other chess composers, he also was a strong player, who created quite a few brilliant games, for instance at the Paris International Master Tournament of 1867.

Loyd was primarily a problemist, who dealt only marginally with endgame studies. His endings accordingly show a close affinity with problems, but fit criteria of endgame construction as well. As many endgame studies have developed from problems with a thematic orientation, Loyd's work can fit either description (for example diagrams 17, 19 and others).

---

* *Lasker's Chess Magazine* (1905, p. 219) touches on both interpretations, but does not favor either, as being too farfetched, preferring linguistic folklore and the colloquial meaning of "to cook", namely to tamper with, to alter; or to garble, to spoil, to ruin—a view shared by Webster's Dictionary, independent of chess usage.

Another born and bred Philadelphian, *Gustavus Charles Reichhelm* (1839–1905), achieved worldwide renown as a player, analyst, writer and composer. He started and conducted a weekly chess column in the Philadelphia *Evening Bulletin* from 1861 to 1870, and from 1880 onwards in the *Philadelphia Times*.

Reichhelm's special forte was positions involving exact tempo play coupled with the crucial question of who had the move and how this fact could be utilized or reversed. The meaning of his stylized settings will emerge clearly from the examples quoted.

As is often the case with researchers who concentrate on a special theme, Reichhelm's compositions may appear somewhat monotonous, but they methodically exhaust many possible aspects of "thematic studies" which he treated in depth—some of them so-called "maximummers" with scores of moves.

Yet he also composed many straight positional studies of individual flair and his influence, if unobtrusive, was steady and profound.

Alain Campbell White (1880–1951) was one of the most generous patrons of chess. He was an American composer and collector of chess games and problems, and between 1905 and 1936 financed and published 44 books as part of a "Christmas Series", mostly sending them as presents to friends all over the world.

Some of these volumes, e.g. *Sam Loyd and his Chess Problems* or *The Golden Argosy* contain many endgame studies as well.

John Griswold White (1845–1928), an earlier namesake, rivalled this munificence with his gift to the Cleveland (Ohio) Public Library, of his extensive collection of manuscripts, books, periodicals and other materials on chess. He augmented his donation with a trust fund, which has enabled the Library to increase the volumes steadily to more than 115,000, and to keep growing.

Unfortunately, this valuable public property does not yet contain Alain C. White's extensively indexed file cabinets with over 10,000 classified compositions of the best known classical problemists. Upon his death, this collection was dispersed among a number of British custodians and has not been reassembled since.

DIAGRAM 1

E. B. COOK

From: H. Keidanz,

THE CHESS COMPOSITIONS OF E. B. COOK

NEW YORK, 1927

Although skeletal and sketchy, the construction contains a thematic idea, called "cross-pinning".

1 P—B6! B×P!	4 B×Q K×B
2 B—Q7!! K—N3	5 P—R4 K—Q3
3 Q×B ch Q×Q ch	6 N—N3 wins

The position is what is called a theoretical or "book" win, and solution and proof need not be carried further.

The date, 1927, is that of Keidanz's publication, but Cook's individual efforts reach back to 1860–1900.

In algebraic notation: 1 c6, ♗:c6; 2 ♗d7, ♚b6; 3 ♕:c6†, ♛:c6†; 4 ♗:c6, ♚:c6; 5 h4, ♚d6; 6 ♘b3+.

DIAGRAM 2

E. B. COOK

From: H. Keidanz,

THE CHESS COMPOSITIONS
OF E. B. COOK

NEW YORK, 1927

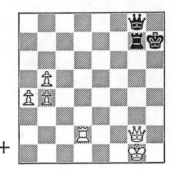

$+$

Another "crosspin". An expert would quickly discover the key move; but also he would have to ponder the consequences very carefully.

1 R—Q7 R×R		3 P—N6!	
2 Q×Q ch K×Q			

The catch. If 3 P—R5, R—Q4; 4 P—R6 (if 4 P—N6?, R—QN4∓), R—Q8 ch; 5 K—B2, R—QR8; 6 K—K3, K—B2; 7 K—Q4, K—K3; 8 K—B5, K—Q2; 9 K—N6, K—B1; 10 K—R7, R—R5; 11 P—N6, R×P; 12 P—N7 ch, K—B2=.

3 ... R—QN2

Wrong is 3 ... R—Q5; 4 P—N5, R×P; 5 P—N7+.

4 P—R5 K—B2	8 K—B2 R—N1
5 P—N5 K—K2	9 P—N6 K—Q2
6 P—R6 R×P	10 P—N7 wins
7 P—R7 R—N3 ch	

Just by one tempo. If 10 ... K—B2; 11 P—R8(Q), R×Q; 12 P×R(Q).

Alg.: 1 ♖d7, ♖:d7; 2 ♕:g8†, ♔:g8; 3 b6, ♖b7; 4 a5, ♔f7; 5 b5, ♔e7; 6 a6, ♖:b6; 7 a7, ♖g6†; 8 ♔f2, ♖g8; 9 b6, ♔d7; 10 b7+.

5

DIAGRAM 3

E. B. COOK

From: H. Keidanz,

THE CHESS COMPOSITIONS
OF E. B. COOK

NEW YORK, 1927

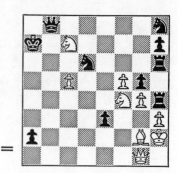

=

One of those long-distance, corner-to-corner double-chases, which are often employed in problems. But mostly they are not flexible enough to allow for draws.

White perpetually threatens mate, while Black in turn keeps preventing it.

1 Q—QR1	Q—N8	3 Q—R1	Q—N8
2 Q×N	Q—N1		

In view of Black's preponderance in material, he might try other means of winning. He has two "tries" but neither of them works.

I. 1 ... Q—N6; 2 Q×N, R×P ch; 3 N×R, R×N ch; 4 K×R, P—K7 dis. ch; 5 K—R2, Q—N6 ch; 6 K×Q, P—K8 (Q) ch; 7 K—R2, N—K1; 8 Q—N2, Q—N8; 9 Q—R3 ch, K—N1; 10 Q—R8 ch, K×N; 11 Q—B6 ch, K—Q1 with a perpetual check.

II. 1 ... N—K5; 2 Q×P ch, K—N2; 3 Q—Q5 ch, K—B1; 4 Q×N=.

Alg.: 1 ♕a1, ♛b1; 2 ♕:h8, ♛b8; 3 ♕a1, ♛b1=.

DIAGRAM 4

E. B. COOK

From: H. Keidanz,

THE CHESS COMPOSITIONS
OF E. B. COOK

NEW YORK, 1927

+

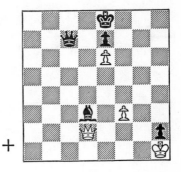

A poignant conception. The White queen's geometrical strides are very forcing. Cook's own notes indicate about 1890 as the date of inception.

1 Q—QN2! Q—KB5!	4 Q—R5 ch K—B1
2 Q—R8 ch Q—B1	5 Q—R8 ch K—B2
3 Q—R5 ch K—Q1	6 Q×Q wins

The black bishop serves to prevent a second solution. Without it the study would be cooked, because of the alternative 1 Q—Q4 with a win after some prolonged play.

In diagram 5, a very similar concept is worked out thirty years later with unsurpassable economy.

Alg.: 1 ♕b2, ♕f4; 2 ♕h8†, ♕f8; 3 ♕h5†, ♚d8; 4 ♕a5†, ♚c8; 5 ♕a8†, ♚c7; 6 ♕:f8+.

D. JOSEPH§

BRITISH CHESS MAGAZINE

1922

DIAGRAM 5

A classic that made the composer immortal!

   1 P—R8(Q) P—R8(Q)   2 Q—N8!

If 2 Q—K8? Q—N2!=.
If 2 Q—B8?, Q—R6; 3 Q—N8, Q—Q3 ch=.

   2 ...   Q—R7!   4 Q—K5 ch K—R1
   3 Q—K8 Q—R5!   5 Q—R8! and wins

Alg.: 1 h8(♛), a1(♛); 2 ♛g8, ♛a2; 3 ♛e8, ♛a4; 4 ♛e5†, ♚a8; 5 ♛h8+.

DIAGRAM 6

E. B. COOK

ILLUSTRATED LONDON NEWS

SEPTEMBER 30, 1854

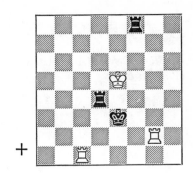

This simple combination constitutes Cook's first true endgame.

A beginner may note the try 1 R—K1 ch, K—Q6; 2 R—Q1 ch, K—K6!; 3 R×R, R—K1 ch!, draw.

1 R—B3 ch R—Q6	2 R—N3 ch R—B6

An aesthetic and elegant symmetry—and a deadly one. Any white rook takes any rook with check and wins!

With two pairs of rooks opposing each other, this *œuvre* goes one giant step further than the ancient prologue to it, transmitted by V. Firdusi (see next diagram, 6 (A)).

Alg.: 1 ♖c3†, ♜d3; 2 ♖g3†, ♜f3; 3 ∞ ♖:♜†+.

DIAGRAM 6 (A)

U. FIRDUSI§

SATRANG-NAMA-i KABIR
(*Vatican Library*)

Abt. 1500 *

+

With stark simplicity, Black threatens mate on the move, or to win one of White's rooks. But the appearance is misleading.

    1 R—KR5! R×R

Now it was White's turn to threaten mate on the move or to win Black's rook.

    2 R—R6 ch! K—any   3 R—R5 ch

winning Black's rook. An astonishing piece of conjuring out of an empty vessel.

---

* Firdusi's diagram is an improvement over position No. 229 in the early 15th century Italian manuscript, "Civis Bononiae," with Black's king on K3 (e6) and "Black to move, White wins" by 1 . . . K—Q3 (d6).

Alg.: 1 ♖h5, ♖:h5; 2 ♖a6†, ♔∞; 3 ♖a5†+.

DIAGRAM 7

E. B. COOK

From: H. Keidanz,

THE CHESS COMPOSITIONS
OF E. B. COOK

NEW YORK, 1927

+

This miniature might be labeled "didactic-analytical". As distinct from problems, composed endings often require a thorough knowledge of endgame theory.

>   1 R×QP!

White has another try at his disposal, which looks very straightforward, but leads nowhere:
>   1 K—K5, R—B4 ch; 2 K—Q6, K—Q5; 3 R×QP, P—K4; 4 K—K6 dis. ch, K—K5; 5 R—Q1, R×P; 6 K×R, K—B6; 7 K—K6, P—K5; 8 K—Q5, P—K6=. White must give up the rook for the advancing pawn.

>   1 ...   R—B4!

to prevent 2 K—K5.

>   2 R—Q4 ch K—B4

If 2 ... K—B6; 3 R—Q3 ch and 4 R—KB3+.

>   3 R—Q5 ch! P×R ch   4 K×R+

If 3 ... R×R; 4 P—B8(Q)+, K—B3; 5 Q—K7 wins the pawn and game (5 ... R—Q3; 6 K—K5+).
>   There are a few positions where the process of winning with

queen *versus* rook and pawn is far more difficult, and one such instance is shown in diagram 8.

Within the strict terminology of problemists, a "miniature" is a setting of seven units or less.

Alg.: 1 ♖:d7! ♖f5! 2 ♖d4†, ♔c5; 3 ♖d5†, e:d5†; 4 ♔:f5+.

DIAGRAM 8

W. KORN

BRITISH CHESS MAGAZINE

1943

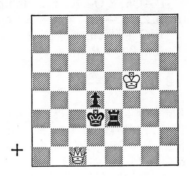

+

For almost a century, this and similar typical positions, analyzed in 1964 by Baron Guretzky-Cornitz, were accepted as won for White if Black were to move and thus in a squeeze, but drawn if White had the move.*

The first breach in established belief was caused by the Czech encyclopedist of endgame study F. Dedrle who, in the 1930s, proved some of the accepted analysis wrong. "Correcting Reuben Fine" was the legend that accompanied diagram No. 8. The move obligation is reversed by the simple means of triangulation, a device often used in "opposition play", thus restoring the starting position but with Black being compelled to move and lose, as shown by the earlier analysts.

(A) 1 Q—R3 ch K—Q7   2 Q—B5 P—Q6

If 2 ... K—Q6; 3 Q—B1! and Black is in *Zugzwang* (†) and succumbs, e.g.

(*a*) 3 ... R—K1; 4 Q—R3 ch, K—K7 (4 ... K—Q7; 5 Q—R4 wins the pawn); 5 Q—R4, R—Q1 (5 ... R—B1 ch; 6 K—K4, P—Q6; 7 Q—N5, R—Q1; 8 Q—R5

---

* e.g. J. Berger: *Theorie und Praxis der Endspiele* (1922) No. 143, or R. Fine: *Basic Chess Endings* (1941) No. 599b.

† See explanation of terms after diagram 17.

ch, K—B8; 9 K—K3+); 6 Q—R5, R—B1 ch; 7 K—K4,
P—Q6; 8 Q—R5 ch, winning the pawn or rook.
(*b*) 3 ... K—K7; 4 Q—B2 ch, K—K8; 5 K—B4, R—K2;
6 Q—B1 ch, K—K7; 7 Q—N2 ch, K—Q6; 8 Q—R3 ch
and 9 Q×R wins.

3 K—B4 R—K7	4 Q—Q4

For 4 Q—B4, R—K1; 5 Q—N5, R—K7; 6 Q—N3, see line (B).
If 5 ... R—QR1 (or 5 ... R—KB1 ch); 6 K—K4 +; or
5 ... R—QB1; 6 K—K4, R—B6; 7 K—Q4 +; or 5 ... R—Q1;
6 Q—R5 ch +; or 5 ... R—KN1; 6 Q—N2 ch, K—K8;
7 Q—B1 ch, K—K7; 8 Q—K3 ch +.

4 ... R—K1

Or 4 ... K—B7; 5 K—B3, R—K8; 6 Q—B4 ch, K—Q7;
7 Q—N4 ch, K—Q8; 8 Q—N2, R—K7; 9 Q—B3, R—Q7;
10 Q—B4 + (Averbakh–Simagin, Tula 1950, with colors.
reversed).

5 Q—N2 ch K—Q8

5 ... K—K8; 6 Q—N5! R—Q1; 7 K—K3, K—B8; 8 Q—B5 +.

6 Q—N5 R—Q1	8 Q—B5 ch K—Q8
7 K—K3 K—B7	9 Q—N6 wins

In 1946–9, André Chéron experimented with the same setting
and, instead of returning the queen to QB1, he demonstrated an
alternative road to victory, which is lengthier, but allows
exploration of further detail; namely (start from diagram 8):

(B) 1 Q—B5 R—K7!	3 K—B4 K—B7
2 Q—R3 ch K—Q7	

(*a*) 3 ... R—K6; 4 Q—N2 ch, K—Q6; 5 Q—N3 ch, K—Q7
(5 ... K—K7; 6 Q—B2 ch, K—K8; 7 Q—B4 +);
6 Q—B4, R—Q6; 7 K—K4+.

(*b*) 3 ... R—K1 (or K8); 4 Q—N4 ch+.
(*c*) 3 ... P—Q6; 4 Q—N3 reverts to the main line.

    4 Q—R2 ch K—Q6   6 Q—B4 P—Q6
    5 Q—N3 ch K—Q7

This position was always taken as drawn, at least with White on the move—the win with Black to move is seen in section (A). Chéron (1949) continues:

    7 Q—N3! R—K8

Black loses upon (*a*) 7 ... R—B7 ch; 8 K—K4, R—K7 ch; 9 K—Q4, or (*b*) 7 ... R—K1; 8 Q—N2 ch, K—K8; 9 Q—N5, R—Q1; 10 K—K3, K—B8; 11 Q—B5 ch, or 8 ... K—Q8; 9 Q—N5, R—Q1; 10 K—K3, K—B8; 11 Q—B5 ch, K—Q8; 12 Q—N6+.

    8 Q—N2 ch K—Q8   11 Q—B4 winning the
    9 K—B3   R—K7   pawn
   10 Q—B3   R—Q7

A last minute pitfall would spell disaster after 11 K—K3, R—K7 ch; 12 K×P??, R—K3 ch!; 13 K×R, stalemate.

But a postscript may be added which illuminates once more how in best faith priorities may be claimed—or overlooked.

The position in line (B) after Black's 6th move (together with a string of related positions) was analyzed and published by the Czech composer, F. Dedrle, in *Národní Osvobození* 1937,* proving a win for White, whoever has the move.

---

  * Also quoted by W. Korn, "Main Types of End-Game Studies", *Chess* (England), July–October 1942.

Alg.: (A) 1 ♛a3†, ♚d2; 2 ♛c5, d3; 3 ♚f4, ♖e2; 4 ♛d4, ♖e8; 5 ♛b2†, ♚d1; 6 ♛b5, ♖d8; 7 ♚e3, ♚c2; 8 ♛c5†, ♚d1; 9 ♛b6†.
    (B) 1 ♛c5, ♖e2; 2 ♛a3†, ♚d2; 3 ♚f4, ♚c2; 4 ♛a2†, ♚d3; 5 ♛b3†, ♚d2; 6 ♛c4, d3; 7 ♛b3, ♖e1; 8 ♛b2†, ♚d1; 9 ♚f3, ♖e2; 10 ♛c3, ♖d2; 11 ♛c4+.

DIAGRAM 9

E. B. COOK

ILLUSTRATED LONDON
NEWS

JUNE 7, 1856

=

Cook reaches for perfection in the composition of studies. All of White's pieces are *en prise*—under threat of capture— and the rook is pinned.

By employing a device called "cross-checking", White saves the situation. All men play an assigned role; there is no super-fluous force standing idly by.

    1 B—B7 ch K—N5   2 B—K6 ch K—B5

The king interposes, unpinning White's rook.

    3 R—B5 ch K—N5 dis. ch   5 B—B7 ch and draws
    4 R—K5 dis. ch! K—R4

Alg.: 1 ♗f7†, ♔g4; 2 ♗e6†, ♔f4; 3 ♖f5†, ♔g4†; 4 ♖e5†, ♔h5; 5 ♗f7=.

E. B. COOK

BALTIMORE SUNDAY NEWS

JULY 3, 1892

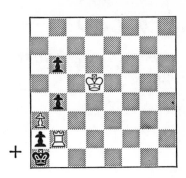

DIAGRAM 10

+

The winning strategy becomes evident later in the play.

1 R×P	P—N4	3 K—B4!	P—R6
2 P—R4	P×P	4 K—N3!!	

A critical line-interference which suspends the threatening stalemate and thus allows a win. The maneuver is labeled the "Indian Theme".

4 ...	K—N8	6 R—KR4 wins	
5 K×P dis. ch	K—R8		

Alg.: 1 ♖:b4, b5; 2 a4, b:a4; 3 ♔c4, a3; 4 ♔b3, ♔b1; 5 ♔:a3†, ♔a1; 6 ♖h4+.

DIAGRAM 11

E. B. COOK

AMERICAN CHESS-NUTS
1868

=

Black's king intends to make short shrift of White's rook pawn and to promote his own pawn. White's king seems tied up far away.

1 K—K7	N—N3 ch	2 K—Q6!

For 2 K—B6 see final note below.

2 ... K—R6		3 K—B5! N—K4!!

a subtle and strong turn. If 4 P—B8 (Q or R or B), N—Q2 ch, wins.

4 P—B8(N)!!	N—Q6 ch	7 N—N6	P—N7
5 K—B4	K×P	8 N—R4 draws!	
6 N—Q7	P—N6		

If 7 ... N—K4 ch; 8 K—Q5, N—Q2; 9 N—B4, N—N3 ch; 10 N×N, P—N7; 11 N—R4=.

Deceptive is (1 K—K7, N—N3 ch) 2 K—B6!?, N—B1; 3 K—K7, and not 3 ... N—N3 ch with a quicker draw for White, but 3 ... N—R2?!; 4 K—Q6, K—R6; 5 K—B5, N—N4!; 6 P—B8(N)!, N—K5 ch; 7 K—B4, N—B6; 8 N—Q7, N×P; 9 N—B5, again drawing by means of the same device as employed in the main line.

Alg.: 1 ♔e7, ♘g6†; 2 ♔d6, ♔a3; 3 ♔c5, ♘e5; 4 f8(♘)), ♘d3†; 5 ♔c4, ♔:a2; 6 ♘d7, b3; 7 ♘b6, b2; 8 ♘a4=.

DIAGRAM 12

E. B. COOK

From: P. R. v. Bilguer,

*HANDBUCH DES
SCHACHSPIELS*

1864

=

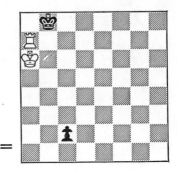

The first experimental *matrix* (i.e. a basic strategic idea or tactical finesse, that can serve as the starting point for artistic elaboration); and it may have its uses in practical end-play.

1 R—N7 ch K—B1	3 R—B5 ch Q×R
2 R—N5! P—B8(Q)	Stalemate!

Cook was a close friend of Loyd's and the next diagram illustrates Loyd's attempt to convert the sketch into a composed ending.

Alg.: 1 ♖b7†, ♚c8; 2 ♖b5, c1 (♛); 3 ♖c5†, ♛:c5 ⊜.

DIAGRAM 13

S. LOYD

AMERICAN CHESS
JOURNAL

1878

$+$

As against the previous diagram, Loyd very soundly turned colors to "White to win", and the stalemate becomes a hidden Black defence, which is refuted by means of an *under-promotion.*

    1 P—B8(R)!

If 1 P—B8(Q), R—B5 ch; 2 Q×R stalemate, as shown on the previous page. After the text, White's pawn wins easily after 1 ... R—B5; 2 R—B8, K—N5; 3 P—B7, K—B4; 4 R—B8 ch and 5 P—B8(Q)+.

Except for the tactical twist in the first move, the ending as such is still too primitive and not sufficiently instructive, but it was a "first".

Alg.: 1 f8(♜)!+.

DIAGRAM 14

F. HEALEY§

SHAKHMATNY LISTOK

1880

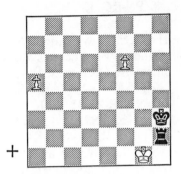

+

This configuration is attributed to the British composer Frank Healey (1828–1906) and it was demonstrated in analytical detail but without source during a series of lectures on "Common Sense in Chess",* given by Dr. Emanuel Lasker in London in 1895.

First, the diagram restores Cook's original concept.

1 P—B7!

White loses after 1 P—R6, but only if Black correctly plays 1 ... R—N7 ch; 2 K—B1, R—N1!; 3 K—K2, K—N5; 4 K—Q3, R—QB1! cutting off White's king from possible defense—with promotion of the rook's pawn.

Lasker's explanation takes off from here, with Black to move.

1 ...	R—N7 ch	3 P—B8(R)	R—QR5
2 K—B1	R—N5	4 R—QR8	K—N5!

White threatened P—R6 and then a check with his rook, queening the pawn. But if now 5 P—R6, then K—B6!, threatening mate, forces the draw, e.g. 6 K—K1, K—K6; 7 K—Q1, K—Q6; 8 K—B1, K—B6; 9 K—N1, R—N5 ch! etc.

---

* Published by McKay, New York 1917, and Dover Publications, 1965.

21

5 K—K2 K—B4   7 K—Q3!
6 P—R6 K—B3!

The decisive operation. Now the king comes to the support
of the pawn, liberates the rook and finds a place of safety
on square QR7 against the checks of Black's rook.

7 ... K—N2; 8 K—B3, K—R2; 9 K—N3, R—R4; 10
K—N4, R—R8; 11 K—N5, R—N8 ch; 12 K—B6, R—B8
ch; 13 K—N7, R—N8 ch; 14 K—R7! K—N2; 15 R—N8,
R—QR8; 16 R—N6, K—B2; 17 K—N7+.

Significantly, the analysis stands up even to later discovery
in 1924–5, made independently by Orrin Frink (b.1902) and
Josef Vančura, that in many positions with the rook's pawn
still on R6, Black better defends "horizontally" with the rook
on KB3 instead of QR8. But in here, the rook is just one move
too late and White's king is too near, e.g. 8 ... R—KB5;
9 R—R7 ch! (9 P—R7? R—QR5 =), K—N3 (9 ... K—B3;
10 R—R7! +); 10 R—QN7 (10 K—N3? R—B3!! =),
R—QR5; 11 P—R7, K—B3; 12 K—N3, R—R8; 13 K—B4,
K—K3; 14 R—KR7, K—Q3; 15 K—N5, R—N8 ch;
16 K—R6, K—B3; 17 R—R1!+.

Alg.: 1 f7, ♖g2†; 2 ♔f1, ♖g4; 3 f8 (♖), ♖a4; 4 ♖a8, ♔g4! 5 ♔e2,
    ♔f5; 6 a6, ♔f6! 7 ♔d3!+.

DIAGRAM 15

G. E. BARBIER§
and
F. SAAVEDRA§

GLASGOW WEEKLY CITIZEN

MAY 4 AND 18, 1895

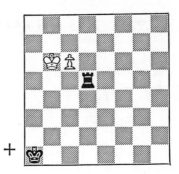

The magnetism of the American Cook's matrix, the Britisher Healey's amendment, and the German Lasker's lecture series in 1895 might have created the mental climate for an extraordinary "multinational" discovery.

For the diagram, as shown, was published by the French-born columnist Barbier—with the verdict "drawn"—only to have a Glasgow resident, the Spaniard Saavedra, send in a winning solution two weeks later.

1 P—B7 R—Q3 ch	4 K—N3 R—Q6 ch
2 K—N5 R—Q4 ch	5 K—B2 R—Q5!
3 K—N4 R—Q5 ch	6 P—B8(R)!!

Barbier noticed only 6 P—B8(Q), R—B5 ch; 7 Q×R stalemate.

6 ... R—QR5	7 K—N3!+

Black cannot avert mate or loss of the rook.

Alg.: 1 c7, ♖d6†; 2 ♔b5, ♖d5†; 3 ♔b4, ♖d4†; 4 ♔b3, ♖d3†; 5 ♔c2, ♖d4; 6 c8(♖), ♖a4; 7 ♔b3+.

DIAGRAM 16

V. and M. PLATOV§

DEUTSCHE
SCHACHZEITUNG
1908

+

In the 20th century, endgame composition developed into a fine art, with high demands on technique by an elite that created brilliant new ideas, and perfected or combined existing matrices.

The Russian brothers Platov showed how Saavedra's solution to an ending can be provided first with an overture (moves 1 and 2), then with an added thematic ingredient (the preventative fork 3 ... R—R1?; 4 B—K5 ch!) and, lastly, a "decoy" which brings about the winning constellation with its own full flavor:

1 K—N4!	R—B4	5 K—N6	R—R3 ch
2 P—B6!	R×P	6 B—Q6!!	R×B ch
3 P—B7	R—R5 ch	7 K—N5	
4 K—N5	R—R4 ch		

and White wins as in diagram 15.

An original idea and perfect technique complementing each other.

Alg.: 1 ♔b4, ♖f5; 2 c6, ♖:h5; 3 c7, ♖h4†; 4 ♔b5, ♖h5†; 5 ♔b6, ♖h6†; 6 ♗d6, ♖:d6†; 7 ♔b5+.

DIAGRAM 17

S. LOYD

CHESS MONTHLY

APRIL, 1858

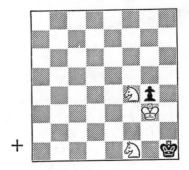

+

"The black pawn is blocked not by a knight, but by White's king which is immobilized, apparently making a mate by two knights out of the question. However, it is possible to obtain a forced mate in three moves by *Zugzwang;* the pawn taking the knight, changes the file and the mating pattern." (Lamarre)

1 N—R3 P×N   3 N—N3 ⧧

2 K—B2 P—R7

In this context, a comparison with the Ponziani diagram 203 is appropriate: it also converts a pawn into an active instrument for mate, using a bishop as the catalyst.

Alg.: 1 ♘h3, g:h3; 2 ♔f2, h2; 3 ♘g3⧧.

The Zugzwang

The comments to diagram 17, taken from Marcel Lamarre's *Fins de Partie* (1924), characterize it as a typical "Zugzwang" for Black, meaning he is under move-compulsion, under duress or "in a squeeze". Specifically, White or Black finds himself in a situation where the choices are so restricted that his obligation to move whether he likes it or not, becomes a disastrous liability, spelling the difference between a win and a draw, or a draw and a loss.

The likelihood of a real "Zugzwang" is rare in practical play, because of the great tactical latitude. It may often be the after-effect of what is also called a blockade. But in a general sense, every composition becomes a "Zugzwang" after White's key move to which Black is to succumb no matter what defense he chooses. Thus this technical term requires careful use, neither too indiscriminate nor with too much sophistication. In the 1940s, a number of chess journals probed into the usage of a native word in preference to the often misspelt expression adopted from German (and pronounced *tsoog-tsvung*), but the term "squeeze" was, instead, incorporated into the arsenal of chess nomenclature as the sophisticated definition for a milder variety of "Zugzwang"! A "reciprocal Zugzwang" is a position wherein each White or Black having the move would find himself in an unpalatable or catastrophic bind. C. B. Jones' diagram 226 is a prominent specimen of this mechanism. The reciprocal "Zugzwang" has similarities with "opposition play" which commands a complex terminology of its own (another reason for not using the word "Zugzwang" indiscriminately), and of which diagrams 76, 91 and other Reichhelm positions are instructive instances.

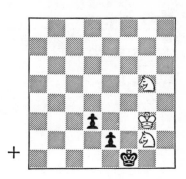

DIAGRAM 18

R. BRIEGER

1973*

+

Given new polish by a latter-day disciple.

1 N—K3 ch	K—N8	6 N—B3 ch	K—R8
2 N—B3 ch	K—R8	7 N—N4	P—Q8(N)!
3 N—N4	P—K8(Q) ch	8 K—R3!	N—K6
4 N×Q	K—N8	9 N—B2 mate	
5 N—K3	P—Q7		

* From: Robert Brieger, *Imagination in the Endgame*, Dallas, Texas, 1973 (Example No. 15)

Alg.: 1 ♘e3†, ♔g1; 2 ♘f3†, ♔h1; 3 ♘g4, e1(♕)†; 4 ♘:e1, ♔g1; 5 ♘e3, d2; 6 ♘f3†, ♔h1; 7 ♘g4, d1(♘); 8 ♔h3, ♘e3; 9 ♘f2‡.

DIAGRAM 19

S. LOYD

CHESS MONTHLY

APRIL, 1858

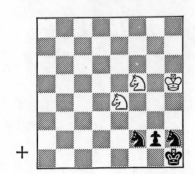

+

Not just a "Zugzwang", but a garotte!

1 N/5—N3 ch K—N8   2 N—N5!

A marvelous symmetry; whichever black knight moves, it gives up control of either one or the other mating square R6 or B6. The pawn is blocked by the knight. If 2 ... N/R—any; 3 N—B3 mate. If 2 ... N/B—any, 3 N—R3 mate.

Two different but interconnected and strictly rectangular mating positions. An amazing parallel.

This "first form" has served as a propellant for other such tries and a breakthrough was achieved in diagram 20.

Alg.: 1 ♘fg3†, ♚g1; 2 ♘g5, ♘f(h)∞; 3 ♘f3(h3)‡.

DIAGRAM 20

A.S.GURVICH[§]

BAKINSKI RABOCHI

BAKU, 1927

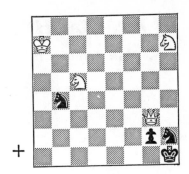

+

Still Loyd's matrix, with a sophisticated introduction by a modern composer.

   1 N—K4 N—Q6   2 Q—B2!!

The crude 2 Q×N only draws after 2 ... P—N8(Q). After 2 Q—B2, P—N8(Q); 3 N—N3 ch, Black loses his new queen— but White's queen is *en prise!*

   2 ...   N×Q   4 N—N5!!
   3 N—N3 ch K—N8

With the same smothered mate as in diagram 19. There the pawn is blocked by the king.

Alg.: 1 ♘e4, ♘d3; 2 ♕f2, ♘:f2; 3 ♘g3†, ♔g1; 4 ♘g5+.

DIAGRAM 21

H. ROMBACH§

CANADIAN CHESS CHAT

1968

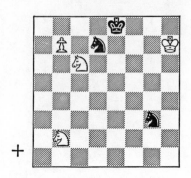

+

The composer, a Canadian who for decades lived, worked, and played chess in the United States as well, was for many years the endgame editor of *Chess Chat*.

    1 N—B4 N—KB4

If Black tries to win the pawn by 1 ... N—K5; 2 K—N7, N—N1! (a blocking sacrifice); 3 N × N, N—B4!; 4 N—Q6 ch!, K any; 5 N—B6 ch and White queens with a neat win.

    2 K—R8!! N—K2

2 ... K—B1; 3 N—N6, N—N1; 4 N × N, again saving the pawn after 4 ... N—Q3; 5 N/8—Q7 ch.

    3 N—Q6 ch K—B1   4 N—K5!! N—QN1

Clearly, if 4 ... N × N; 5 P—N8(Q) ch; whereas Black's knight on K2 must stay put to prevent N—N6 mate.

    5 K—R7!!

Upon either move of Black's knights, White mates.

    In its lucid clarity, this rendering is as convincing as the interpretation of the same motif in diagram 20.

Alg.: 1 ♘c4, ♘f5; 2 ♔h8, ♘e7; 3 ♘d6†, ♔f8; 4 ♘e5, ♘b8; 5 ♔h7+.

DIAGRAM 22

S. LOYD—
S. ROSENTHAL

PARIS INTERNATIONAL
TOURNAMENT

1867

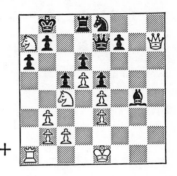

+

Motifs from composition may occur in practical play, but rarely does a composer duplicate a study theme in a tournament game!

Loyd did, in striking fashion, in the one big tournament he participated in, and against a very competent international master.

From the diagrammed position, the game went:

27 R×P!!	N—B2	30 Q—B1	B—B6
28 R—R5	Q—B3	31 N—N6	Q—R5 ch
29 Q—R1	R—R1	32 K—Q2	Q—N5

The stage is set. The finish is shown on the next page.

If 27 ... P × R; 28 N—B6 ch wins the queen.

Alg.: 27 ♖:a6, ♘c7; 28 ♖a5, ♕f6; 29 ♕h1, ♖h8; 30 ♕f1, ♗f3;
    31 ♘b6, ♕h4 †; 32 ♔d2, ♕g4.

SUB-DIAGRAM 22(A)

S. LOYD—
S. ROSENTHAL

Position after Black's 32nd Move

White starts a brilliant combination with a decoy—diverting Black's queen from guarding Black's square Q2.

33 Q×B!!	Q×Q	35 N—B6 dis. ch	N—R3
34 N—Q7 ch!	K—R1	36 N—N6	mate

A kind of smothered mate.

Alg.: 33♕:f3, ♕:f3; 34 ♘d7†, ♚a8; 35 ♘c6†, ♘a6; 36 ♘b6‡.

S. LOYD

BOSTON GLOBE

1876

DIAGRAM 23

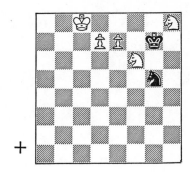

+

As a next step, Loyd tries his hand at a multiple knight promotion.

1 P—K8(N) ch! K×N	3 N—B7 mate
2 P—Q8(N) N—any	

Three white Knights on the board. Or

1 P—K8(N) ch K—B1	3 N—N6 mate
2 P—Q8(N) K (or N)—any	

Four white knights on the board.

The idea is well usable in study composition, although Loyd's technique was geared to problems and his original construction could (and did) equally carry the demand: mate in three.

But others utilized the same blueprint for endgame studies proper.

Alg.: 1 e8(♘)†, ♚:h8; 2 d8(♘), ♘∞; 3 ♘f7♯ or 1..., ♚f8; 2 d8(♘), ♚ (or ♘)∞; 3 ♘g6♯.

DIAGRAM 24

V. A. KOROL'KOV§

"*64*" (U.S.S.R.)

1937

1st and 2nd Prize *ex aequo*

A revelation. To begin with, Black threatens mate not by queening, but by "knighting": 1 ... P—B8(N) ch; 2 K—R1, N/7—N6 mate.

White parries the threat by a threefold under-promotion, crowned by a mate with five white knights on the board—and it all looks very natural!

1 N—B4 ch K—R3

If 1 ... K—R5 or N4; 2 P—Q8(Q) ch.

2 P—N8(N) ch K—R2	6 N—K6 ch K—B2
3 N/N8—B6 ch K—R3	7 P—Q8(N) ch K—K2
4 N×P ch K—R2	8 P—B8(N) mate
5 N/8—B6 ch K—N2	

The next portrait no longer resembles a plausible game position, but is a supreme record instead—an eightfold promotion to knight, the maximum possible.

Alg.: 1 ♞f4†, ♚h6; 2 g8(♞)†, ♚h7; 3 ♞gf6†, ♚h6; 4 ♞:g4† ♚h7; 5 ♞ef6†, ♚g7; 6 ♞e6†, ♚f7; 7 d8(♞)†, ♚e7; 8 c8 (♞)‡.

DIAGRAM 25

W. A. SHINKMAN

DEUTSCHE
SCHACHZEITUNG

1903

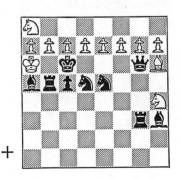

+

William Anthony Shinkman (1847–1933) was an early disciple of Loyd's; he came to be known as "The Wizard of Grand Rapids", Michigan.

With this diagram, his magnificent imagination created the first typical pattern for eight consecutive under-promotions to a knight. Such intensive treatment of an idea is called a *Task*, when the composer tries to achieve a new record in a particular theme.

1 P—N8(N) ch R×N	5 P×B(N) ch K—B3
2 RP×R(N) ch K—Q3	6 P—N8(N) ch Q×N
3 P—B8(N) ch K—K3	7 RP×Q(N) ch R×N
4 P—Q8(N) ch B×N	8 P×R(N) mate

Unfortunately, the technical execution contains some flaws. White's captures on the 7th and 8th moves can be reversed and thus the sequence becomes inexact. Furthermore, the first three moves are indisputably the only ones leading to a win, but on the 4th, 5th, 6th and 8th moves of the above solution, White has other winning moves at his disposal as well, and could break the envisioned "promotional" winning pattern. Thus, the promotions become somewhat voluntary maneuvers, implying mutual cooperation by both sides. The factor of one winning choice only, which is of overriding importance in classifying a work as a true endgame composition, is missing. But let us turn to the next presentation.

Alg.: 1 b8(♘)†, ♖:b8; 2 a:b8(♘)†, ♔d6; 3 c8(♘)†, ♔e6; 4 d8(♘)†, ♗:d8; 5 e:d8(♘)†, ♔f6; 6 g8(♘)†, ♕:g8; 7 h:g8(♘)†, ♖:g8; 8 f:g8(♘)#.

DIAGRAM 26

A. CHÉRON§

(Amending a study by W. A. Shinkman)

JOURNAL DE GENÈVE

FEBRUARY 4, 1964

+

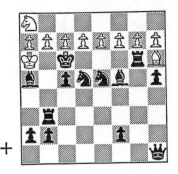

White to move and win.

Almost sixty years after publication of Shinkman's pioneering model (diagram 25), the French mathematician and international master of endgame composition, André Chéron, constructed a technically perfect prototype:

1 P—N8(N) ch	R × N	5 P × B(N) ch	K—B3
2 RP × R(N) ch	K—Q3	6 P—N8(N) ch	R × N
3 P—B8(N) ch	K—K3	7 RP × R(N) ch!	K—N3
4 P—Q8(N) ch	B × N	8 P—B8(N)	mate

None of the above moves can be interchanged without jeopardizing the win: the solution is unequivocal. The march of time . . .

Alg.: 1 b8(♘)†, ♖:b8; 2 a:b8(♘)†, ♚d6; 3 c8(♘)†, ♚e6; 4 d8(♘)†, ♗:d8; 5 e:d8(♘)†, ♚f6; 6 g8(♘)†, ♖:g8; 7 h:g8(♘)†! ♚g6; 8 f8(♘)‡.

DIAGRAM 27

E. B. COOK

NEW YORK ALBION

1852

+

Black's preponderance in material is enormous, but it serves merely as playground for a leapfrogging knight.

1 Q—B7 ch	K×Q!	5 N—K8 ch	K—B3
2 P×B(N) ch	K—K1	6 N—K5 ch	K—N4
3 N—N7 ch	K—Q1	7 N—B7 ch	K×P
4 N—B7 ch	K—B2	8 N—B4	mate

A very clean-cut improvement over an earlier—famous but somewhat "leaky"—inspiration. See diagram 28.

Alg.: 1 ♕f7†, ♔:f7; 2 g:h8(♘)†, ♔e8; 3 ♘g7†, ♔d8; 4 ♘f7†, ♔c7; 5 ♘e8†, ♔c6; 6 ♘e5†, ♔b5; 7 ♘c7†, ♔:a5; 8 ♘c4#.

DIAGRAM 28

A. D. PETROV§

SHAKHMATNAYA IGRA

1824

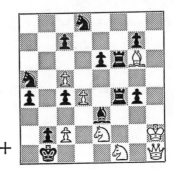

"Napoleon's retreat from Moscow to Paris"

+

The Russian analyst dedicated this romantic enterprise to the French champion Labourdonnais, but it ruffled patriotic feelings. The composition was classified as symbolic. It has kept making the round, although it is basically "cooked" on move six—an impurity nowadays not tolerated.

1 N—Q2 dbl ch K—R7	4 N—R2 ch K—N4
2 N—B3 ch K—R6	5 N—R3 ch K—R3
3 N/2—N1 ch K—N5	6 N—N4 ch!? K—R2

White could have mated very simply with 6 Q—R8, but that would have violated the built-in condition and tacit agreement of chase-and-be-chased.

7 N—N5 ch K—N1	12 N—Q7 ch K—N1
8 N—R6 ch K—B1	13 N—K7 ch K—R1
9 N—R7 ch K—Q2	14 K—N2 (or
10 N—N8 ch K—K2	N3) dis. ch and mate
11 N—B8 ch K—B1	

Alg.: 1 ♘d2†, ♚a2; 2 ♘c3†, ♚a3; 3 ♘db1†, ♚b4; 4 ♘a2†, ♚b5;
5 ♘a3†, ♚a6; 6 ♘b4†, ♚a7; 7 ♘b5†, ♚b8; 8 ♘a6†, ♚c8;
9 ♘a7†, ♚d7; 10 ♘b8†, ♚e7; 11 ♘c8†, ♚f8; 12 ♘d7†, ♚g8;
13 ♘e7†, ♚h8; 14 ♘b2 ‡.

DIAGRAM 29

E. B. COOK

*CHESS PLAYERS'
CHRONICLE*

1852 (AMENDED)

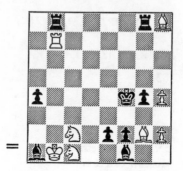

=

"The Circus"

Cook's motto alludes to the amusingly symmetrical movements —knights and king circling the ring. This type of composition was classified as "picturesque".

1 N—Q3 ch K—B4	5 N—K6 ch K—B5
2 N—K3 ch K—K3!	6 N—Q6 ch K—Q6
3 N—B4 ch K—Q3	7 N—B5 ch K—K6
4 N—B5 ch K—B4	

If 7 ... K—Q7; 8 N—B4 ch, K—Q8 (8 ... K—K8; 9 N—Q3 ch, K—Q8; 10 N×P ch, K—K1; 11 N—Q3 ch=); 9 N—K3 ch, K—K8; 10 N—B2 ch, K—Q7; 11 N—K4 ch, K—Q6; 12 N—N4 ch, K—B5; 13 N—Q2 ch, K—B4; 14 N—K4 ch=.

8 N—B4 ch K—B5   9 N—Q3 ch drawn

The mechanics are impeccable.

Alg.: 1 ♘d3†, ♚f5; 2 ♘e3†, ♚e6; 3 ♘f4†, ♚d6; 4 ♘f5†, ♚c5; 5 ♘e6†, ♚c4; 6 ♘d6†, ♚d3; 7 ♘c5†, ♚e3; 8 ♘c4†, ♚f4; 9 ♘d3†, etc.=.

DIAGRAM 30

E. B. COOK

AMERICAN CHESS-NUTS

1868

=

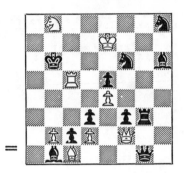

Another merry-go-round, but with a subtle sub-valiant added.

1 R—B3 dis. ch!		7 R—B3 (R3) ch	
1 ...	K—N2!*	7 ...	K—N4
2 R—N3 ch	K—R1 (B1)	8 R—N3 ch	K—R5 (B5)
3 R—R3 (B3) ch		9 R—R3 (B3) ch	
3 ...	K × N	9 ...	K—N5
4 R—N3 ch	K—B2	10 R—N3 ch!	K × R
5 R—B3 ch	K—N2	11 Q—N6 ch	Q × Q
6 R—N3 ch	K—B3 (R3)	Stalemate	

If 11 ... K—R7?; 12 Q—R5 ch, K—N6; 13 Q—N5 ch, K—R7; 14 Q—R4 mate.

* The subtle sub-variant appears after the plausible 1... Q×Q?; 2 R—N3 ch!, K—R2; 3 N—B6 ch, K—R3 (3... K—R1?; 4 R—N8 mate!); 4 N—N8 ch, K—R4; 5 N—B6 ch, K—R3 (5... K—R5?; 6 R—N4 mate) =. 2... K—B2 leads to an "echo" of the same variations, called the "star-flight" theme.

Alg.: 1 ♖c3†, ♔b7; 2 ♖b3†, ♔a8 (c8); 3 ♖a3 (c3)†, ♔:b8; 4 ♖b3†, ♔c7; 5 ♖c3†, ♔b7; 6 ♖b3†, ♔c6 (a6); 7 ♖c3 (a3)†, ♔b5; 8 ♖b3†, ♔a4(c4); 9 ♖a3 (c3)†, ♔b4; 10 ♖b3†, ♔:b3; 11 ♕b6†, ♕:b6☖

DIAGRAM 31

H. M. LOMMER[§]

MAGYAR SAKKÉLET

1965

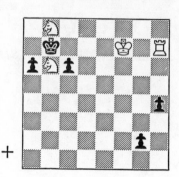

4th–6th Hon. Mention *ex aequo*

$+$

One hundred years after Cook had indicated the problem theme of a "star flight" in a sub-variation leading to a draw in diagram 30, another famous chess magician forged it into a massive fourfold mate in five moves in the corner, on the rank, and in the center.

    1 K—K6 dis. ch K × N/3

If 1 ... K × N/1; 2 R—KN7, P—R6; 3 K—Q6, P—R7; 4 K × P, P—N8/Q; 5 R—N7 mate.

    2 R × P! P—N8(Q)   3 R—N4 ch with mate

(*a*) 3 ... K—R4; 4 N × P mate.
(*b*) 3 ... K—B4; 4 N × P mate.
(*c*) 3 ... K—R2; 4 N × P ch, or,
(*d*) 3 ... K—B2; 4 N × P ch and mate next move.

    Lommer constructed another, even more game-like version for *Die Schwalbe*, October 1965 (Position 31a):
White: K on KB4; Q on KB7; R on KR4; N on QN1.
Black: K on QN5; Q on Q4; R on KR4; Ps on QR6 and QB6.
    White wins by 1 K—K3 dis. ch, K—N6!; 2 R × R, Q × Q; 3 R—N5 ch.

Alg.: 1 ♔e6†, ♚:b6; 2 ♖:h4, g1 (♛); 3 ♖b4† and mate in 2.

DIAGRAM 32

J. E. PECKOVER

L'ITALIA SCACCHISTICA

1965

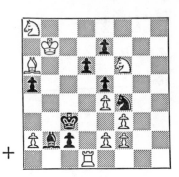

+

2nd Prize

The ancient model, revived by modern man.

1 N—Q5 ch N×N	7 R—N3 ch K—B4
2 R—Q3 ch K—N5	8 R—N5 ch K—Q5
3 R—N3 ch K—B4	9 P—K3 ch K—B6
4 R—N5 ch K—Q5	10 R—N3 ch K—Q7
5 R×N ch K—B6	11 R×B wins
6 R—Q3 ch K—N5	

"The main idea is clear: to win, White's rook chases Black's king around twice. Had it been achieved with quiet moves instead of checks, the composition would have had greater value." (Tourney Judge F. Bondarenko) A thematic heavyweight in contemporary style. Joseph Edmund Peckover, endgame columnist for the *American Chess Quarterly* 1961–65, creator of well over a hundred first rate works, is here at his best. Every theme commands its specific mechanics and here—in our view—the checks are typical, even including the opener.

Alg.: 1 ♘d5†, ♘:d5; 2 ♖d3†, ♚b4; 3 ♖b3†, ♚c5; 4 ♖b5†, ♚d4; 5 ♖:d5†, ♚c3; 6 ♖d3†, ♚b4; 7 ♖b3†, ♚c5; 8 ♖b5†, ♚d4; 9 e3†, ♚c3; 10 ♖b3†, ♚d2; 11 ♖:b2+.

DIAGRAM 33

S. LOYD

AMERICAN CHESS-NUTS

1868

=

Black's king is kept in a cage by White's opposing king. The bishop watches the pawn chain and provides the needed waiting moves. An early specimen of the staircase pattern in simple form.

1 B—Q7 ch	K—R6	3 K—B2	P—QR3
2 B—B6	K—R7	4 B—R1	drawn

Alg.: ♗d7†, ♚a3; 2 ♗c6, ♚a2; 3 ♔c2, a6; 4 ♗h1, etc.=.

Ladders, Walls and Other Structures

Diagram 33 and the next group of (fourteen) artistic creations have a feature in common which more or less distinctly resembles various ladder-like patterns. These typical stratagems can often be embodied in a study in various shapes and become part and parcel of its strategy. The same concept may enter into "pawn chains" and they are also included in order to illustrate the trait.

These scale-like patterns, with their ascending or descending movements, have been described eloquently as "Ferris wheels", or "steeplechases", or "staircases", or "escalators", or "*Treppenschach*", etc. They may range from simply "threading the needle" to complex and repetitive line interferences, with pinnings and cross-pinnings involved and they are of a romantic and attractive zigzag design.

Imposed or self-inflicted imprisonment is another design with a touch of humor. Variously described as "walking in" or "shutting in" or, most vividly, as "blocking in", it occurs in diagrams 52–8 and on later occasions and works both ways— White forces his own stalemate, or lures Black into stalemate, to salvage a draw; or he succeeds in caging in Black's King, ready for the kill.

DIAGRAM 34

B. HORWITZ§

DEUTSCHE
SCHACHZEITUNG

1872

+

A "ladder" of slightly broader scope. White wins by a curiously involuted process with three distinct steps. White's bishop climbs up the ladder, his king down.

Step 1: 1 P—B3 ch K—B4   3 P—B4 ch K—R3
             2 N—R4 ch K—N4   4 B—B6   B—N8

Step 2: 5 K—B2, B—any; 6 K—Q1, 7 K—K2, 8 K—B1, 9 K—N2, 10 K—R3, 11 K—N4, 12 K—B5, 13 K—K6, 14 K—Q7; 15 K—B8, B—any.

Step 3: The last move is simple: 16 B—N7 mate.

Alg.: 1 c3†, ♚c5; 2 ♘a4†, ♚b5; 3 c4†, ♚a6; 4 ♗c6, ♗g1; 5 ♚c2, ♗∞;   6 ♚d1—e2—f1—g2—h3—g4—f5—e6—d7—c8, ♗∞; 16♗ b7#.

DIAGRAM 35

The Editors of

CHESS REVIEW, 1936

and

*AMERICAN CHESS
BULLETIN*, 1930

"A didactic lesson"

This stairway actually dates back to the co-authors Kieseritzky and Lippmann Palamède 1848, No. LXII), and is thus shopworn thrice. But the logic of the solution is rather compelling, once the demand "to win" is faced squarely

1 P—B3! P×P	3 P—K4! P×P
2 K—B1! P—B7	

The method is clear, the outcome will impress itself on the solver with endgame experience

4 K×P	P—K6 ch	8 K—Q2	P—Q6
5 K—K1	P—K7	9 P—B6	P×P
6 P—Q5	P×P	10 K×P	P—B4
7 K×P	P—Q5		

Now enters a subtle pawn ending. Black can also play 10 ... K—N2 first, but without gaining anything, e.g. 11 K—B4, K—R1; 12 K—B5, K—N2; 13 K—Q6!, P—B4; 14 P—R8(Q) ch, K×Q; 15 K—B7+.

11 K—B4	K—N2	14 P—R8(Q) ch	K×Q
12 K—Q5!	P—B5	15 K—B7	P—B7
13 K—Q6!	P—B6	16 P—N7 ch and mate in three moves	

And in the nick of time!

Alg.: 1 f3, e:f3; 2 ♔f1, f2; 3 e4, d:e4; 4 ♔:f2, e3†; 5 ♔e1, e2; 6 d5, c:d5;
7 ♔:e2, d4; 8 ♔d2, d3; 9 c6, b:c6; 10 ♔:d3, c5; 11 ♔c4, ♔b7;
12 ♔d5, c4; 13 ♔d6, c3; 14 a8(♕)†, ♔:a8; 15 ♔c7, c2; 16 b7†+.

DIAGRAM 36

G. C. REICHHELM

LASKER'S CHESS
MAGAZINE

NEW YORK, 1904

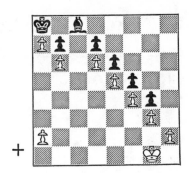

+

A thematic elaboration of diagram 35. Slightly amended forms of other, earlier works, are frowned upon as being "anticipated". But reworking a known idea, with marked technical improvement, or with significant changes in material, is artistically legitimate. It adds spice.

1 P—R3	P×P		12 P—R5	B—B3
2 K—R1	P—R7		13 K—K3	B—Q2
3 P—N4	P×P		14 K—K4	B—B1
4 K×P	P—N6 ch		15 K—K5	B—Q2
5 K—N1	P—N7		16 K—B6	B—B1
6 P—B5	P×P		17 K—K7	P—K4
7 K×P	P—B5		18 P—Q7	B×P
8 P—R4!	P—B6 ch		19 K×B	P—K5
9 K—B1	P—B7		20 K—B7	P—K6
10 P—K6	P×P		21 P—R6 wins	
11 K×P	B—Q2			

Just *en passant*, 1 P—R4!? also forces 1 ... P × P and in diagram 35 White can equally play 1 P—B4. The dual can be eliminated by starting the position at move 2.

Alg.: 1 h3, g:h3; 2 ♔h1, h2; 3 g4, f:g4; 4 ♔:h2, g3†; 5 ♔g1, g2; 6 f5, e:f5; 7 ♔:g2, f4; 8 a4, f3†; 9 ♔f1, f2; 10 e6, d:e6; 11 ♔:f2. ♝d7; 12 a5, ♝c6; 13 ♔e3, ♝d7; 14 ♔e4, ♝c8; 15 ♔e5, ♝d7; 16 ♔f6, ♝c8; 17 ♔e7, e5; 18 d7, ♝:d7; 19 ♔:d7, e4; 20 ♔c7, e3; 21 a6,+.

DIAGRAM 37

G. T. ROBERTSON

CINCINNATI COMMERCIAL

PROBLEM TOURNEY,

1882–83

"Special prize for the best
endgame study"

+

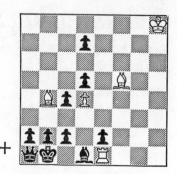

1 B—B8	K—B8	4 K—N6 P—B6
2 B—R6 ch	K—N8	5 K—N5 K—B8
3 K—N7	P—Q3	

White's king interferes with his bishop on R6. Typically, this recurs on descending levels.

6 K—N4 dis. ch K—N8	11 R—N1	P—K8(Q) ch
7 K—B4	K—B8	12 K×Q	B—any
8 K—B3 dis. ch K—N8	13 K—B2 dis. ch	B—Q8
9 K—K3	K—B8	14 R×B mate
10 K—B2 dis. ch K—N8	

The first known case of such a special prize specifically awarded to an "endgame study" in an American problem tourney.

Alg.: 1 ♗f8, ♚c1; 2 ♗h6†, ♚b1; 3 ♔g7, d6; 4 ♔g6, c3; 5 ♔g5, ♚c1;
  6 ♔g4†, ♚b1; 7 ♔f4, ♚c1; 8 ♔f3†, ♚b1; 9 ♔e3, ♚c1; 10 ♔f2†,
  ♚b1; 11 ♖g1, e1(♛)†; 12 ♔:e1, ♗∞; 13 ♔f2†, ♗d1; 14 ♖:d1 ‡.

DIAGRAM 38

H. KEIDANZ

*HALPERN'S CHESS
SYMPOSIUM, VOL. I*

NEW YORK, 1904

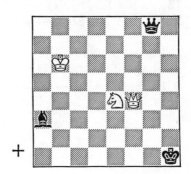

Hermann Keidanski, born in Europe in 1865, spent his most fruitful years of chess publicity in New York where he arrived in 1902. Changing his name, Keidanz wrote a monograph on the *Rice Gambit* (1905) and edited a scholarly posthumous anthology of Eugene B. Cook's compositions (1927).

1 N—N3 ch K—R7!

If 1 ... K—N7; 2 Q—B1 ch, K—R7; 3 Q—R1 ch, K×N; 4 Q—N1 ch, winning the queen. This kind of "ambush", whereby Black loses if he captures, or is forced to capture, the knight, is idiomatic for this type of queen-and-knight *versus* queen.

2 Q—R4 ch K—any	4 Q—B1 ch K—K6
3 Q—R1 ch K—B7	5 Q—K2 ch K—B5

If 5 ... K—Q5; 6 Q—Q2 ch, K—K4; 7 Q—K3 ch, K—Q3; 8 N—B5 ch, K—Q2; 9 Q—Q4 ch, K—K1; 10 Q—K5 ch, K—Q2; 11 Q—B7 ch, etc., as in the main line.

6 N—R5 ch K—B4	10 Q—B6 ch K—Q2
7 Q—B3 ch K—N3	11 Q—B6 ch K—K2
8 Q—N4 ch K—B2	12 Q—B7 ch K—B1
9 Q—B5 ch K—K2	

Another recurring finesse, which governs Black's retreat: If 12 ... K—K3?; 13 Q—B4 ch, wins the queen, just as 12 ... K—K1; 13 N—B6 ch. The sequel is all forced.

13 Q—Q8 ch K—B2	17 N—B5 ch K—B1!
14 Q—B6 ch K—K1	18 Q—B8 ch K—B2
15 N—N7 ch K—Q2	19 N—R6 ch wins
16 Q—B6 ch K—K2!	

Alg.: 1 ♘g3†, ♚h2; 2 ♕h4†, ♚ ∞; 3 ♕h1†, ♚f2; 4 ♕f1†, ♚e6; 5 ♕e2†, ♚f4; 6 ♘h5†, ♚f5; 7 ♕f3†, ♚g6; 8 ♕g4†, ♚f7; 9 ♕f5†, ♚e7; 10 ♕f6†, ♚d7; 11 ♕c6†, ♚e7; 12 ♕c7†, ♚f8; 13 ♕d8†, ♚f7; 14 ♕f6†, ♚e8; 15 ♘g7†, ♚d7; 16 ♕c6†, ♚e7; 17 ♘f5†, ♚f8; 18 ♕c8†, ♚f7; 19 ♘h6†+.

DIAGRAM 39

G. C. REICHHELM

LASKER'S CHESS
MAGAZINE

NEW YORK, 1904

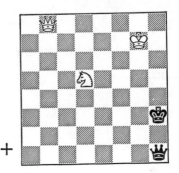

+

In the previous diagram, White's task was difficult enough: to win with a bare knight ahead, when only queens are left on the board. Black had another bishop, seemingly to balance the forces, but it was completely ineffective.

Reichhelm tackles the same subject more economically.

1 Q—R8 ch	K—N7	9 Q—Q6 ch	K—N7
2 N—B4 ch	K—N8	10 Q—Q5 ch	K—R7
3 N—K2 ch	K—N7	11 Q—K5 ch	K—N7
4 Q—R8 ch!	K—R7	12 Q—K4 ch	K—R7
5 Q—N8 ch	K—N7	13 Q—R4 ch	K—N7
6 Q—N7 ch	K—R7	14 N—B4 ch	K—N8
7 Q—B7 ch	K—N7	15 Q—K1 ch	K—R7
8 Q—B6 ch	K—R7	16 Q—B2 ch and mate	
		next move.	

Alg.: 1 ♕h8†, ♔g2; 2 ♘f4†, ♔g1; 3 ♘e2†, ♔g2; 4 ♕a8†, ♔h2; 5 ♕b8†, ♔g2; 6 ♕b7†, ♔h2; 7 ♕c7†, ♔g2; 8 ♕c6†, ♔h2; 9 ♕d6†, ♔g2; 10 ♕d5†, ♔h2; 11 ♕e5†, ♔g2; 12 ♕e4†, ♔h2; 13 ♕h4†, ♔g2; 14 ♘f4†, ♔g1; 15 ♕e1†, ♔h2; 16 ♕f2†+.

DIAGRAM 40

W. A. SHINKMAN

MOORE'S GEMS OF CHESS

1872

A tuneful humoresque.

   1 K—B2! R—QN8

If 1 ... R—K8 (or R—B8); 2 P—R7, R—K1; 3 B—N8+.

   2 P—R7 R×P ch   3 K—Q1

If 3 K—B3, R—N6 ch; 4 any, R—QR6=.

3 ...	R—N8 ch	6 K—N2	R—N7 ch
4 K—K2	R—N7 ch	7 K—R1	R—N8 ch
5 K—B1	R—N8 ch	8 B—N1	wins

Black's apparently useless knight becomes very active if White tries the obvious 1 P—R7, K—N8; 2 B—N8, N—N3; 3 P—N4, N—K2; 4 P—N5, N—Q4 ch; 5 K—B4, N—N3 ch; 6 K—B5, N—B1; 7 P—N6, N×NP; K×N, R×P=.

Alg.: 1 ♔c2, ♜b1; 2 a7, ♜:b2†; 3 ♔d1, ♜b1†; 4 ♔e2, ♜b2†; 5 ♔f1, ♜b1†; 6 ♔g2, ♜b2†; 7 ♔h1, ♜b1†; 8 ♗g1+.

DIAGRAM 41

B. S. BARRETT

*THE DUBUQUE CHESS
JOURNAL*

1874

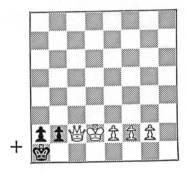

+

One of the oldest "serpentine" themes on record. Note the peculiar ascent—and descent—of White's queen.

1 Q—B3 K—N8   2 Q—Q3 ch K—R8

The crude but clear design emerges—for a while the ascent continues, but in reverse:

3 Q—Q4	K—N8		8 Q—N6 ch	K—R8
4 Q—K4 ch	K—R8		9 Q—N7	K—N8
5 Q—K5	K—N8		10 Q—R7 ch	K—R8
6 Q—B5 ch	K—R8		11 Q—R8!	K—N8
7 Q—B6	K—N8		12 Q—R1 mate	

Alg.: 1 ♕c3, ♚b1; 2 ♕d3†, ♚a1; 3 ♕d4, ♚b1; 4 ♕e4†, ♚a1; 5 ♕e5, ♚b1; 6 ♕f5†, ♚a1; 7 ♕f6, ♚b1; 8 ♕g6†, ♚a1; 9 ♕g7, ♚b1; 10 ♕h7†, ♚a1; 11 ♕h8, ♚b1; 12 ♕h1‡.

DIAGRAM 42

G. C. REICHHELM

1899

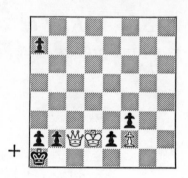

Compared to the previous position, this innocuous change of scenery signals a remarkable artistic advance. It employs Barrett's formula, but adds a wider dimension.

1 Q—B3	K—N8	5 Q—K5	K—N8
2 Q—Q3 ch	K—R8	6 Q—B5 ch	K—R8
3 Q—Q4	K—N8	7 Q—B6	K—N8
4 Q—K4 ch	K—R8	8 Q—N6 ch	K—R8

So far the familiar tune—but it is merely an overture.

    9 Q—N7 P—R3

A new figure. Black's king does not doom itself so easily.

10 Q—R8 P—R4	12 Q—R8 P—R6
11 Q—N7 P—R5	

Black's pawn-tempi are exhausted—but that is not all.

    13 Q—N7 P—K8(Q) ch

Now White must block off the rank on which he expected the queen to mate Black's king.

    14 K×Q K—N8   15 K—Q2!!

If now 15 ... P—R8(Q); 16 Q—N8, any; 17 Q—N1 mate. Or
15 ... P—R8(N); 16 Q—N8, N—N6 ch; 17 Q×N, K—R1;
18 K—B2 and mate next move.

Alg.: 1 ♕c3, ♚b1; 2 ♕d3†, ♚a1; 3 ♕d4, ♚b1; 4 ♕e4†, ♚a1; 5 ♕e5,
♚b1; 6 ♕f5†, ♚a1; 7 ♕f6, ♚b1; 8 ♕g6†, ♚a1; 9 ♕g7, a6;
10 ♕h8, a5; 11 ♕g7, a4; 12 ♕h8, a3; 13 ♕g7, e1(♕)†; 14 ♔:e1,
♚b1; 15 ♔d2+.

DIAGRAM 43

D. L. SILVERMAN

From: David L. Silverman,

YOUR MOVE—Section "Chess and Variations"*

1971

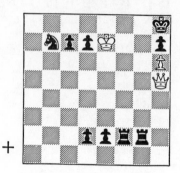

+

To quote the programmer's lingo as an example of this particular technique of teaching:

> "White is confronted with a strong threat against which he can again achieve a perpetual check. However he has the initiative, and with proper planning can use it to mate Black's king.
> While not exactly simple, the solution is within range of the average chess novice for this reason: against Black's threats, White cannot afford a single waiting move but must keep Black constantly in check until he is able to deliver the checkmate. White to play and win."

As is usual with frames of instruction, the book quotes the solution to the frame overleaf, thus:

> "If unhindered by Black's rooks, White plans to navigate the route by checking the black king along a diagonal. From the start of White's queen's trek, he can handle rook interference without difficulty."

---

* ibid. *A treasury of 100 decision making problems designed to challenge your insight* (McGraw-Hill, New Jersey, 1971). The original uses a classical descriptive notation for elementary clarity.

1 Q—K5 ch K—N1		7 Q—N2 ch K—N1	
2 Q—Q5 ch K—R1		8 Q—R2 ch K—R1	
3 Q—Q4 ch K—N1		9 Q—R1 ch K—N1	
4 Q—B4 ch K—R1		10 Q—R8 ch N—Q1	
5 Q—B3 ch K—N1		11 Q×N ch R—B1	
6 Q—N3 ch K—R1		12 Q×R mate	

lg.: 1 ♕e5†, ♚g8; 2 ♕d5†, ♚h8; 3 ♕d4†, ♚g8; 4 ♕c4†, ♚h8; 5 ♕c3†, ♚g8; 6 ♕b3†, ♚h8; 7 ♕b2†, ♚g8; 8 ♕a2†, ♚h8; 9 ♕a1†, ♚g8; 10 ♕a8†, ♘d8; 11 ♕:d8†, ♖f8; 12 ♕:f8♯.

DIAGRAM 44

K. REGAN

CHESS LIFE & REVIEW

1972

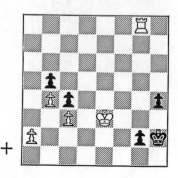

**Special Prize, 1972–73 U.S.C.F.
Study Tourney**

$+$

1 K—B2 P—R6   2 P—R4!

2 R—N3?, P—N8(Q) ch; 3 R × Q turns into a familiar stalemate.

2 ...	P×P
3 P—N5	P—R6
4 P—N6	P—R7

| 5 P—N7 | P—R8(Q) |
| 6 R × P ch! | K—R8! |

Evidently, if 6 ... P × R; 7 P—N8(Q) ch and mate next move. Now the well-known ladder makes its entrance. 6 P—N8(Q) ch, K—R8 loses for White.

7 R—R2 ch	K × R
8 P—N8(Q) ch	K—R8
9 Q—N7 ch	K—R7
10 Q—B7 ch	K—R8
11 Q—B6 ch	K—R7
12 Q—Q6 ch	K—R8
13 Q—Q5 ch	K—R7

14 Q—K5 ch	K—R8
15 Q—K4 ch	K—R7
16 Q—B4 ch	K—R8
17 Q—B3 ch	K—R7
18 Q—N3 ch	K—R8
19 Q×P	mate

Composed at the age of 12, it is a first of promise.

Alg.: 1 ♔f2, h3; 2 a4, b:a4; 3 b5, a3; 4 b6, a2; 5 b7, a1(♕); 6 ♖:g2†, ♔h1; 7 ♖h2†, ♔:h2; 8 b8(♕)†, ♔h1; 9 ♕b7†, ♔h2; 10 ♕c7†, ♔h1; 11 ♕c6†, ♔h2; 12 ♕d6†, ♔h1; 13 ♕d5†, ♔h2; 14 ♕e5†, ♔h1; 15 ♕e4†, ♔h2; 16 ♕f4†, ♔h1; 17 ♕f3†, ♔h2; 18 ♕g3†, ♔h1; 19 ♕:h3#.

DIAGRAM 45

G. C. REICHHELM

From: Reichhelm and Shipley,

CHESS IN PHILADELPHIA

1898

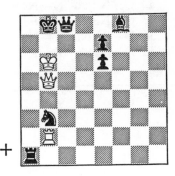

One year before diagram 42, Reichhelm concocted this most sophisticated shuttle. LeLionnais* quotes Barrett's diagram 41 together with Reichhelm's above, as typical of the staircase theme, commenting: "Here is a more elaborate example. This artistic *étude* by a major specialist (Reichhelm) in this theme, manages to have the queen descend four times and then ascend the same staircase once." Let the action make it clear:

1	Q—K5 ch	K—R1	16	Q—K4 ch	K—N1
2	Q—K4 ch	K—N1	17	Q—B4 ch	K—R1
3	Q—B4 ch	K—R1	18	Q—B3 ch	K—N1
4	Q—B3 ch	K—N1	19	Q—N3 ch	K—R1
5	Q—N3 ch	K—R1	20	Q—N2 ch	K—N1
6	Q—N2 ch	K—N1	21	Q—R2 ch	B—Q3!
7	Q—R2 ch	P—K4!	22	Q×B ch	K—R1
8	Q×P ch	K—R1	23	Q—Q5 ch	K—N1
9	Q—K4 ch	K—N1	24	Q—K5 ch	K—R1
10	Q—B4 ch	K—R1	25	Q—K4 ch	K—N1
11	Q—B3 ch	K—N1	26	Q—B4 ch	K—R1
12	Q—N3 ch	K—R1	27	Q—B3 ch	K—N1
13	Q—N2 ch	K—N1	28	Q—N3 ch	K—R1
14	Q—R2 ch	P—K4	29	Q—N2 ch	K—N1
15	Q×P ch	K—R1	30	Q—R2 ch	K—R1

* F. LeLionnais et E. Maget: *Dictionnaire des Échecs*, Paris 1967. The otherwise superb opus erroneously classifies Reichhelm as a German national.

31 R—R2 ch	N—R4!	36 Q—K4 ch	K—N1
32 Q—N2 ch	K—N1	37 Q—K5 ch	K—R1
33 Q—N3 ch	K—R1	38 Q×N ch	Q—R3 ch
34 Q—B3 ch	K—N1	39 Q×Q ch	K—N1
35 Q—B4 ch	K—R1	40 Q—N7	mate

Alg.: 1 ♕e5†, ♔a8; 2 ♕e4†, ♔b8; 3 ♕f4†, ♔a8; 4 ♕f3†, ♔b8; 5 ♕g3†, ♔a8; 6 ♕g2†, ♔b8; 7 ♕h2†, e5; 8 ♕:e5†, ♔a8; 9 ♕e4†, ♔b8; 10 ♕f4†, ♔a8; 11 ♕f3†, ♔b8; 12 ♕g3†, ♔a8; 13 ♕g2†, ♔b8; 14 ♕h2†, e5; 15 ♕:e5†, ♔a8; 16 ♕e4†, ♔b8; 17 ♕f4†, ♔a8; 18 ♕f3†, ♔b8; 19 ♕g3†, ♔a8; 20 ♕g2†, ♔b8; 21 ♕h2†, ♗d6; 22 ♕:d6†, ♔a8; 23 ♕d5†, ♔b8; 24 ♕e5†, ♔a8; 25 ♕e4†, ♔b8; 26 ♕f4†, ♔a8; 27 ♕f3†, ♔b8; 28 ♕g3†, ♔a8; 29 ♕g2†, ♔b8; 30 ♕h2†, ♔a8; 31 ♖a2†, ♘a5; 32 ♕g2†, ♔b8; 33 ♕g3†, ♔a8; 34 ♕f3†, ♔b8; 35 ♕f4†, ♔a8; 36 ♕e4†, ♔b8; 37 ♕e5†, ♔a8; 38 ♕:a5†, ♕a6†; 39 ♕:a6†, ♔b8; 40 ♕b7♯.

DIAGRAM 46

W. A. SHINKMAN
and
O. WURZBURG

CHESS WEEKLY

1909

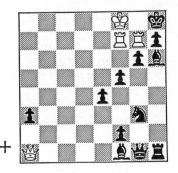

Otto Wurzburg (1875–1951) was Shinkman's talented nephew. The construction here has also the faint flavor of a problem.

1 K—K7 B—N4 ch   2 K—Q6 B—B5 ch

If White's king enters a white square, e.g. 1 K—K8 or 2 K—Q7, then Black's queen's bishop, checking, wins the day.

3 K—B5 B—K6 ch   5 K×P B—B8 ch
4 K—N4 B—Q7 ch   6 K—N4 B—Q7 ch

6 Q×B, B—B5! was taboo.

7 K—B5 B—K6 ch   10 K—B8! B—R3
8 K—Q6 B—B5 ch   11 Q—R8! B×R ch
9 K—K7 B—N4 ch   12 K—K7 dis. ch and
                        mate next move

Really a winding road!

Alg.: ♔e7, ♗g5†; 2 ♔d6, ♗f4†; 3 ♔c5, ♗e3†; 4 ♔b4, ♗d2†; 5 ♔:a3, ♗c1†; 6 ♔b4, ♗d2†; 7 ♔c5, ♗e3†; 8 ♔d6, ♗f4†; 9 ♔e7, ♗g5†; 10 ♔f8, ♗h6; 11 ♕a8, ♗:g7†; 12 ♔e7†+.

DIAGRAM 47

A. C. WHITE

Reproduced from A. Rueb's
BRONNEN VAN DE
SCHAAKSTUDIE

1952

+

Again, a halfbreed between problem and study, but the continual linear deployment reminds us of a study rather than of a multivariation problem. The idea is to show a win, in distinct fashion, by minimal White force against all of Black's, across the full length of two diagonals—and on the double!

1 R—B2 dbl ch K—K6		7 R—B5 dbl ch K—N3
2 R—B3 dbl ch K—K5		8 R—B6 dbl ch K—N2
3 R—K3 dbl ch K—Q5		9 R—N6 dbl ch K—R2
4 R—K4 dbl ch K—Q4		10 R—N7 dbl ch K—R1
5 R—Q4 dbl ch K—B4		11 R—R7 dbl ch K—N1
6 R—Q5 dbl ch K—B3		12 R—R8 mate

Alg.: 1 ♖f2†, ♔e3; 2 ♖f3†, ♔e4; 3 ♖e3†, ♔d4; 4 ♖e4†, ♔d5; 5 ♖d4†, ♔c5; 6 ♖d5†, ♔c6; 7 ♖c5†, ♔b6; 8 ♖c6†, ♔b7; 9 ♖b6†, ♔a7; 10 ♖b7†, ♔a8; 11 ♖a7†, ♔b8; 12 ♖a8‡.

DIAGRAM 48

D. GURGENIDZE[§]

MOLODEZH GRUZII

1970

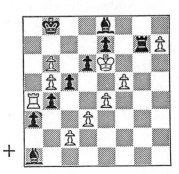

4th Prize

Reaching the peak, but a century after diagram 33 and seventy years after Reichhelm's diagram 36.

1 R—R8 ch K—N2   2 R—N8 ch K×R

After this introduction, the corkscrew starts turning. Only at the very end does the purpose of the introduction become apparent. We first witness a game of switch-on and switch-off.

3 P—R8(Q) R—N3 ch!

White keeps threatening Q×B ch, with mate to follow, Black keeps defending by a succession of checks that uncover a threat by Black's bishop to capture the queen.

4 P—B6	R×P ch	8 P—Q4	R×P ch
5 K—Q5	R—B4 ch	9 K—N3	R—Q6 ch
6 P—K5	R×P ch	10 P—B3	R×P ch!
7 K—B4	R—K5 ch	11 K—R4!!	

White wins by escaping into a loophole, where he is no longer exposed to checks. In the initial position this loophole was "blocked" by a white rook. With his "introduction", White compellingly vacated, or "unblocked", the square QR4 which is to become vital for the final outcome. This maneuver also serves to conceal the solution and thus adds to the difficulty, complexity and beauty of the composition. Without it, White's remaining course would have been 11 K—R2?, P—N6 ch; 12 K×P (if 12 K×B, R—B8 mate), P—N7 dis. ch; 13 K—R2, P—N8(Q) ch; 14 K×Q, R—B8 ch; 15 K×R, B×Q; 16 R—KN4, B—B2; with a won endgame for Black.

Alg.: 1 ♖a8†, ♔b7; 2 ♖b8†, ♔:b8; 3 h8(♕), ♖g6†; 4 f6, ♖:f6†; 5 ♔d5, ♖f5†; 6 e5, ♖:e5†; 7 ♔c4, ♖e4†; 8 d4, ♖:d4†; 9 ♔b3, ♖d3†; 10 c3, ♖:c3†; 11 ♔a4!+.

DIAGRAM 49

C. E. DIESEN

CHESS REVIEW

1968

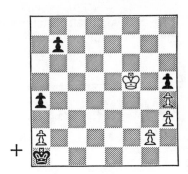

+

Another two-way switch—the play is genteel, prolonged and very logical in the two echo variations that arise after each of Black's two defences.

1 P—N4!

Black draws after 1 P—R3, P—N4; 2 P—N4, P×P; 3 P×P, K—N7; 4 P—R5, K×P; 5 P—R6, P—N5; 6 P—R7, P—N6; 7 P—R8(Q), P—N7=. After the text, the defender has the choice of:

(A)

1 ...	P×P	9 Q—B7 ch	K—R6
2 K×P!	K×P	10 Q—K7 ch	K—R7
3 P—R5	P—N4	11 Q—K6 ch	K—R6
4 P—R6	P—N5	12 Q—Q6 ch	K—R7
5 P—R7	P—N6	13 Q—Q5 ch	K—R6
6 P—R8(Q)	P—N7	14 Q—B5 ch	K—R7
7 Q—N8 ch	K—R6!	15 Q—B2	P—R6
8 Q—B8 ch	K—R7		

With Black's last move, which is forced, White gains a tempo towards bringing his king within active range.

16 K—B3!	K—R8	18 Q—B3	K—N8
17 Q—N3	P—R7!	19 Q—Q3 ch	K—B8

If 19 ... K—R8; 20 Q—Q4, K—N8; 21 Q—Q1 mate.

20 K—K2 P—N8(N)   21 Q—Q4 wins

The next alternative echoes the queen's sweep along the diagonals adjoining those in variant A.

C. E. DIESEN

BLACK'S MOVE

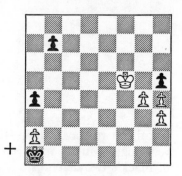

+

(B)

1 ...	P—N4	11 Q—K6 ch K—R8
2 P×P!	K×P	12 Q—K5	K—R7
3 P—R6	P—N5	13 Q—Q5 ch K—R8
4 P—R7	P—N6	14 Q—Q4	K—R7
5 P—R8(Q)	P—R6	15 Q—B4 ch K—R8
6 P—R5	P—N7	16 Q—B3	K—R7
7 Q—N8 ch K—R8		17 Q—B2	K—R8
8 Q—N7	K—R7	18 P—R6	P—N8(Q)
9 Q—B7 ch K—R8		19 Q×Q ch wins
10 Q—B6	K—R7	

Alg.: 1 g4, (A) 1..., h:g4; 2 ♔:g4, ♚:a2; 3 h5, b5; 4 h6, b4; 5 h7, b3; 6 h8(♕), b2; 7 ♕g8†, ♚a3; 8 ♕f8†, ♚a2; 9 ♕f7†, ♚a3; 10 ♕e7†, ♚a2; 11 ♕e6†, ♚a3; 12 ♕d6†, ♚a2; 13 ♕d4†, ♚a3; 14 ♕c5†, ♚a2; 15 ♕c2, a3; 16 ♔f3, ♚a1; 17 ♕b3, a2; 18 ♕c3, ♚b1; 19 ♕d3†, ♚c1; 20 ♔e2, b1(♘); 21 ♕d4+. Or

(B) 1... b5; 2 g:h5, ♔:a2; 3 h6, b4; 4 h7, b3; 5 h8(♕), a3; 6 h5, b2; 7 ♕g8†, ♚a1; 8 ♕g7, ♚a2; 9 ♕f7†, ♚a1; 10 ♕f6, ♚a2; 11 ♕e6†, ♚a1; 12 ♕e5, ♚a2; 13 ♕d5†, ♚a1; 14 ♕d4, ♚a2; 15 ♕c4†, ♚a1; 16 ♕c3, ♚a2; 17 ♕c2, ♚a1; 18 h6, b1(♕); 19 ♕:b1†+.

DIAGRAM 49 (B)

C. E. DIESEN

*THE CHESS
CORRESPONDENT*

1959

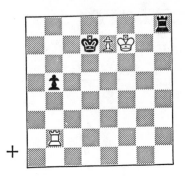

+

On a smaller scale, another climb uphill till the peak is reached.

If 1 P—K8(Q) ch? R×Q; 2 R—Q2 ch, K—B3; 3 K×R, K—B4; 4 K—K7, K—B5; 5 K—K6, K—B6; 6 R—KR2, P—N5; 7 K—K5, P—N6; 8 K—K4, P—N7 =. If 1 R×P, R—R2 ch; 2 K—B1, R—R1 ch; 3 K—N7, R—R7 =.

1 R—KR2 R—QN1!	2 R—R5!

Threatening 3 R×P, R×R; 4 P—K8(Q) ch winning. A droll roundabout, repeated in the next move.

2 ... P—N5	3 R—R4

Not now 3 R—QN5? R—KR1; 4 R×P, R—R2 ch with a definite theoretical draw; or 4 R—N7 ch, K—Q3; 5 R×P, R—R2 ch; 6 K—B8, R×P; 7 R—Q4 ch, K—K4 =.

3 ...	P—N6	7 K—B8	R—R1ch
4 R—QN4	R—KR1	8 K—N7	R—K1
5 R—N7 ch	K—Q3	9 K—B6 wins	
6 R × P!	R—R2 ch		

Alg.: 1 ♖h2, ♖b8; 2 ♖h5, b4; 3 ♖h4, b3; 4 ♖b4, ♖h8; 5 ♖b7†, ♚d6; 6 ♖:b3, ♖h7†; 7 ♔f8, ♖h8†; 8 ♔g7, ♖e8; 9 ♔f6+.

DIAGRAM 50

S. LOYD

CHESS MONTHLY

1958

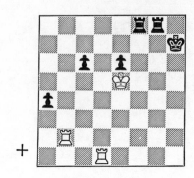

+

An early rook ending, with interesting side lines, already an accomplished classic.

1 R—R1 ch K—N2   3 R—B1 ch K—K1
2 R—N1 ch K—B2

All forced, else Black is mated. If 3 ... K—K2; 4 R—N7 ch, K—Q1; 5 K—Q6!, K—B1; 6 KR—N1, R—Q1 ch; 7 K×BP+.

4 R×R ch R×R   5 K×P wins

If 4 ... K×R; 5 K—B6+.

The positional imitation of a symmetrical mating variation on the queen's or king's side alternatively, as shown above, is known as an "echo". As the crucial mating squares also take turns between black- and white- colored ones (c8, c6 and f8, f6) respectively, the experts qualify this mechanism further as a "chameleon echo".

Alg.: 1 ♖h1†, ♔g7; 2 ♖g1†, ♔f7; 3 ♖f1† ♔e8; 4 ♖:f8†, ♖:f8; 5 ♔:e6+.

DIAGRAM 51

F. BOWLY

AMERICAN CHESS-NUTS

1868

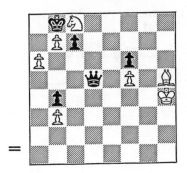

=

In probing for the possible solution, the solver may notice that 1 B—B3, Q×B would end in stalemate, but for White's three men in the far left corner of the board. How does White dispose of them?

    1 P—R7 ch K×P   **2 P—R8(Q) ch K×Q**

The stage is set—almost! Just one more piece needs to "annihilate" itself. These heroic "annihilation keys"—in this case shown in a multiple chain—are standard in composition.

    3 N—N6 ch! P×N   **4 B—B3! Q×B stalemate**

Alg.: 1 a7†, ♔:b7; 2 a8(♕)†, ♔:a8; 3 ♘b6†, c:b6; 4 ♗f3, ♕:f3=.

S. LOYD

CHESS MONTHLY

1860

DIAGRAM 52

=

Returning to another one of Loyd's themes of "shutting in", a draw seems unattainable.

  1 B—Q7 P—R7   2 B—B6 ch K—N8

If 2 ... N—B6 ch; 3 K—K2, P—R8(Q); 4 B×N ch, draw. Now Black threatens 3 ... N—N7 with an easy win.

  3 B—R1!! K×B

Forcing Black to wall himself in. If 3 ... N—N7 ch; 4 K—K2, N—B5 ch; 5 K—K1, etc.; or 4 ..., K×B; 5 K—B1 also draw.

  4 K—B2! drawn

A well-established theoretical book draw as Black's knight cannot dislodge White's king from the squares B1—B2, and cannot liberate Black's king from his prison. It is the prerequisite of a study that it shall succeed against insuperable odds.

    After 4 K—B1?, N—B6; 5 K—B2, N—Q7!; 6 K—any, K—N8, Black would have won.

    As also transpires, White loses after the immediate 1 B—B6

ch?, K—N8; 2 B—R1!?, K×B; 3 K—B1, K—R7; 4 K—B2, N—N3; 5 K—B1, K—N6; 6 K—N1, N—K4; 7 K—R1, N—N5; 8 K—N1, N—B7+.

In the main line, White also maintains equality after Black's

1 ...	N—B6 ch!?	5 B—N7	N—B4 ch
2 K—K2	N—Q5 ch	6 K—K2	N—R5
3 K—K3	P—R7	7 B—R1!	N—N7
4 B—B6 ch	K—N6!	8 K—B1	draw

Alg.: 1 ♗d7, h2; 2 ♗c6†, ♔g1; 3 ♗h1, ♔:h1; 4 ♔f2=.

DIAGRAM 53

A. S. GURVICH§

IZVESTYA

1928

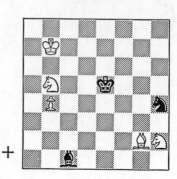

1st Prize

+

Inconspicuously, White shifts a piece to the rook's square and eight moves later Black, taking it, is mated.

| 1 B—R1!! | B—Q7 | 3 N—B6 ch | K—B5 |
| 2 N—R7! | B × P | 4 N × B | K—N6 |

At this point it may be realized that another first move of White's would have secured Black a draw right here and now, e.g. 1 B—B1 (or 1 B—R3), B—Q7; 2 N—R7, B×P; 3 N—B6 ch, K—B5; 4 K—N6=. Or 1 B—B6, B—Q7; 2 N—N4 ch, K—B4!; 3 B—Q7 ch, K—N4=. Or 1 B—B3, B—Q7; 2 N—R7, B×P; 3 N B6 ch, K—B5; 4 N×B, N×B=. Or 1 N—B3 ch, N×N; 2 B×N, B—Q7; 3 N—R7, B×P; 4 N—B6 ch, K—B5=.

| 5 N—B1 ch | K—B7! | 6 N—Q2 | N—N7 |

Shutting in the white bishop, and if 7 B × N, K × B draws.

| 7 N—Q3 ch | K—N8 | 9 N—B2 mate |
| 8 N—B3 ch | K × B | |

A rare sight (but not quite forced—Black can choose the prosaic loss 8 ... K—B8; 9 K—B6, N—K6; 10 K—B5).

Alg.: 1 ♗h1, ♝d2; 2 ♘a7, ♝:b4; 3 ♘c6†, ♚f4; 4 ♘:b4, ♚g3; 5 ♘f1†, ♚f2; 6 ♘d2, ♞g2; 7 ♘d3†, ♚g1; 8 ♘f3†, ♚:h1; 9 ♘f2♯.

DIAGRAM 54

A. H. BRANTON

EG

MAY, 1973

1st Hon. Mention *Assiac* **Jubilee Tourney of** *E.G.* **Magazine 1972 (amended)*** +

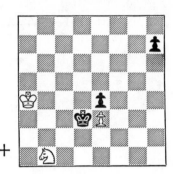

The main solution holds out and stands up throughout a whole labyrinth of treacherous sidelines. The same theme of "shutting in", as in diagrams 52 and 53, is manipulated by White so as to rescue himself from imminent defeat.

1 K—N3 P—R4	2 N—B3 K×P

If 2 ... P—R5; 3 N—Q5, K—K7; 4 N—B4 ch, K×P; 5 N—N2 ch, K—B7; 6 N×P, P—K6; 7 N—N6, P—K7; 8 N—B4, P—K8(Q); 9 N—Q3 ch and 10 N×Q=.

3 K—B2 P—R5	4 K—Q1!

Black forces a win after 4 N—Q1 ch?, K—B6; 5 K—Q2, P—R6; 6 K—K1, P—K6 (6 ... P—R7?; 7 N—B2! as in the main line); 7 K—B1, P—K7 ch, wins.

4 ...	P—R6	7 N—B2	P—K6
5 K—K1	P—R7!	8 K—B1!	K—N6
6 N—Q1 ch	K—B6		

8 N—R1?, K—N7; 9 K—K2, K×N wins. After the text, 8 ... P×N is stalemate.

---

* The first submission had White's king on square QR5, and Black's king on KB5, with the first move 1 K—R4, K—Q3 containing a dual solution. *Assiac* is the pseudonym of Heinrich Fraenkel, chess columnist of the *New Statesman*, London.

9	N—R1 ch	K—B6	12	K—K2	K—N7
10	N—B2	K—N6	13	K×P	K×N
11	N—R1 ch	K—R6	14	K—B2 stalemate	

Alg.: 1 ♔b3, h5; 2 ♘c3, ♚:e3; 3 ♔c2, h4; 4 ♔d1, h3; 5 ♔e1, h2; 6 ♘d1†, ♚f3; 7 ♘f2, e3; 8 ♔f1, ♚g3; 9 ♘h1†, ♚f3; 10 ♘f2, ♚g3; 11 ♘h1†, ♚h3; 12 ♔e2, ♚g2; 13 ♔:e3, ♚:h1; 14 ♔f2 (=).

DIAGRAM 55

J. SCHLESINGER

AMERICAN CHESS-NUTS

1868

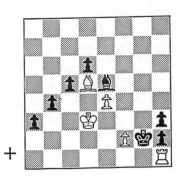

+

1 K—K2! K×R

A must. As may easily be seen, the presence of a white pawn on square KB2 is also a must, as otherwise the king, swaying to and from N6—N7—N6 would hold the draw.

2 K—B1!	P—B5	5 B×P	B—Q5
3 B×P	P—R7	6 P—K5	any move
4 B×P	P—N6	7 B—Q5 mate	

During this early stage of endgame theory, the technical execution of original ideas was casual. For one, Black's pawn sacrifices ... P—B5; ... P—N6; and ... P—R7 are interchangeable at will. Also, the final clearing of the diagonal Q5—R1 can be reached by various means, e.g. 6 B—Q5, B any; or 5 ... P—Q4; 6 B×P, B any. For a simple, monolithic theme, the texture is too loose. Later on, technique was to become tighter.

Alg.: 1 ♔e2, ♚:h1; 2 ♔f1, c4; 3 ♗:c4, a2; 4 ♗:a2, b3; 5 ♗:b3, ♝d4; 6 e5, ∞; 7 ♗d5#.

DIAGRAM 56

"FROM A CONTEST"

AMERICAN CHESS BULLETIN

1905

+

Another "suffocation", discovered by the magazine's editor, Herman Helms, when adjudicating an adjourned game between anonymous players. The masterly flow of the analysis and the economy of the material have all the earmarks of a cohesive composition.

1 N—B5	P—N7	8 N—Q6	K×P
2 N—Q6 ch	K—Q5	9 K—B2	K—R8
3 N—N7!	P—N8(Q)	10 N—B5	K—R7
4 B—B5 ch	K×P	11 N—K3	K—R8
5 B×Q	K—B6	12 N—B1	P—R7
6 K—Q2	K—N7	13 N—N3 mate	
7 K—K2	K×B		

An episode reminiscent of Barbier and Saavedra's synthesis (diagram 15).

Alg.: 1 ♘f5, g2; 2 ♘d6†, ♔d4; 3 ♘b7, g1(♕); 4 ♗c5†, ♔:e4; 5 ♗:g1, ♔f3; 6 ♔d2, ♔g2; 7 ♔e2, ♔:g1; 8 ♘d6, ♔:h2; 9 ♔f2, ♔h1; 10 ♘f5, ♔h2; 11 ♘e3, ♔h1; 12 ♘f1, h2; 13 ♘g3 ‡.

G.KOLTANOWSKI

DIAGRAM 57

SAN FRANCISCO
CHRONICLE

1960

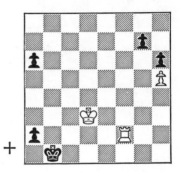

+

Gregarious "Kolty", international master, world blindfold champion, international umpire, chess columnist, popular lecturer and TV-commentator, and so on, and so forth, concocted this naive-looking little ending which appears dead drawn.

If 1 K—K4, P—R8(Q); 2 R—B1 ch, K—N7; 3 R×Q, K×R; 4 K—B5, P—R4; 5 K—N6, P—R5; 6 K×P, P—R6; 7 K×P, P—R7; 8 K—N7, K—N7; 9 P—R6, P—R8(Q); 10 P—R7 with a book draw. Or 1 R—B1 ch, K—N7; 2 R—B2 ch, K—N6; 3 R—B1, K—N7; 4 R—B2 ch, etc.=.

But a sudden and deadly artistic turn decides for White:

1 R—B1 ch	K—N7	3 K—B2
2 R—QR1!!	K×R	

The same attribute as in diagrams 52 to 56, but using different equipment in each case.

3 ...	P—R4	6 K—B1	P—N4
4 K—B1	P—R5	7 P×P *e.p.*	wins
5 K—B2	P—R6		

It's a throwback to old times—but instructive, and popular with the teacher's pupils.

Alg.: 1 ♖f1†, ♔b2; 2 ♖a1, ♔:a1; 3 ♔c2, a5; 4 ♔c1, a4; 5 ♔c2, a3;
    6 ♔c1, g5; 7 h:g6 e.p.+.

DIAGRAM 58

G. POLERIO§

TRATTATO DE' SCACCHI
(*Ludovisi*)

1590

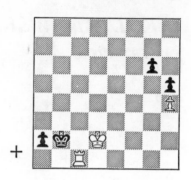

+

The progenitor's basic prototype for diagram 57.

1 R—QR1 K×R   2 K—B2!

Not 2 K—B1, else Black promotes with a check as seen below:

2 ...	P—N4	5 P—N7	P—R7
3 P×P	P—R5	6 P—N8(Q)	P—R8(Q)
4 P—N6!	P—R6	7 Q—N7 ch and mate	
		next move	

This core of an idea was first shaped into a study by R. Williams (1894) (Position 58a):

White: K on Q3, R on K2, P on QN5.
Black: K on QN8, P's on QR2 and QR7.
Solution: 1 R—K1 ch, K—N7; 2 R—QR1!, K—N6; 3 K—Q2, K—N7; 4 K—Q1, K × R (Black's capture was forced. If 4 ... K—N6; 5 K—B1!); 5 K—B2, P—R4; 6 P—N6, P—R5; 7 P—N7, P—R6; 8 K—Q2!!, K—N7; 9 P—N8(Q) ch, wins. The same maneuver was used by Pachman versus Welling, simul., Amsterdam 1972.

Alg.: I. (POLERIO) 1 ♖a1, ♚:a1; 2 ♔c2, g5; 3 h:g5, h4; 4 g6, h3; 5 g7, h2; 6 g8(♛), h1(♛); 7 ♛g7†+.
II. (WILLIAMS) 1 ♖e1†, ♚b2; 2 ♖a1, ♚b3; 3 ♔d2, ♚b2; 4 ♔d1, ♚:a1; 5 ♔c2, a5; 6 b6, a4; 7 b7, a6; 8 ♔d2, ♚b2; 9 b8(♛)†+.

DIAGRAM 58 (A)

PH. STAMMA§

*THE NOBLE GAME OF
CHESS*

LONDON, 1745

$+$

For chess historians' consumption, Stamma's adaptation is exactly midway between Polerio (1590) and Williams (1894) and subject-wise is also in between. Stamma called it a mate in seven moves because of the definite limitation to that maximum number.

    1 R—K1 ch R—KN8   2 R—QB1!!

A tight squeeze that leaves Black with only two equally restricted choices—but they give it the character of an endgame.

    2 . . .   R × R ch   3 K × R   P—R4

The other choice was the immediate 2 . . . P—R4; 3 P × P, P—N5; 4 P—R6, P—N6; 5 P—R7, P—N7; 6 P—R8(Q) mate, or the deferred capture 5 . . . R × R ch; 6 K × R, P—N7; 7 P—R8(Q) mate.

    4 P × P P—N5   6 P—R7 P—N7
    5 P—R6 P—N6   7 P—R8(Q) mate

In this setting, the squeeze applies the other way round. Instead of Black's king being forced into the corner by . . . K × R, as in diagrams 57 and 58, it is White's king which keeps Black in the corner by compelling the exchange of rooks.

Alg.: 1 ♖e1†, ♖b1; 2 ♖c1, ♖:c1†; 3 ♔:c1, h5; 4 g:h5, g4; 5 h6, g3; 6 h7, g2; 7 h8(♕)‡.

DIAGRAM 59

TH.
LICHTENHEIN

AMERICAN CHESS-NUTS

1868

+

Still a construction with a look as if derived from a game, and the course of the game vacillates between the features of a combination and a study. But the quiet sacrificial key comes as a surprise:

    1 B—N2!

It is all over, but each finale is different and carries an interesting point of its own.

    If 1 ... B×B; 2 B—Q5 wins.

    If 1 ... K—R2; 2 B—B5 ch, K—N1; 3 Q—K6 ch, K—B1; 4 B×B ch, K×B; 5 Q—K7 ch, K—N1; 6 Q—R7 ch, K—B1; 7 Q—R8 ch wins.

    If 1 ... Q—K1; 2 B×B ch, K×B; 3 Q—K5 ch, K—N3; 4 B—B5 ch, K—B2; 5 B—N6 ch, wins.

The structure of this study, cast into the fashionable framework of actual play, becomes understandable once it is realized that Lichtenhein was one of the champions of the period. In the great First American Chess Congress, New York, 1857, he was placed third, after P. Morphy and L. Paulsen.

Yet there is more to it than just a combinative flair, and that little finesse can only be discovered if one important lesson is learned sooner rather than later: that neither composer nor solver can ever be sure that even the best study is really sound or fully explored—and never to take a given solution for granted.

The skeptic might probe further and discover 1 B—N2, B × B; 2 B—Q5, Q × B; 3 Q × Q, N—N5; 4 Q—R8 ch, K—R2; 5 Q × P ch, B—N2; 6 Q × NP, B—Q5; 7 K—N3!? P—KR4! and Black has in an ingenious manner set up an impregnable fortress. Black's king-side pawns are invulnerable, so is his queen side—and White's king is unable to cross over! But to qualify the solution further, White is unable to cross unless he prevents Black's setting up the barrier. He can do that by 7 Q—B7 ch, K—N3; 8 Q—Q6 ch, K—N2 (if 8 ... K—R4; 9 K—R3! and Black's king must retreat to avoid being mated); 9 Q—K7 ch, K—N3; 10 Q—K6 ch, K—N2; 11 K—R3! and White penetrates Black's king side, winning the rook's pawn, e.g. 11 ... P—R4 !? 12 Q—B5, K—R3; 13 K—N2! wins. *Zugzwang*.

Alg.: 1 ♗b2+.

DIAGRAM 60

J. B. RICHARDSON

AMERICAN CHESS-NUTS

1868

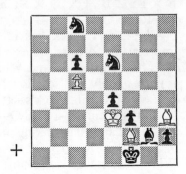

+

Black threatens to queen; White prevents it by synchronized mating threats on the other diagonal as shown:

   1 B×N! B—R8   2 B×N K—N7

Now follows a waiting move which forces the king back into captivity. If 2 ... B—N7; 3 B—R6 mate.

   3 B—Q7! K—B8   6 P—B6 B—N7
   4 B×P   K—N7   7 P—B7
   5 B—Q7 K—B8

Re-opening the conduit for the mating threat ... B—N4.

   7 ...   B—R8   8 P—B8(Q) and mate next
                                       move

In this specimen Black's king is confined not to the rook's but to the bishop's square. But, applying the lesson taught in the preceding diagram, O. Frink observes that this solution is slightly blurred by the alternative 6 B—K6! K—N7; 7 P—B6, K—B8; 8 P—B7, K—N7; 9 P—B8(Q), K—B8; 10 B—R3 ch, B—N7; 11 Q—B1 mate.

Alg.: 1 ♗:e6, ♗h1; 2 ♗:c8, ♔g2; 3 ♗d7, ♔f1; 4 ♗:c6, ♔g2; 5 ♗d7, ♔f1; 6 c6, ♗g2; 7 c7, ♗h1; 8 c8(♕)+.

DIAGRAM 61

E. B. COOK

SATURDAY EVENING
GAZETTE

1859

+

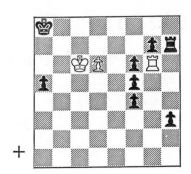

To recite H. Keidanz' impression: "The strategy of this endgame, the solution of which is not very difficult, consists first of the forced directing of the black rook to h8 (KR1) and back to h7 (KR2); then in the capture of that rook by White's queen after an interesting zigzag maneuver, by means of which White is able to frustrate Black's queening."

| 1 P—Q7 | R—R1 | 2 R×NP | P—R7 |

If 2 ... P—B6; then 3 R—K7, etc., winning.

3 R—R7!	R×R!	8 Q—N3 ch	K—R2
4 P—Q8(Q) ch	K—R2	9 Q—R2 ch	K—N1
5 Q×P ch	K—N1	10 Q—N8 ch	K—R2
6 Q—N4 ch	K—R1	11 Q×R ch	wins
7 Q—R3 ch	K—N1		

Alg.: 1d7, ♜h8; 2 ♖:g7, h2; 3 ♖h7, ♜:h7; 4 d8(♕)†, ♚a7; 5 ♕:a5†, ♚b8; 6 ♕b4†, ♚a7; 7 ♕a3†, ♚b8; 8 ♕b3†, ♚a7; 9 ♕a2†, ♚b8; 10 ♕g8†, ♚a7; 11 ♕:h7†+.

DIAGRAM 62

S. LOYD

MUSICAL WORLD

APRIL, 1859

+

Like diagram 56, this is another endgame study naturally created from practical play in postmortem—that is after-game—analysis.

The position is the end result of a blindfold encounter between S. Loyd and members of the Hudson City Chess Club. Loyd as Black, was offered a draw, which he accepted.

Turning the table, he demonstrated a win, missed by his erstwhile opponents:

1 R—B8 ch	R×R		5 K—B7	K—R3
2 N—R7!	R—B8		6 P—N8(Q)	K—R4
3 N—B6 ch	R×N		7 Q—N3	K—R3
4 K×R	K—R2		8 Q—R4 mate	

Alg.: 1 ♖c8†, ♖:c8; 2 ♘a7, ♖c1; 3 ♘c6† ♖:c6; 4 ♔:c6, ♔a7; 5 ♔c7, ♔a6; 6 b8(♕), ♔a5; 7 ♕b3, ♔a6; 8 ♕ a4♯.

E. B. COOK

From: H. Keidanz,

THE CHESS COMPOSITIONS
OF E. B. COOK

NEW YORK, 1927

DIAGRAM 63

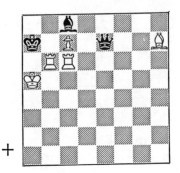

+

In this fragment, published posthumously, Cook toyed with a knight under-promotion. The construction is crude, but the idea comes through lucidly.

In view of Black's threats, White takes drastic measures.

1 R—R6 ch B×R	3 R—R7 ch! K×R
2 R×B ch K—N2	

3 ... K—B1 fails, because of 4 B—B5 ch—proving the *raison d'être* of the seemingly forlorn white bishop.

4 P—B8(N) ch K—any	5 N×Q wins

Mastery of under-promotion can be also of practical conse-quence, as seen in diagram 64.

Alg.: 1 ♖a6†, ♗:a6; 2 ♖:a6†, ♔b7; 3 ♖a7†, ♔:a7; 4 c8(♘)†, ♔∞; 5 ♘:e7+.

DIAGRAM 64

O. H. LABONE§—AMATEUR§

From W. Steinitz'

INTERNATIONAL CHESS
MAGAZINE

JUNE, 1887
Paris Tournament, 1887

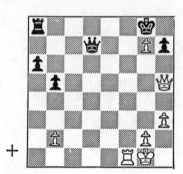

+

A practical tactical turn, with the authorship often misquoted in chess columns and manuals. A likely analogue given in Tattersall (1911) No. 822 is from a game similarly won by Dr. J. W. Hunt at Oxford in 1891, but Tattersall's No. 949, quoted without a source, is just an apocryphal duplication. Em. Lasker's *Common Sense in Chess* (1896), p. 113, contains an almost identical illustration, but without a bibliographical reference.

1 R—B8 ch R×R	3 P×R(N) ch
2 Q×P ch! K×Q	

and White wins back the queen, and the game.

Alg.: 1 ♖f8†, ♖:f8; 2 ♕:h7†, ♔:h7; 3 g:f8(♘)†+.

DIAGRAM 65

W. A. SHINKMAN

THE GOLDEN ARGOSY

1929

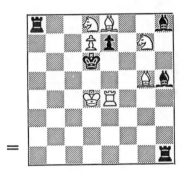

=

Two leapfrogging knights, reminders of Cook's Circus (diagram 29) but without the embroidery and thus coming closer to modern technique.

1 B—B6 ch	P—K4 ch	7 N—N8 ch	K—N4
2 B×P ch	K—K2	8 N—R7 ch	K—B4
3 N—B6 ch	K—B1	9 N—R6 ch	K—K3
4 N—K6 ch	K—N1	10 N—N5 ch	K—K2
5 N—K7 ch	K—R2	11 N—B5 ch	K—B1
6 N—B8 ch	K—R3	etc.	

A *perpetuum mobile.*

Alg.: 1 ♗f4†, e5†; 2 ♗:e5†, ♔e7; 3 ♘c6†, ♔f8; 4 ♘e6†, ♔g8; 5 ♘e7†, ♔h7; 6 ♘f8†, ♔h6; 7 ♘g8†, ♔g5; 8 ♘h7†, ♔f5; 9 ♘h6†, ♔e6; 10 ♘g5†, ♔e7; 11 ♘f5†, ♔f8; etc.=

DIAGRAM 66

E. B. COOK

ILLUSTRATED LONDON NEWS

MARCH 24, 1855

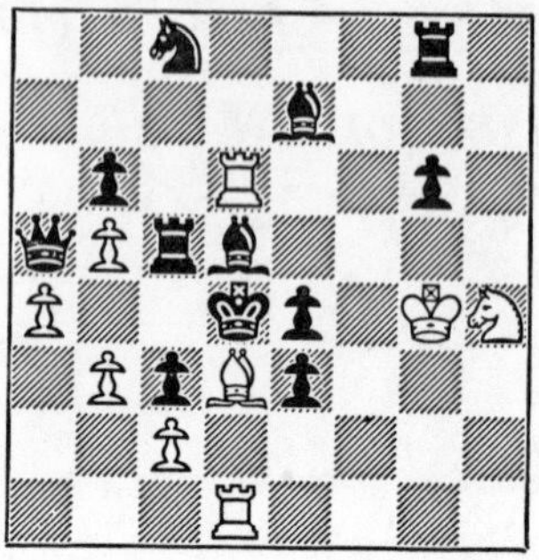

"The Treadmill"

=

1 N—B3 ch	P×N	5 R—K4 ch	K—B4
2 B—B5 dis ch	K—K4	6 R—B4 ch	K—Q3
3 R/1×B ch	R×R	7 R—B6 ch	
4 R—K6 ch	K—Q5	with perpetual check	

This type of decorative motion was much in vogue in the 19th century. It made room for more exacting creations, but the basic principle remains the same. The next diagram shows the same quadrangular outline in its pure abstraction.

The theme reminds one of a revolving door.

Alg.: 1 ♘f3†, e:f3; 2 ♗f5†, ♚e5; 3 ♖d1: d5†, ♖:d5; 4 ♖e6†, ♚d4;
  5 ♖e4†, ♚c5; 6 ♖c4†, ♚d6; 7 ♖c6† =.

DIAGRAM 67

D. L. PONZIANI§

IL GIUOCO INCOMPARABILE
DEGLI SCACCHI

MODENA, 1769

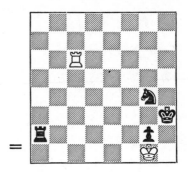

By an old master!

1 R—R6 ch K—N6	4 R—B5 ch K—R3
2 R—R3 ch! K—B5	5 R—R5 ch K—N3
3 R—B3 ch K—N4	6 R—N5 ch draw

In here, if 3 ... K—K4; 4 R—KN3=.

As one of the ending's fine points, 1 R—B3 ch is supposed to fail after ... K—R5; 2 R—R3 ch, K—N4; 3 R—R5 ch, K—B3; 4 R—B5 ch, K—K3!; 5 R—B3, R—K7!; and Black wins. If 1 R—R6 ch, K—N6; 2 R—R6?, R—R8 ch!; 3 R×R, N—R7 (or K4) and White is lost!

The demonstration of an acute point, with White's force restricted to two and Black's material almost equally austere, is called a "minimal". Diagrams 12, 52 and so forth, are of that *genre*.

But the point is no longer acute! In 1974, O. Frink pointed out that the study has two solutions, because 1 R—B3 ch, K—R5; 2 R—R3 ch, K—N4; 3 R—R5 ch, K—B3; 4 R—B5 ch, K—K3; 5 R—B4 also draws.

Alg.: 1 ♖h6†, ♔g3; 2 ♖h3†, ♔f4; 3 ♖f3†, ♔g5; 4 ♖f5†, ♔h6; 5 ♖h5†, ♔g6; 6 ♖g5†=.

DIAGRAM 68

E. B. COOK

From: H. Keidanz,

THE COMPOSITIONS OF
E. B. COOK

1927

+

An enormously flexible piece of clockwork of massive pro-
portions that keeps going indefinitely.

(A) 1 R×R Q×R

This reply winds the mechanism and the minute hand starts
moving. Upon the minor variant 1 ... B×R; 2 Q—R1 ch,
K—Q5; 3 Q—R1 ch, K any; 4 Q—R8 ch, or R1 ch, etc., White
draws as shown in the main line.

   2 Q—R1 ch K—K4

or 2 ... K—Q5; 3 Q—R1 ch, K—Q4; 4 Q—R8 ch, K—K4;
5 Q—R8 ch, K—K5; 6 Q—R1 ch, etc., with a perpetual check
clockwise.

   3 Q—R8 ch K—Q4   6 Q—R1 ch K—K4
   4 Q—R8 ch K—Q5   7 Q—R8 ch etc.
   5 Q—R1 ch K—K5

with perpetual movement anti-clockwise.

(B) 1 R×R B—K6 ch?!   3 Q—R1 ch K×P
   2 P×B B×R   4 Q—B3 ch K—Q7

If 4 ... K—Q5; 5 Q—Q3 ch, K—B4; 6 Q×NP ch, K—Q5; 7 Q—Q3 ch=.

   5 Q—Q3 ch   K—K8

5 ... K—B8; 6 Q—R3 ch, K—B7 (6 ... Q—N7 also draws); 7 Q—Q3 ch, K—N7; 8 Q×P ch, Q×Q; 9 B×Q=.

After the text the sweep-second starts spinning around.

6 Q—Q1 ch K—B7	8 Q—B3 ch K—Q7
7 Q—B1 ch K—K6!	9 Q—Q3 ch K—K8

again drawn by perpetual check.

Alg.: (A) 1 ♖:e6, ♕:e6; 2 ♕h1†, ♔e5; 3 ♕h8†, ♔d5; 4 ♕a8†, ♔d4;
     5 ♕a1†, ♔e4; 6 ♕h1†, ♔e5; 7 ♕h8†=.
   (B) ♖:e6, ♗e3†; 2 d:e3, ♗:e6; 3 ♕h1†, ♔:e3; 4 ♕f3†, ♔d2;
     5 ♕d3†, ♔e1; 6 ♕d1†, ♔f2; 7 ♕f1†, ♔e3; 8 ♕f3†, ♔d2;
     9 ♕d3†, ♔e1=.

DIAGRAM 69

E. B. COOK

From: H. Keidanz,

THE CHESS COMPOSITIONS
OF E. B. COOK

1927

=

This early try contains an echo variation. In the main line the king is exposed, in the secondary line the queen.

1 P × N(Q) ch	K × Q	4 B—K3	Q—K4 ch
2 B—K3	Q—B2 ch	5 B—B4 drawn	
3 B—B4	Q—B4		

or

1 ...	Q × Q	3 B—K3 ch	K—N1
2 B—B4 ch	K—R2	4 B—B4 ch	drawn

Alg.: 1 b:a8(♕)†, ♚:a8; 2 ♗e3, ♛c7†; 3 ♗f4, ♛c5; 4 ♗e3, ♛e5†;
    5 ♗f4= or 1..., ♛:a8; 2 ♗f4†, etc.=.

94

DIAGRAM 70

H. OTTEN

From W. Steinitz'

INTERNATIONAL CHESS
MAGAZINE

NEW YORK, 1886

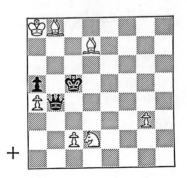

+

An ingenious piece of total surveillance of the queen by two minor pieces (and just two pawns), on a practically empty board. The theme is called "domination".

1 B—Q6 ch! K×B   2 P—B3!! wins

Amazing in its simplicity. The queen has nowhere to go without being taken promptly, or exposed to the knight forking king and queen.

World Champion Steinitz was the first editor who in his magazine's column on composition clearly differentiated between "problems", "game endings", and "ending studies", as he called them at that time.

Black threatens to win the knight, and if 1 N—N3, K—N3! If 1 B—B4, K—N3; 2 P—B4, Q—K2 +. The technical setback of the study is the juxtaposition of the kings, with White's king in Black's area and vice versa.

Alg.: 1 ♗d6†, ♚:d6; 2 c3+.

DIAGRAM 71

H. OTTEN

From W. Steinitz'

INTERNATIONAL CHESS MAGAZINE

NEW YORK, 1890

+

Another effective and very harmonic "domination".

   1 N—Q7!   R—N5!

For the moment, the safe square. If 1 ... R—N7; 2 N × P ch, K—Q5; 3 B—N7 ch+.

   2 N×P ch K—B6   4 B—R6 ch K—B6
   3 B—N7 ch K—Q7

If 4 ... K—Q8; 5 N—Q6+.

   5 K—K1

Threatens 6 B—Q2 ch, followed by a forking check.

   5 ...   R—N1

If 5 ... K—N7; 6 N—Q3 ch, K×N; 7 B—B8+.
5 ... K—Q5; 6 N—B2 ch, K×N; 7 B—B8 ch+.

   6 B—N7 ch K—N5   7 N—R6 ch+

This study provided the subject for two compositions (one in 1927 and one in 1935) by the famed A. Troitsky.

Alg.: 1 ♘d7, ♖b4; 2 ♘:c5†, ♚c3; 3 ♗g7†, ♚d2; 4 ♗h6†, ♚c3; 5 ♚e1, ♖b8; 6 ♗g7†, ♚b4; 7 ♘a6†+.

DIAGRAM 72

EMANUEL LASKER

HALPERN'S CHESS SYMPOSIUM, VOL. 2

NEW YORK, 1905

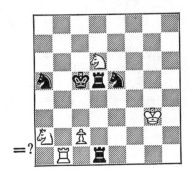

=?

A position appropriated by the New York master Halpern from one of Lasker's sporadic lectures in New York between 1893 and 1904. Lasker then left for his native Europe, but returned to the United States for good in 1936. The study also dealt with "domination".

1 R—N5 ch K×N	3 N—B3?!
2 R×R ch R×R!	

The rook has nowhere to go without becoming victim of a fork and at that time the ending with two knights was considered drawn. Really, the attractive looking study as reproduced by Halpern turns out to be a Greek gift and the horses are Trojan. Due to the single white pawn, Black still wins by a procedure first thoroughly analyzed by Troitsky in 1913 but not known around 1900.

Moreover, some of these special endings—which may be found in all advanced works on the theory of endings—require more than fifty moves to reach the mate and only recently exceptions to this rule have been officially allowed, so as to include such special occurrences.

Continuing from and improving on Halpern's solution:

3 ... N/R—B5	5 P—B3 K—K5
4 N×R K×N	

presents a clear and easy "book" win for Black.

It is interesting for modern technicians to note that even 1 R—N5 ch, K—B3!?; 2 N—N4 ch, K×N; 3 N×R, R×N; 4 R×R, K×R; 5 P—B4 ch!, K—K5; 6 P—B5, N/R—B3 still leaves Black with a theoretical win, even though the pawn is now further advanced and has been stopped on the fifth instead of the third rank. The instructive procedure is demonstrated in treatises on endings. Anyhow, Black need not defer capturing by 1 ... K×N. Compare also diagram 222.

Alg.: 1 ♖b5†, ♔:d6; 2 ♖:d5†, ♖:d5; 3 ♘c3=? 3..., ♘ac4; 4 ♘:d5, ♔:d5; 5 c3, ♔e4+.

DIAGRAM 73

H. MATTISON§

RIGAER TAGEBLATT

1914

=?

A champion of composition once fell into the same trap as Halpern. The assumed and accepted solution of this jewel was:

1 B—R2	N—B6	4 N—B3	N—Q5 ch
2 B—N1!	N×B	5 K—N4!	N×N
3 N—K5	N—K7	6 K—R3	drawn!?

If 6 ... P—N8 (B); 7 K—N2, draws; or 6 ... P—N8 (R or Q) stalemate, and, as then assumed, 6 ... P—N8 (N) drawing because two solitary knights cannot win.

It took the progress of time till 1968 to discover that White's treacherous left-over pawn on KB2 secures a win for Black after all.

Fortunately, a famous Dutch composer repaired the cook, in the next diagram 74.

Alg.: 1 ♗h2, ♘f3; 2 ♗g1, ♘:g1; 3 ♘e5, ♘e2; 4 ♘f3, ♘d4†; 5 ♔g4, ♘:f3; 6 ♔h3=(?).

DIAGRAM 74

C. J. FEIJTER§

(amending H. K. Mattison)

*E.G.**

JANUARY, 1968

+

Quite a feat of correction and improvement over the celebrated diagram 73 achieved by turning the liability into a valuable asset!

1 P×P	B—R2	5 N—K5 ch	K—N4
2 N—B6!	B—N1	6 N×N	K—R3!
3 N×B	N—Q5	7 P—N8(N) ch wins!	
4 N—Q7	N—B3		

If 7 P—N8 (B, R or Q), Black draws, as shown in diagram 73. Feijter's amendment also adds an interesting try that fails, namely 7 N—R5!? (or N—Q8), K—R2; 8 K—N7, P—B4; 9 K—B6, P—B5; 10 K—K5, P—B6; 11 K—Q6, P—B7!; (not 11 ... K—N1?; 12 K—B6, P—B7; 13 K—N6, wins); 12 K—B7, P—B8(Q) ch; 13 N—B6 ch, Q×N; 14 K×Q, K—N1 draws. A difference of one tempo!

---

* Abbreviation for "End Game", a magazine edited by A. J. Roycroft, London.

Alg.: 1 c:b7, ♗a7; 2 ♘c6, ♗b8; 3 ♘:b8, ♘d4; 4 ♘d7, ♘c6; 5 ♘e5†, ♔b5; 6 ♘:c6, ♔a6; 7 b8 (♘)†+.

DIAGRAM 75

G. C. REICHHELM

From: Reichhelm and Shipley,

CHESS IN PHILADELPHIA

1894

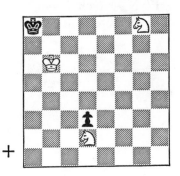

+

Reichhelm as composer and teacher. In 1894 and before, it was an eccentric chance to win such a position of two knights against a pawn. The task here seemed especially difficult because Black's pawn was too far advanced and the knights were away from Black's king. The analyst in Reichhelm provides the "algorithm" for treating such a case—prior to Troitsky (compare the remarks to diagram 72).

1 N—R6 K—N1		3 K—B6 K—N1	
2 N—B7 K—B1			

Black's king is turned back, and the knight comes even closer.

4 N—Q6 K—R2	8 K—B7 K—R2
5 K—N5 K—R1	9 N—N7! K—R3
6 K—R6 K—N1	10 K—B6 K—R2
7 K—N6 K—R1	

Now White gets his king and active knight on to the squares which will allow the other knight to become active effectively.

11 N—B5 K—R1	14 K—B8 K—R2
12 K—Q7 K—N1	15 K—B7 K—R1
13 K—Q8 K—R1	

All is ready for the kill.

16 N—B4!	P—Q7	19 N—Q7	P—Q8(Q)
17 N—N6 ch	K—R2	20 N—N6 mate	
18 N—B8 ch	K—R1		

Alg.: 1 ♘h6, ♚b8; 2 ♘f7, ♚c8; 3 ♚c6, ♚b8; 4 ♘d6, ♚a7; 5 ♚b5, ♚a8; 6 ♚a6, ♚b8; 7 ♚b6, ♚a8; 8 ♚c7, ♚a7; 9 ♘b7, ♚a6; 10 ♚c6, ♚a7; 11 ♘c5, ♚a8; 12 ♚d7, ♚b8; 13 ♚d8, ♚a8; 14 ♚c8, ♚a7; 15 ♚c7, ♚a8; 16 ♘c4, d2; 17 ♘b6†, ♚a7; 18 ♘c8†, ♚a8; 19 ♘d7, d1(♛); 20 ♘b6 ♯.

G. C. REICHHELM

LASKER'S CHESS MAGAZINE

NEW YORK, 1904

DIAGRAM 76

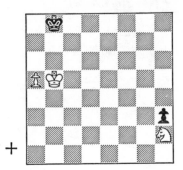

+

Another case of a too distant knight, tied to the blockade of Black's advanced pawn. The upper left hand corner indicates a clear book draw of a king against the rook's pawn. A casual look reveals that White only draws in variation I, e.g.:

I

1 K—N6	K—R1	5 N—K8	P—R8(Q)
2 P—R6	K—N1	6 N—B7 ch	K—N1
3 N—N4	K—R1	7 P—R7 ch	K—B1
4 N—B6	P—R7	8 P—R8(Q) ch Q × Q draw	

But there enters a neat simple twist based on the theory of "corresponding squares" and opposing kings, and Reichhelm was one of its great exponents. Variation II is a didactic case in point. It is known as (regular) triangulation.

II

1 K—R6!	K—R1	3 P—R6	K—R1
2 K—N6	K—N1	4 N—N4	K—N1

Deceptively, White has won one immensely important tempo. As distinct from variation I, Black's king is now on square N1 and it matters greatly.

Clearly, if 4 ... P—R7; 5 N×P, K—N8; 6 N—N4, K—R1; 7 N—B6, K—N1; 8 N—K8, K—R1; 9 N—B7 ch, wins.

5 P—R7 ch	K—R8		7 N—K8	P—R8(Q)
6 N—B6	P—R7		8 N—B7	mate

Alg   1 ♔b6, ♚a8; 2 a6, ♚b8; 3 ♘g4, ♚a8; 4 ♘f6, h2; 5 ♘e8, h1(♛); 6 ♘c7†, ♚b8; 7 a7†, ♚c8; 8 a8(♛)†, ♛:a8=.
II.   1 ♔a6, ♚a8; 2 ♔b6, ♚b8; 3 a6, ♚a8; 4 ♘g4, ♚b8; 7 a7†, ♚a8; 6 ♘f6, a7; 7 ♘e8, a8(♛); 8 ♘c7#.

DIAGRAM 77

H. KEIDANZ

LASKER'S CHESS MAGAZINE

NEW YORK, 1909

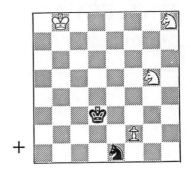

$+$

The magazine's endgame section editor (Keidanz himself) states in his preamble:

"The question arises, how can White force a win after

1 P—B4 N—N7	3 P—B6 N—N5
2 P—B5 N—K6	4 P—B7 N—K4!?"

Obviously, 5 P—B8 (Q or R or B), N—Q2 ch! loses White's newly promoted piece. The right move is of course

5 P—B8 (N)!

Black's sole knight is powerless to prevent mate by White's three knights.

White may try to remove the threat of a fork first, but the attempt is in vain, e.g. 1 K—B7!?, K—K7!; 2 P—B4, N—N7; 3 P—B5, N—K6; 4 P—B6, N—Q4 ch drawn; and if 1 K—B8, N—B6! (a bold blocking sacrifice—if 2 N×N, K—K7; and 3 ... K×P=); 2 N—R3! (if 2 N/8—B7, K—K7; 3 N—K4, N—Q7; 4 N/7—N5, N×N; 5 N×N, K—B6=), K—K5!; 3 N—B7, K—B4; 4 K—Q7, K—N5=.

Alg.: 1 f4, ♘g2; 2 f5, ♘e3; 3 f6, ♘g4; 4 f7, ♘e5! 5 f8 (♘)!+.

DIAGRAM 78

H. OTTEN

THE BOY'S OWN PAPER

1892

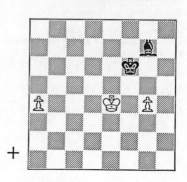

+

An immortal which served as an incentive.

  1 P—R5 B—B1   2 K—Q5 B—R3

The bishop swings over—Black will be content with the pendulum of white king to Q5 to K4 and back.

  3 P—N5 ch?! B×P   5 K—B3! wins
  4 K—K4   B—R5!

Alg.: 1 a5, ♗f8; 2 ♔d5, ♗h6; 3 g5†, ♗:g5; 4 ♔e4, ♗h4; 5 ♔f13 +

DIAGRAM 79

J. MASON

THE PRINCIPLES OF CHESS IN THEORY AND PRACTICE

1894

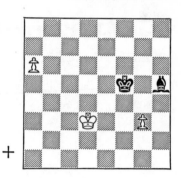

+

James Mason, born in Ireland in 1849, migrated to the United States in 1854, then took up residence in London in 1878. He reduced Otten's study to a didactic instruction piece, somewhat extending the white king's influence.

1 P—N4 ch	B × P	3 K—B2	wins
2 K—K3	B—R6		

This matrix, also called a "thematic aggregation", served as an added element in the Platov diagram 80.

Alg.: 1 g4†, ♗:g4; 2 ♔e3, ♗h3; 3 ♔f2+.

DIAGRAM 80

V. and M. PLATOV§

WIENER SCHACHZEITUNG

1912

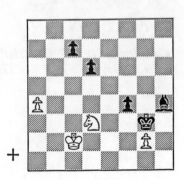

+

Twenty years later, a melodious tune was added to the libretto of diagram 78.

    1 P—R5 B—B3   2 N × P!

Vacating the square Q3 for White's king to enter, and threatening (2 ... B—Q5); 3 N—K2 ch.

2 ...	K×N	5 K—K2	B—R7
3 K—Q3!	B—R5	6 K—B1	wins
4 P—N3 ch!	B×P		

Alg.: 1 a5, ♗f6; 2 ♘:f4, ♚:f4; 3 ♚d3, ♗h4; 4 g3†, ♗:g3; 5 ♚e2, ♗h2; 6 ♚f1+.

A. MOUTERDE§

SYDSV. DAGBL.
SNÄLLPOSTEN

1914

DIAGRAM 81

4th Prize

$+$

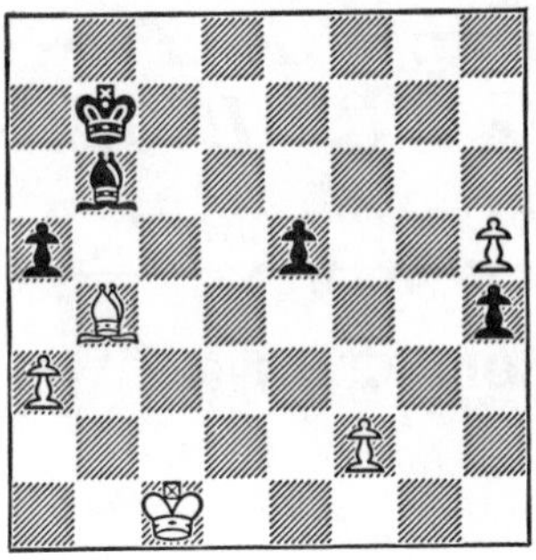

Two years after diagram 80 was published, a Frenchman paraphrased Otten's and the Platovs' theme by combining it with an intriguing blockade as the clincher, thereby increasing the range of action.

> 1 P—R6 B—Q5

The programmatic move! Lengthily but surely White wins after 1 ... B—Q1; 2 P—R7, B—B3; 3 B—K7, B—N2; 4 B×P!, P—R5; 5 K—Q2, K—B3; 6 K—Q3, K—Q4; 7 P—B3, B—R1; 8 B—K1, B—N2; 9 B—B3, B—R1; 10 P—B4+. Or 4 ... K—B3; 5 P—R4, K—B4; 6 B—K7 ch, K—B5; 7 K—B2, B—R1; 8 B—R3, K—Q5; 9 P—B4+.

2 B—B5	B—R8	5 B—Q4!	B×B
3 K—N1	B—B6	6 K—Q3	B—N7
4 K—B2	B—R8	7 K—K4!	wins

Perfect wheelwork.

Alg.: 1 h6, ♗d4; 2 ♗c5, ♗a1; 3 ♔b1, ♗c3; 4 ♔c2, ♗a1; 5 ♗d4, ♗:d4; 6 ♔d3, ♗b2; 7 ♔e4+.

DIAGRAM 82

E. EVERTZ§—
G. KIENINGER§

GERMAN MASTER
TOURNAMENT

SOLINGEN, 1964

Black to play.

Replicas of study themes occur often over the board. In this game White is lost after, e.g., 1 ... P—B5; 2 B—B2, K—B4! But Black thought it simpler and safer to play:

   1 ... B×P

and if 2 P—R6, P—B5; 3 P—R7, P—B4 winning. He did not reckon with the "blockade":

  2 B—B4!!

and the rook pawn cannot be stopped. Black resigned after 2 ... K×B; 3 P—R6, K—K5; 4 P—R7, P—B5; 5 P—R8(Q), P—B6; 6 Q—R1, K—K6; 7 Q—K1 ch, K—B5; 8 K—Q3, B—K4; 9 Q—K4 ch, K—N6; 10 K—K3.

Alg.: 1... ♗:d4; 2 ♗f4+.

E. B. COOK

*AMERICAN CHESS
MONTHLY*

1858

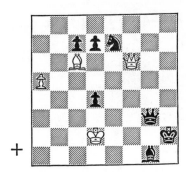

DIAGRAM 83

+

Reaching once more back into the past, this composite embroidery uses the identical blocking pattern in the final stage. In the prelude, White conceives a fine strategic maneuver to win with a pawn after capture of the black knight by a tempo, and a cleverly forced exchange of queens. Moreover, the ladder reappears as the intermediate stratagem.

1 Q—R8 ch	Q—R6	7 Q—K5 ch	K—R5
2 Q—K5 ch	Q—N6	8 Q—R8 ch	K—N6
3 Q—R5 ch	Q—R6	9 Q×Q ch	K×Q
4 Q—K2 ch	K—N6	10 K—Q3	P×B
5 Q—K5 ch	K—R5!	11 P—R6	P—B4
6 Q×N ch	K—N6	12 P—R7	wins

A showpiece. The reprint of this study in *American Chess-Nuts* (1868) replaced White's queen on KB6 with a pawn on KR7, changing the key move to the less obtrusive 1 P—R8(Q) ch.

Alg.: 1 ♕h8†, ♕h3; 2 ♕e5†, ♕g3; 3 ♕h5†, ♕h3; 4 ♕e2†, ♔g3;
5 ♕e5†, ♔h4; 6 ♕:e7†, ♔g3; 7 ♕e5†, ♔h4; 8 ♕h8†, ♔g3;
9 ♕:h3†, ♔:h3; 10 ♔d3, d:c6; 11 a6, c5; 12 a7+.

DIAGRAM 84

B. MARKOV§

SHAKHMATNA MIS'L

1948

Another artful diversion operates in this setting.

1 B—K1!! K—B5!

To prevent 2 B—B3+.

2 B—N3! K—Q4

The original position seems restored—but the bishop's regrouping is of delicate importance.

3 P—R6 P—R7		5 P—R7	P—R8(Q)
4 B×P!! K×B		6 P—R8(Q) ch wins	

The bishop sacrifice serves to entice Black's king to enter the critical square K4 (e5), a deflection known as a "decoy". As a result, Black's king obstructs the diagonal needed for his new queen to guard KR1 (h8) and White queens with a check immediately after.

Alg.: 1 ♗e1, ♔c4; 2 ♗g3, ♔d5; 3 h6, a2; 4 ♗:e5, ♔:e5; 5 h7, a1(♕); 6h8(♕)†+.

DIAGRAM 85

W. KORN

CHESS LIFE

MAY 20, 1957

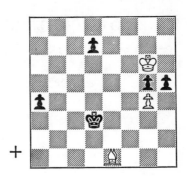

+

Quite independently, another version of line interference, with an additional side-variation.

1 P×P	P—R6	7 K—B5	P—N5
2 P—R6!	P—R7	8 K—K4	P—N6
3 B—B3!	K×B	9 K—Q3	P—N7
4 P—R7	K—N7	10 K—B2	P—N8(Q)
5 P—R8(Q) ch	K—N8	11 Q—N2	mate
6 Q—N8 ch	K—R8		

But if White plays 2 B—B3?, P—N5!; 3 P—R6, P—N6; 4 P—R7, P—N7; 5 B—Q4, P—R7; 6 P—R8(Q), P—R8(Q); 7 Q—R3 ch, K—B5! draws.

Alg.: 1 g:h5, a3; 2 h6, a2; 3 ♗c3, ♚:c3; 4 h7, ♚b2; 5 h8(♕)†, ♚b1; 6 ♕b8†, ♚a1; 7 ♔f5, g4; 8 ♔e4, g3; 9 ♔d3, g2; 10 ♔c2, g1(♕); 11 ♕b2‡.

W. A. SHINKMAN

DETROIT FREE PRESS

1881

DIAGRAM 86

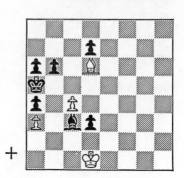

This, and some of the following constructions, rank among the more difficult exercises in endgame study, but they also have a considerable relationship to practical play. The stratagems involve simple tempo play, knowledge of "corresponding squares" and of the right opposing moves by either king.

In the diagram, Black's bishop seems able to shuttle eternally between B6 and K8, thus guarding against a mate by White's bishop. As long as the White king must move forth and back between Q1, R1, and N2, and Black's bishop between B6, Q7 and K8, all is in balance; but there is one odd square that upsets that balance . . .

1 K—B1	B—K8	4 K—R1 B—B6 ch
2 K—N2	B—Q7	5 K—N1 B—Q7
3 K—R2!	B—K8	6 K—N2! B—K8

The (white) square N2 and (Black's) K8 no longer "correspond". Black's equilibrium is now disturbed.

7 K—B1	B—B6	10 K×Q B—K8
8 K—Q1	P—Q7	11 K×B P—N4
9 K—B2	P—Q8(Q) ch	12 B—B7 mate

Alg.: 1 ♔c1, ♝e1; 2 ♔b2, ♝d2; 3 ♔a2, ♝e1; 4 ♔a1, ♝c3†; 5 ♔b1, ♝d2; 6 ♔b2, ♝e1; 7 ♔c1, ♝c3; 8 ♔d1, d2; 9 ♔c2, d1(♛)†; 10 ♔:d1, ♝e1; 11 ♔:e1, b5; 12 ♝c7#.

DIAGRAM 87

W. A. SHINKMAN

CHESS RECORD

1874

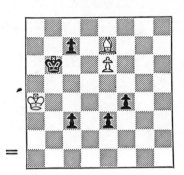

=

A crisp, clear distillate of a positional miniature with three variations.

1 B—B5 ch   K×B

After 1 ... K—B3; 2 P—K7, K—Q2; 3 K—N3 White draws easily.

2 P—K7   P—B7   4 Q—K5 ch K—B3
3 P—K8(Q) P—B8(Q)

If 4 ... K—N3; 5 Q—N2 ch, Q×Q stalemate.
If 4 ... K—B5; 5 Q×QBP ch, K—any; 6 Q×Q wins.
After the text, the third variation goes into effect.

5 Q—B3 ch   Q×Q

Stalemate.

Alg.: 1 ♗c5†, ♚:c5, 2 e7, c2; 3 e8(♛), c1(♛); 4 ♛e5†, ♚c6; 5 ♛c3†, ♛: Ⓓ.

115

DIAGRAM 88

G. C. REICHHELM

LASKER'S CHESS MAGAZINE

1904

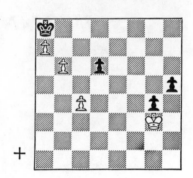

$+$

White gives up material for space . . .

1 K—B4	K—N2	2 P—B5! P×P	

. . . and gains access to the key square K5.

3 K—K5	P—N6	7 P—N7 ch	K—R2
4 K—Q6!	P—N7	8 P—N8(Q) ch	K—R3
5 P—R8(Q)	K × Q	9 Q—N6 mate	
6 K—B7	P—N8(Q)		

Easy looking, but it is the timing that matters.

Alg.: 1 ♔f4, ♚b7; 2 c5!, d:c5; 3 ♔e5, g3; 4 ♔d6, g2; 5 a8(♕)†, ♚:a8;
6 ♔c7, g1(♕); 7 b7†, ♚a7; 8 b8(♕)†, ♚a6; 9 ♕b6‡.

DIAGRAM 89

G. C. REICHHELM

PHILADELPHIA EVENING
BULLETIN

1873

=

It is not always self-evident that two pawns win against one—nor that the side with one pawn can draw.

Scrupulous count of the available tempi and of opposition play proves that neither party on the move can win.

Var. I

1 K—B3	P—R4!		4 P—R3	K—K4
2 K—K3	K—K4		5 K—B3	K—B4
3 P—N3	K—B4		6 P—R4	K—K4 draw

Var. II

1 K—B1	K—B5		4 P—R3 ch	K—N4!
2 P—N3 ch	K—N5		5 K—B3	K—B4 draw
3 K—N2	P—R4			

Alg.: Var. I. 1 ♔f3, h5!; 2 ♔e3, ♚e5; 3 g3, ♚f5; 4 h3, ♚e5; 5 ♔f3, ♚f5; 6 h4, ♚e5=.
  Var. II. 1 ♔f1, ♚f4; 2 g3†, ♚g4; 3 ♔g2, h5; 4 h3†, ♚g5! 5 ♔f3, ♚f5=.

DIAGRAM 90

EMANUEL LASKER

MANCHESTER EVENING NEWS

1900

+

A module that created a sensation, especially when supported by Reichhelm's further artistic improvement in changing the king's position (see next diagram).

Inspired by a setting of Locock's (1892), Lasker is reported to have shown his own rendering to Reichhelm at Chicago in 1901. The same year Reichhelm published an amended version, (diagram 91) which deepened the thematic content of these almost architectural constructions that became the backbone of the "Theory of Corresponding Squares".

1 K—N2! K—R2

If ... K—N1; 2 K—B2, K—B1; 3 K—Q2, K—Q1; 4 K—B3, K—B2; 5 K—Q3, K—N2 (5 ... K—B1; 6 K—B4+); 6 K—K3, and 7 K—B3, 8 K—N3, 9 K—R4 and 10 K—R5+.

2 K—N3 K—N2

If 2 ... K—R3; 3 K—B2!+.

3 K—B3 K—B2	5 K—B4 wins
4 K—Q3 K—Q2	

Or 4 ... K—N3(N2); 5 K—K3+.

White's king victoriously outflanks Black via the king's wing in the manner shown in the first sideline above.

Alg.: 1 ♔b2, ♚a7; 2 ♔b3, ♚b7; 3 ♔c3, ♚c7; 4 ♔d3, ♚d7; 5 ♔c4+.

DIAGRAM 91

G. C. REICHHELM

CHICAGO TRIBUNE

1901

+

Offering more variety than diagram 90.

1 K—N1!

If 1 K—N2?, K—R1!; 2 K—R2, K—N2!; 3 K—N1, K—R2;
4 K—B2, K—N1; 5 K—Q2, K—B1!; 6 K—Q3, K—B2!;
7 K—B3, K—N2!; 8 K—B4, K—N3!; 9 K—Q3, K—B2!;
10 K—K3, K—Q2=.

1 ...   K—N2

If 1 ... K—R1; 2 K—N2!, K—N2; 3 K—B3!, K—N3;
4 K—B4!, K—N2; 5 K—N5+.

2 K—B1   K—B2   3 K—Q1   K—Q2 (or Q1)

If 3 ... K—B1; 4 K—Q2!, K—B2; 5 K—Q3, K—N2; 6
K—K3+.

4 K—B2! K—B1   7 K—Q3! K—N2
5 K—Q2! K—Q2   8 K—K3 wins
6 K—B3   K—B2

If 7 ... K—Q2; 8 K—B4+.

Both diagrams 90 and 91 are often captioned "Lasker and
Reichhelm" indiscriminately.

Alg.: 1 ♔b1, ♚b7; 2 ♔c1, ♚c7, 3 ♔d1, ♚d7; 4 ♔c2, ♚c8; 5 ♔d2,
♚d7; 6 ♔c3, ♚c7; 7 ♔d3, ♚b7; 8 ♔e3+.

DIAGRAM 92

J. J. DOLAN

LITERARY DIGEST

1903

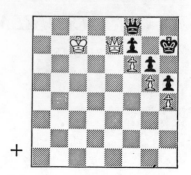

+

Diagrams 90 and 91 are the acme of opposition play of the kings. The projection by Dolan, secretary of the Mechanics Institute Chess Club of San Francisco, applies the same principle to queens.

This is the comment by C. E. C. Tattersall in his *A Thousand Endgames* (1911):

"The most difficult study in the whole of the collection. Black repeatedly menaces stalemate by sacrificing his queen and in consequence White has to play with the greatest exactness— in fact he rarely has an alternative move that will win the game. The side-variations, when at first sight obscure, will usually be found to lead back to the main play."

    1 K—Q7 Q—KN1

If 1 ... K—N1; 2 Q×Q ch, K×Q; 3 K—Q8, K—N1; 4 K—K8, K—R1; 5 K×P+.

    2 Q—Q6! Q—B1

Upon 2 Q—B5? or 2 Q—K8? or 2 Q—Q8? Black draws.

3 Q—Q5! K—R1	7 K—K7 Q—QN1!
4 Q—K5! K—N1	8 Q—B6! Q—QR1
5 Q—K7! K—R2	9 Q—B7! Q—QN1
6 Q—Q6! Q—QR1!	

If 9 ... K—N1; 10 Q—Q8 ch, K—R2; 11 K—K8, Q—K5 ch (11 ... Q—R7; 12 K—B8, K—R1; 13 Q—Q7, Q—B5; 14 Q×P+); 12 K—B8, Q—N5 ch; 13 Q—K7, Q—N1 ch; 14 Q—K8, Q—N5 ch; 15 K×P+.

10 Q—Q6! Q—N6!

Not 10 ... Q—N2 ch; 11 K—B8, winning in all lines.

11 Q—Q7!	Q—B5	17 Q—K6!	Q—Q1 ch
12 K—B8!	K—R1	18 K—B7!	K—R2
13 Q×P	Q—B4 ch	19 Q—K4!	Q—Q2 ch
14 Q—K7	Q—B1 ch	20 Q—K7!	Q—B1
15 Q—K8!	Q—Q2	21 Q—R7!	Q—QR1
16 Q—K5!	Q—B2	22 Q—Q7!	Finis!

To quote a news item from the *British Chess Magazine* 1909, p. 212: "... J. J. Dolan has earned fame in the chess world through his celebrated endgame."

Alg.: 1 ♔d7, ♛g8; 2 ♕d6, ♛f8; 3 ♕d5, ♚h8; 4 ♕e5, ♚g8; 5 ♕e7, ♚h7; 6 ♕d6, ♛a8; 7 ♔e7, ♛b8; 8 ♕c6, ♛a8; 9 ♕c7, ♛b8; 10 ♕d6, ♛b3; 11 ♕d7, ♛c4; 12 ♔f8, ♚h8; 13 ♕:f7, ♛c5†; 14 ♕e7, ♛c8†; 15 ♕e8, ♛d7; 16 ♕e5, ♛c7; 17 ♕e6, ♛d8†; 18 ♔f7, ♚h7; 19 ♕e4, ♛d7†; 20 ♕e7, ♛c8; 21 ♕a7, ♛a8; 22 ♕d7+.

DIAGRAM 93

ED. LASKER

From: Eduard Lasker,

CHESS STRATEGY

1915

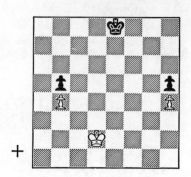

+

Despite equal pawns, exacting opposition play breaks the symmetry and wins.

1 K—K2!	K—K2	3 K—K4	K—B3
2 K—K3	K—K3	4 K—B4!	

If 4 K—Q5, K—B4; 5 K—B5, K—N5; 6 K × P, K × P; 7 K—B4, K—N6; 8 P—N5, P—R5, etc., drawn.

4 ...	K—K3	5 K—N5 wins	

Alg.: 1 ♔e2, ♚e7; 2 ♔e3, ♚e6; 3 ♔e4, ♚f6; 4 ♔f4, ♚e6; 5 ♔g5+.

DIAGRAM 94

C. E. DIESEN

CHESS REVIEW

1967

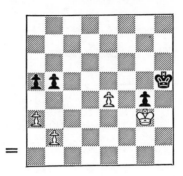

=

At a first glance, White's advancing passed pawn will be captured and Black's king will be on his way to take White's pawn on the queen's side, while White will be occupied taking Black's king's knight pawn.

Yet White saves the game by accurate temporizing which is persuasive in its simplicity.

    1 P—R4 P—N5!

White gets away with a draw after 1 ... P×P; 2 P—K5, K—N4; 3 P—K6, K—B3; 4 K×P, K×P; 5 K—B4, K—Q4; 6 K—K3, K—B5; 7 K—Q2, K—N6; 8 K—B1, K—R7; 9 K—B2=.

2 K—B2!	K—R5	7 K×P	K—Q4
3 K—N2	K—N4	8 K—B3	K—B5
4 K—N3	P—N6	9 K—K4	K—N5
5 P—K5	K—B4	10 K—Q4	K×P
6 P—K6	K×P	11 K—B4	stalemate

Alg.: 1 a4, b4; 2 ♔f2, ♚h4; 3 ♔g2, ♚g5; 4 ♔g3, b3; 5 e5, ♚f5; 6 e 6, ♔:e6; 7 ♔:g4, ♚d5; 8 ♔f3, ♚c4; 9 ♔e4, ♚b4; 10 ♔d4, ♚:a4; 11 ♔c4 (=).

DIAGRAM 95

O. FRINK

THE CHESS AMATEUR

1928

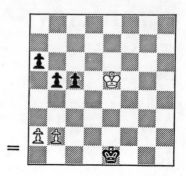

=

The earlier nucleus of the idea, before Diesen fashioned the broader tapestry of diagram 94.
If 1 K—Q5, P—B5; 2 K—B5, K—Q7; 3 P—R4!=.

1 P—R4! P—N5	3 K×P P—N6!
2 K—Q5 K—Q7	

Not 3 ... P—R4?; 4 K—N5, K—B7; 5 K×P, P—N6; 6 K—N6, K×P; 7 P—R5, K—B6; 8 P—R6, P—N7; 9 P—R7, P—N8(Q) ch; 10 K—B7=.

4 K—N4 K—B7	5 K—R3 P—R4
	stalemate

Alg.: 1 a4, b′ ; 2 ♔d5, ♚d2; 3 ♔:c5, b3; 4 ♔b4, ♚c2; 5 ♔a3, a5 Ⓔ.

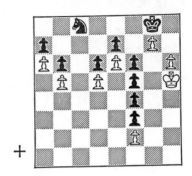

DIAGRAM 96

C. G. REICHHELM

LASKER'S CHESS MAGAZINE

NEW YORK, 1904

+

Black, with an immobile knight, is utterly helpless, but neither can White utilize his passed pawns, as 1 K—N6 would stalemate. Innocuously, White retreats from the scene!

1 K—R4 K—R2	4 K—R1 K—N1	
2 K—R3 K—N1	5 K—N1!	
3 K—R2 K—R2		

The square that gains an extra tempo for White's king, which starts marching back.

5 ... K—R2	8 K—R4 K—N1	
6 K—R2 K—N1	9 K—R5	
7 K—R3 K—R2		

The initial position, but with Black having the move—and he is stuck for a good one!

9 ... K—R2	13 K—K8 K×P	
10 P—N8(Q) K×Q	14 K—Q8 K—R4	
11 K—N6 K—R1	15 K×N K—R5	
12 K—B7 K—R2	16 K—Q7 K—R6	

17 K×P	K—N7	22 Q—R6 ch	K—N7
18 K×BP	K×P	23 Q×P	P—B8(Q)
19 P—K7	K—N8	24 Q×Q ch	K×Q
20 P—K8(Q)	P—B7	25 K×P	wins
21 Q—N6 ch	K—R7		

The distinctly Reichhelmian touch.

Alg.: 1 ♔h4, ♚h7; 2 ♔h3, ♚g8; 3 ♔h2, ♚h7; 4 ♔h1, ♚g8; 5 ♔g1, ♚h7; 6 ♔h2, ♚g8; 7 ♔h3, ♚h7; 8 ♔h4, ♚g8; 9 ♔h5, ♚h7; 10 g8(♕), ♚:g8; 11 ♔g6, ♚h8; 12 ♔f7, ♚h7; 13 ♔e8, ♚:h6; 14 ♔d8, ♚h5; 15 ♔:c8, ♚h4; 16 ♔d7, ♚h3; 17 ♔:e7, ♚g2; 18 ♔:f6, ♚:f2; 19 e7, ♚g1; 20 e8(♕), f2; 21 ♕g6†, ♚h2; 22 ♕h6†, ♚g2; 23 ♕:f4, f1(♕); 24 ♕:f1†, ♚:f1; 25 ♔:f5+.

DIAGRAM 97

H. KEIDANZ
and A. CHÉRON§

CATALONIAN ENDGAME
TOURNEY

1914

=

A sample and a formula of principal importance for tournament practice, and a study demolished, but restored.

1 R—R8 P—Q7

If 1 ... P—B6; 2 R—K8 ch, K—Q5; 3 K—B4, P—B!7; 4 R—Q8 ch, K—B6; 5 R—B8 ch, K—Q7; 6 K—K4 draw. Also 1 ... K—K5 only draws, whereas 1 ... P—Q7! is Black's aggressive reach for a win and it seems difficult to parry.

2 R—K8 ch	K—Q5		5 R—K8 ch	K—B7!
3 K—B4	K—Q6!		6 R—Q8	P—B6
4 R—Q8 ch	K—K7		7 R—Q3!!	

The equalizing move! Black threatened 7 ... K—K7; 8 R—Q8, K—Q8; and 9 ... P—B7 winning. As a sequel, Black's king will try to escape and queen the pawns, but White draws by shuttling his rook.

7 ...	K—K7		10 R—N3 ch	K—R7
8 R—K3 ch!	K—B8		11 R—Q3	draw
9 R—B3 ch	K—N7			

The complexity of these stratagems is underlined by the fact that the first setting of this prize-winner was proved inaccurate. Keidanz' initial tourney submission had the rook on square KB2(f2). Forty years later, in 1953, the Soviet theoretician

127

N. Kopayev showed an easier way for White to draw even, by
1 R—B5 ch, K—K5; 2 R—B4 ch, K—K6; 3 R×P, P—Q7;
4 R—B3 ch, K—K5; 5 R—B4 ch, K—K4; 6 R—B8=.

But André Chéron restored Keidanz' intended solution
by moving White's rook to the king rook file and eliminating
Kopayev's adroit "twin" option (Lille, 1952).

Alg.: 1 ♖h8, d2; 2 ♖e8†, ♔d4; 3 ♔f4, ♔d3; 4 ♖d8†, ♔e2; 5 ♖e8†,
♔f2; 6 ♖d8, c3; 7 ♖d3, ♔e2; 8 ♖e3†, ♔f1; 9 ♖f3†, ♔g2;
10 ♖g3†, ♔h2; 11 ♖d3=.

DIAGRAM 98

H. KEIDANZ

DEUTSCHE
SCHACHZEITUNG

1925

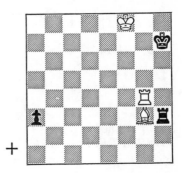

$+$

Slowly moving into the era of the modern positional endgame study, this piece is economical and precise, and has a pungent thematic point.

1 B—B4 R—Q6

If 1 ... P—R7; 2 R—N7 ch, K—R1; 3 B—K5+.

2 R—N7 ch	K—R1	5 K—K6	R—R3 ch
3 B—K5	R—Q1 ch	6 K—B5	R—R3
4 K—K7	R—R1		

The one and only square where Black's rook is immune from a discovered check. But White has a waiting move in store.

7 B—Q4!! P—R7   8 B—R1! wins

Black's rook has no safe haven left.

Alg.: 1 ♗f4, ♖d3; 2 ♖g7†, ♔h8; 3 ♗e5, ♖d8†; 4 ♔e7, ♖a8; 5 ♔e6, ♖a6†; 6 ♔f5, ♖h6; 7 ♗d4!, a2; 8 ♗a1+.

DIAGRAM 99

W. STEINITZ

THE PAWN

MARCH, 1910

First published in *NUOVA RIVISTA DEGLI SCACCHI* **1880**

+

Nowadays one would call this bagatelle a "study-like pawn ending" and class it among the didactic positions found in treatises on endings.

But, once upon a time, there was a beginning to all that studious perfection . . .

1 P—R7 ch	K—N2	4 B—B6 ch	R × B ch
2 P—R8(Q) ch!	K × Q	5 K × R	wins
3 K—B7!	R—B8 ch		

Alg.: 1 h7†, ♚g7; 2 h8(♕)†, ♚:h8; 3 ♚f7, ♜f1†; 4 ♗f6†, ♜:f6†; 5 ♚:f6+.

DIAGRAM 100

I. A. HOROWITZ and I. KASHDAN

CHESS AMATEUR

MARCH, 1928, and reprinted in
CHESS REVIEW

FEBRUARY, 1933

+

A masterpiece in precision narrated in the magazine's endgame column as an "analysis of a position that occurred in actual play recently between two fairly strong amateurs".

The king's straight march forward achieves nothing: 1 K—K7, K—N5; 2 K—Q6, P—R4; 3 K—Q5, P—R5; 4 N—B4, K—N4! Black maintains the opposition and cannot be dislodged, e.g. 5 K—Q4, K—N5; 6 K—Q3 (or 6 N—K3), K—N6=. Therefore:

    1 N—N3 K—B5

If 1 ... K—N5; 2 N—R1, P—R4; 3 K—K7, P—R5; 4 K—Q6, P—R6; 5 N—B2+.

    2 N—R1! K—Q6   4 K—Q6 K—B8
    3 K—K7 K—Q7

If 4 ... P—R4; 5 K—B5!, P—R5; 6 K—N4, K—B8; 7 K—R3, K—N8; 8 N—N3!, P×N; 9 K×P+.

    5 P—N4 K—N7   6 K—B6!

If 6 K—B5, K—B6!; 7 N—B2, K×N; 8 K—N6, K—B6=.

    6 ...   K—B6   7 K—B5! wins

Alg.: 1 ♘b3, ♚c4; 2 ♘a1, ♚d3; 3 ♔e7, ♚d2; 4 ♔d6, ♚c1; 5 b4, ♚b2; 6 ♔c6, ♚c3; 7 ♔c5+.

DIAGRAM 101

P. A. LARSEN§

SKAKBLADET

JANUARY, 1933

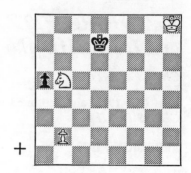

+

An elaboration of diagram 100 but not different enough to stand on its own.

Professional practice requires an altered alignment to be labeled "after a position by Horowitz and Kashdan". By the same token, an apparent "replica" appearing in a separate place may just as well be one of the rare but nevertheless periodic cases of curious coincidence—of two artists hitting upon the same idea in different places at almost the same time.

Also in this work, activating the king at once fails: 1 K—N7?, K—B3; 2 N—Q4 ch, K—B4; 3 N—N3 ch, K—B5; 4 N×P ch, K—N5=.

1 N—Q4! K—Q3	5 K—B6 K—Q6
2 N—N3! P—R5	6 K—K5 K—Q7
3 N—R1 K—Q4	7 K—Q4 K—B8
4 K—N7 K—Q5	8 K—B3 wins

In comparison to diagram 100, the introductory down-the-staircase by-play is more prolonged and hence pleasing, and White's king is even further away. But there is a gap of five years in priority.

Alg.: 1 ♘d4, ♚d6; 2 ♘b3, a4; 3 ♘a1, ♚d5; 4 ♚g7, ♚d4; 5 ♚f6, ♚d3; 6 ♚e5, ♚d2; 7 ♚d4, ♚c1; 8 ♚c3+.

DIAGRAM 102

O. WEINBERGER

BRITISH CHESS MAGAZINE

1961

+

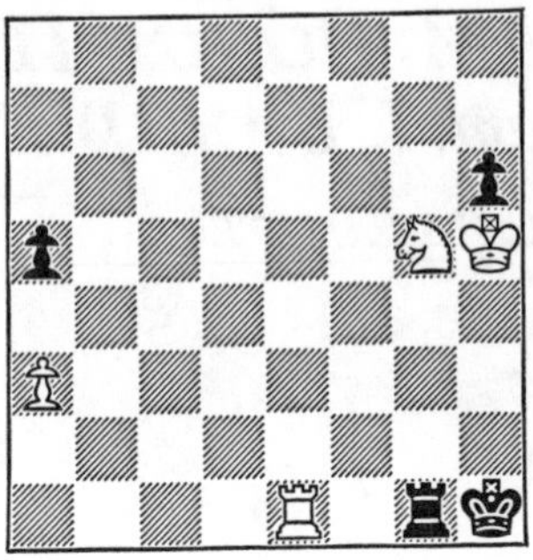

1 N—B3 R×R	6 N×P K—B7
2 N×R K—N8	7 P—R4 K—B6
3 N—Q3 K—B8	8 N—N3 K—N5
4 N—B1! K—K8	9 P—R5 wins
5 N—N3 K—Q8	

Less assuming than diagram 100 but also typical for its punctual knight moves.

If 1 R×R ch, K×R; 2 N—K6, K—B7; 3 N—Q4, K—K6; 4 N—N3, K—Q6; 5 N×P, K—B6. Black wins the pawn and draws.

An amusing trifle.

Alg.: 1 ♘f3, ♖:e1; 2 ♘:e1, ♔g1; 3 ♘d3, ♔f1; 4 ♘c1, ♔e1; 5 ♘b3, ♔d1; 6 ♘:a5, ♔c2; 7 a4, ♔c3; 8 ♘b3, ♔b4; 9 a5+.

DIAGRAM 103

I. A. HOROWITZ and I. KASHDAN

CHESS AMATEUR

1929

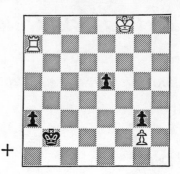

$+$

Three advanced black pawns, two of them passed; White's king a great distance away; Black's king on White's side of the board, eventually threatening to capture White's lone pawn—what more does Black need to prevail?

However, White has an unexpected surprise up his sleeve.

    1 K—K7 P—R7   2 K—Q6

A momentary respite. If the rook pawn queens, the white rook takes and the king captures the pawn on K4. First, Black pushes the centre pawn out of reach:

    2 ...   P—K5   3 K—B5 P—K6

White cannot chase this pawn any further and looks stymied. But another mechanism comes into play:

    4 K—N4 P—K7   7 R—K1 ch K—N7
    5 R—K7! P—R8(Q)   8 R×Q   K×R
    6 R×P ch K—N8 (or   9 K—B3 wins
            B8)

The white king captures Black's pawn with a won endgame. An amazing criss-crossing of the board, but understandable if one is also familiar with the concept depicted in the next diagram.

Alg.: 1 ♔e7, a7; 2 ♔d6, e4; 3 ♔c5, e3; 4 ♔b4, e2; 5 ♖e7, a1 (♕); 6 ♖:e2†, ♔b1; 7 ♖e1†, ♔b2; 8 ♖:a1, ♔:a1; 9 ♔c3+.

134

DIAGRAM 104

R. RÉTI§

KAGAN'S NEUESTE
SCHACHNACHRICHTEN

1921

=

This is the primary origin of the theme utilized in the foregoing study. Black's pawn is far ahead, White's pawn one square away from capture and the white king is out in the cold. Yet, this impression of distance is a one-dimensional illusion—White's king can choose a path which permits either one of two different maneuvers centering on the critical intersection KB6 and/or K5 (algebraically: f6 and e5). It must be seen to be believed:

1 K—N7! P—R5   2 K—B6!

Suddenly, neither of Black's plausible replies suffices to win. After 2 ... P—R6 White protects his pawn: 3 K—K6!, P—R7; 4 P—B7, K—N2; 5 K—Q7=.

Upon 2 ... K—N3; 3 K—K5!! White again resorts to either of two maneuvers:

On 3 ... K×P; 4 K—B4! The King catches Black's pawn; and on 3 ... P—R6 protects the pawn by 4 K—Q6 and both pawns then queen for a draw. Had Black played 1 ... K—N3; then 2 K—B6, P—R5; 3 K—K5, as above. It is amazing to see such a practical proof of the Pythagorean theorem of the right-angled triangle exemplified on the chess board (i.e. the sum of the squares of the two shorter sides, here KR8—K5 and K5—R2 is equal to the square of the hypotenuse, KR8—KR2). Réti's theme is also known as "extended triangulation".

Alg.: 1 ♔g7, h4; 2 ♔f6, h3; 3 ♔e6, h2; 4 c7, ♚b7; 5 ♔d7= or 2 ..., ♚b6; 3 ♔e5, ♔:c6; 4 ♔f4=.

DIAGRAM 104 (A)

F. D. YATES—
F. MARSHALL

MASTER TOURNAMENT

KARLSBAD, 1929

What result?

Superficially, the outcome of this game has been dubbed a typical Marshall "swindle", with that somewhat deprecating tenor that emphasizes the element of a lucky escape at the expense of innate vision.

With hindsight, one can indeed win here by 1 Q—B2, P—R6; 2 K—B3, K—R8; 3 Q—N3, P—N8(Q); 4 Q×P ch, Q—R7; 5 Q×Q ch, K×Q; 6 P—B4. But Yates "simplified" that seemingly over-refined handling of a basic ending:

1 K—B4 P—N8(Q)		3 K—N4
2 Q×Q ch K×Q		

All rather elementary? Black's pawn falls and White's one marches. The post-Rétian innocent would now resign, the pre-Rétian grandmaster continues.

   3 ...   K—N7!!

Naïvely playing for 4 ... P—R6, although White can, and must, take the pawn; but it's all a "feint".

   4 K×P   K—B6!!

Black's king has caught up with the effective corner square of the triangle—within which the white pawn can be diagonally reached and stopped—5 P—B4, K—Q5; 6 P—B5, K—K4, drawn.

Alg.: 1 ♚c4, b1(♛); 2 ♛:b1†, ♚:b1; 3 ♚b4, ♚b2; 4 ♚:a4, ♚c3; 5 f4, ♚d4; 6 f5, ♚e5=.

DIAGRAM 105

M. F. PALMER

IOWA NEWS

1917

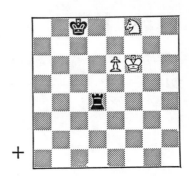

+

A forerunner to the next diagram.

1 P—K7   R—Q3 ch

If 1 ... R—K5; 2 N—K6, K—Q2; 3 N—B5 ch, wins, if
1 ... R—Q1!?; 2 K—B7!+.

2 K—N7!

If 2 K—B7, R—Q1! and White is in a squeeze with Black able
to draw.

2 ...   R—Q1   3 K—B7!

Now it is Black who, on the move, must lift the blockade and
loses.

Alg.: 1 e7, ♖d6†; 2 ♔g7, ♖d8; 3 ♔f7+.

DIAGRAM 106

R. RÉTI§

TAGESBOTE

1928

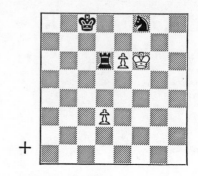

+

Fourteen years after Marvin F. Palmer's diagram 105, Réti published his own adaptation.

    1 P—Q4 R×QP

If 1 ... K—B2; 2 P—Q5, R×QP; 3 P—K7+.

    2 P—K7 R—Q3 ch   4 K—B7 wins
    3 K—N7 R—Q1

Réti can hardly have seen a piece by an unknown amateur published in the heart of the American midwest during the yet undigested war years. Réti's piece is slightly more sophisticated, but, in a strict sense, must also be considered anticipated by diagram 105.

Alg.: 1 d4, ♖:d4; 2 e7, ♖d6†; 3 ♔g7, ♖d8; 4 ♔f7+.

DIAGRAM 107

"KRUSOS"§

TIJDSCHRIFT VON DEN KON.
NEDERLANDSCHEN
SCHAAKBOND

1914

+

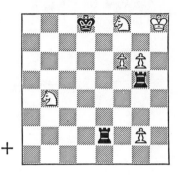

However, either Réti, or Palmer, or both, or neither of the two, may have seen the even earlier sketch drawn by "Krusos", the pseudonym of J. D. Tresling.

The difference between this diagram on the one hand, and diagrams 105–6 on the other, was in moving the vital pawn from the bishop's to the king's file, thus expanding the field of the white king's action. It transformed this merely indicative exercise into a larger, artistic effort.

    1 P—B7

Playing over 1 P—N7, R/4×P/7 soon discloses that each rook will capture each of the two remaining pawns, and the solitary two knights will only draw.

    1 ...   R/4×P/7   3 N—K6 ch R×N
    2 P—N7 R×P   4 K×R   R—K1

The familiar maneuver. White's next move prevents the rook's return to K2 with a pin.

    5 N—Q5 K—Q2!?   6 N—B6 ch wins

And this last maneuver again recalls a still earlier, yet simpler matrix by the Nestor of endgame theory, J. Berger:* (107a)

  * J. Berger, *Theorie und Praxis der Endspiele*, 1922, Example No. 339 with colors reversed.

White: K on Q8; N on K8; P on KB6.
Black: K on KR1; R on KN3.
White wins by 1 P—B7, R—N1; 2 K—K7, K—R2; 3 N—B6 ch.

Alg.: 1 f7, ♖g:g2; 2 g7, ♖:g7; 3 ♘e6†, ♖:e6; 4 ♔:g7, ♖e8; 5 ♘d5, ♔d7; 6 ♘f6†+.
   1 f7, ♖g8; 2 ♔e7,♔h7; 3 ♘f6†+.

DIAGRAM 108

M. F. PALMER

THE CHECKERIST

1926

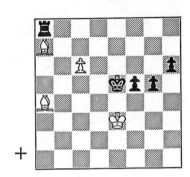

+

1 P—B7 R—QB1   2 B—Q7!

After the "natural" follow up 2 B—N8, K—Q3; 3 K—B3, P—B5! Black draws by shuttling his king between Q3 and K3. If 3 B—N5, P—R4; 4 B—R6, K—Q2; 5 B×R ch, K×B; 6 K—B2, K—N2; 7 any, K—B1=.

2 ...   R×P   4 B—R4 P—R4
3 B—N8 K—Q3

If 4 ... P—B5 ch; 5 K—B2!, P—N5; 6 K—N2, P—B6 ch; 7 K—B2, P—R4; 8 K—N3, P—R5 ch; 9 K—B2, P—R6; 10 K—N3+.

5 K—B2! P—R5   6 K—N1!! wins

Distant opposition as the focal point of the study—or, rather, a king's tempo-play against the pawns. It provides White with the needed leeway. If 6 ... P—N5; 7 K—N2, P—B5; 8 K—N1!+. All Black's pawns will fall to the solitary king and, finally, Black's king must move and abandon his rook.

Alg.: 1 c7, ♖c8; 2 ♗d7, ♖:c7; 3 ♗b8, ♚d6; 4 ♗a4, h5; 5 ♔f2, h4; 6 ♔g1, g4; 7 ♔g2, f4; 8 ♔g1 +.

D. L. PONZIANI §

IL GIUOCO INCOMPARABILE
DEGLI SCACCHI

1769

DIAGRAM 109

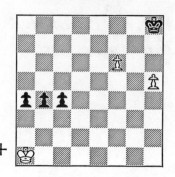

+

In diagram 108 Palmer ingeniously molds an artistic work by using an ancient device first shown by the eighteenth century Italian analyst and player Domenico Lorenzo Ponziani.

Ponziani and earlier compatriots—e.g. Damiano, Salvio del Rio, Lolli, and Cozio—and the Arabian Phillip Stamma laid a sound and often brilliant foundation of endgame theory

    1 P—R6 K—N1   2 K—N1!!

Black's pawns will outpace themselves, be stopped and fall, e.g.

2 ...	P—N6	3 K—N2! or
2 ...	P—R6	3 K—R2! or
2 ...	P—B6	3 K—B2!

Alg.: 1 h6, ♔g8; 2 ♔b1, b3; 3 ♔b2 + or 2 ... a3 (c3) 3 ♔a2 (c2)+.

DIAGRAM 110

ED. LASKER—
K. MOLL

BERLIN CHAMPIONSHIP

1909

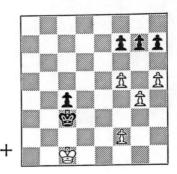

+

This again illustrates how theoretical knowledge, or the lack of it, may win or lose a practical game.

1 ...   P—R3?

Black's actual move, underestimating the danger inherent in the position. White, however, equally unaware of a hidden resource, played 2 P—B4, whereupon 2 ... P—B3!; 3 P—N5, K—Q5 lost him the game. It should have been the other way round:

2 P—B6! P×P		6 P×P K—B3
3 P—B4 K—Q5		7 K—B2 P—B6
4 P—N5 BP×P		8 K×P wins
5 P×P K—K4		

Alg.: 1 ..., h6; 2 f6, g:f6; 3 f4, ♔d4; 4 g5, f:g5; 5 f:g5, ♔e5; 6 g:h6, ♔f6; 7 ♔c2, c3; 8 ♔:c3+.

DIAGRAM 111

W. STEINITZ

*INTERNATIONAL CHESS
MAGAZINE*

1885

An Analysis by Editor

Upon adjournment of a tournament game at the Galveston (Texas) Chess Club, the above position was submitted to the then World Chess Champion for adjudication.

Steinitz's keen insight turned the game into a gem with two ingenious variations.

1 P—N6 ch K—N1

An amazing refutation meets 1 ... P×P?; 2 P—R7, K—N2; 3 P×P, K—R1; 4 K—K4, K—N2; 5 K—B4, K—R1; 6 K—K5!, K—N2! (if 6 ... P—Q6; 7 K—B6, P—Q7; 8 K—B7, P—Q8 (Q); 9 P—N7 ch, wins); 7 K—K6!!, P—Q6; 8 P—R8(Q), K×Q; 9 K—B7 wins. The final finesse recalls the identical wind-up in Steinitz' diagram 99.

2 P—B6   P×P   4 K—B3!! wins
3 K—K4! P—N4

White holds both of Black's passed pawns. Black's king is totally tied to the square which he now occupies. If he moves, either white pawn queens, but whichever of Black's pawns moves, White's king catches up. A strangling "squeeze" reminiscent of the Ponziani diagram 109.

Alg.: 1 g6†, ♚g8; 2 f6, h:g6; 3 ♚e4, g5; 4 ♚f3+.

144

DIAGRAM 112

A. J. ROYCROFT§

*TEST TUBE CHESS**

1972

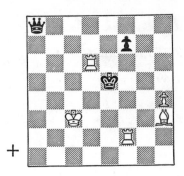

+

1 R—Q5 ch

Black planned 1 ... K×R or 1 ... Q—R6 ch. If 1 R—Q3?, Q—R4 ch; 2 K—B4, Q—R3 ch=.

   1 ... Q×R

If 1 ... K×R; 2 B—N2 ch, and 3 B×Q+.

2 R—B5 ch	K—Q3	5 P—R6	K—B3
3 R×Q ch	K×R	6 B—B5!	any move
4 P—R5	K—K4	7 P—R7 wins	

A distinctive silhouette.

---

*see Bibliography.

Alg.: 1 ♖d5†, ♕:d5; 2 ♖f5†, ♔d6; 3 ♖:d5†, ♔:d5; 4 h5, ♔e5; 5 h6, ♔f6; 6 ♗f5, ∞; 7 h7+.

DIAGRAM 113

R. E. BURGER

THE PROBLEMIST

1969

=

It needs courage to try to revive, or to get away from an ancient Ponziani, but Black's queen's knight's pawn adds new flavor in a different constellation.

1 BP×P	K—R1	7 K—N1	P—B6
2 P—R6	K—N1	8 K—R1	P—B7
3 P—N7	K—R2	9 P—R7 ch	K×P
4 P—N6 ch	K—N1	10 P—R8(Q) ch	K×Q
5 K—B1	P—R6	11 P—N7 ch	K×P
6 K—B2	P—N6 ch		stalemate

Alg.: 1 c:b6, ♚a8; 2 a6, ♚b8; 3 b7, ♚a7; 4 b6†, ♚b8; 5 ♔f1, h3; 6 ♔f2, g3†; 7 ♔g1, f3; 8 ♔h1, f2; 9 a7†, ♚:b7; 10 a8(♕)†, ♚:a8; 11 b7†, ♚:b7(=).

DIAGRAM 114

G. KOLTANOWSKI

SCHAKEND NEDERLAND

1966

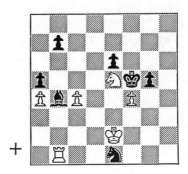

+

Another exploit by the same versatile player-composer as met in diagram 57, but more refined and seasoned

    1 P×P K×N

Preferring a knight capture to a pawn capture which would not help either, e.g. 1 ... K×P; 2 R×N, B×R; 3 N—B3 ch and 4 N×B wins.

    2 R×B P×R   4 P—R5
    3 K×N K—B4

If 4 P—B5?, P—K4; 5 P—B6, P×P; 6 P—R5, P—N6; 7 K—Q1, P—K5; 8 P—R6, P—K6; 9 P—R7, P—N7; 10 K—B2, P—N8(Q) ch!; 11 K × Q, P—K7=.

    4 ...   P—K4   5 P—R6! P×P

Necessary—but Black thus gives White a tempo.

    6 P—B5 P—N6   8 P—B6 P—K6
    7 K—Q1 P—K5   9 P—B7 wins

If 9 ... P—K7 ch; 10 K×P, P—N7; 11 P—B8(Q), promoting with a check. White's and Black's mutual pawn advances echo each other. They also illustrate an intriguing motif occasionally occurring in composition and in practice of an "opposing" echo. Here the tug of war is between pairs of pawns spread even wider apart than in diagrams 109, 113, etc. (The solution originally supplied by the author, was further elaborated by *Schakend* editor Spinhoven.)

Alg.: 1 f:g5, ♔:e5; 2 ♖:b4, a:b4; 3 ♔:e1, ♔f5; 4 a5, e5; 5 a6, b:a6; 6 c5, b3; 7 ♔d1, e4; 8 c6, e3; 9 c7+.

DIAGRAM 115

W. A. SHINKMAN

THE GOLDEN ARGOSY

1929

Black is a rook up and 1 Q—B3 ch, B—B4 dis. ch; or 1 R—Q6 ch, R × R; 2 Q × R ch, Q—K3; or 1 B—R4 ch, K—K3; 2 Q—N4 ch, B—B4 dis. ch are of no help to White.

    1 B × P ch! K—K3

If 1 ... K—B4; 2 Q—R5 ch, K—K5; 3 Q—K2 ch, K × R; 4 Q × P ch, K—K3; 5 Q—K8 ch with a perpetual spin in the outer sphere.

    2 R—Q6 ch, R × R   3 Q × R ch K—B4

3 ... K—B2; 4 Q—B6 ch, K—K1; 5 Q—B6 ch, etc., etc., draws by repetitive queen checks.

    4 Q—B6 ch K—K5   5 Q—B4 ch K—Q4

5 ... K—Q6; 6 Q—Q4 ch, K—K7; 7 Q—N4 ch, K—K8 (7 ... K—Q7; 8 Q—B4 ch, K—Q8; 9 Q—B1 ch =); 8 B—B3 ch, K—B7; 9 Q—B4 ch, K—K7; 10 Q—N4 ch, K—K6; 11 Q—Q4 ch, K—K7; 12 Q—N4 ch =.

    6 Q—Q4 ch K—K3   7 Q—Q6 ch K—B4

with a perpetual check in the inner orbit. Another case of revolving doors.

Alg.: 1 ♗:e5†, ♔e6; 2 ♖d6†, ♖:d6; 3 ♕:d6†, ♔f5; 4 ♕f6†, ♔e4; 5 ♕f4†, ♔d5; 6 ♕d4†, ♔e6; 7 ♕d6†, ♔f5=.

DIAGRAM 116

H. OTTEN

THE BOY'S OWN PAPER

1890

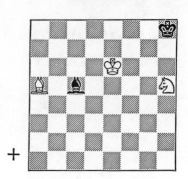

+

Another example from early days and still much alive as a forerunner of later efforts, as will be shown in the following two diagrams.

   1 B—B3 ch   K—R2

Clearly not 1 ... K—N1; 2 N—B6 ch, K—N2 (or B1); 3 N—Q7 dis. ch, winning.

   2 K—B7   B—R6

It is fascinating to watch how White dominates the scene with such frugal means. If Black tries to get away with 2 ... K—R3, then 3 N—B6 threatens 4 B—Q2 mate. Upon 3 ... K—N4; 4 N—K4 ch or 3 ... B—K6; 4 N—N4 ch, White captures the bishop. The same turn works if first 2 ... B—K6 (or B7); 3 N—B6 ch and 4 N—N4 dis. ch.

    Therefore, Black's bishop moves out of range and out of reach—but also out of action

   3 N—B6 ch   K—R1   5 B—N7 wins
   4 N—K8 dis. ch K—R2

Alg.: 1 ♗c3†, ♔h7; 2 ♔f7, ♗a3; 3 ♘f6†, ♔h8; 4 ♘e8†, ♔h7; 5 ♗g7+.

DIAGRAM 117

J. E. PECKOVER

GUNST* MEMORIAL TOURNEY

1959

1st Hon. Mention

+

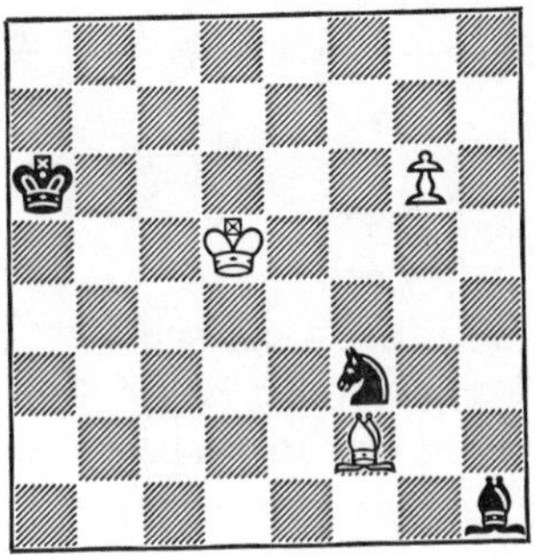

Here the constellation is different from diagram 116, with the knight for the defense.

   1 P—N7 N—R5 dis. ch   2 K—B5

White's king must remain in the vicinity of his square Q5, to prevent Black's bishop from occupying it and foiling the pawn promotion. (However, 2 K—B4 serves the same purpose and constitutes what is known as a "minor dual"—a dual that may be condoned if all other facets of the study are as impeccable as here.)

   2 ...   B—Q4!!

A bait, which is forced upon Black as the only means of stopping the pawn for the time being; but it also lures White's king on to a square that is becoming critical in another respect. For a similar distraction see diagrams 84 and 85.

   3 K×B N—B4!   4 P—N8(N)!!

Obviously 4 P—N8 (R or Q) would have allowed a draw by 4 ... N—K2 ch, as the outcome of White's king standing on Q5 (d5). The under-promotion to a knight creates a miniature of one versus two minor pieces, usually drawn.

151

But Black's night is immobilized by the bishop on the lower part, and by White's knight on the upper part of the playing field. All its escape routes are being cut off in circular motion.

4 ...	K—N2	6 N—B6!	
5 K—K5	N—N2		

Effecting a change-over in the sphere of domination. Now the knight controls the white-colored flight squares. With everything else in suspense, only the king is left with some limited freedom of movement.

6 ...	K—B2	7 B—R4!	

A grand waiting move and at the same time a stalking killer. 7 ... K—Q1 fails for 8 N—R5 dis. ch+. Black's struggle is fading out.

7 ...	K—B1	9 B—R6 wins	
8 B—N5	K—B2		

* Finnish composer 1896–1958.

Alg.: 1 g7, ♘h4†; 2 ♔c5, ♗d5; 3 ♔:d5, ♘f5; 4 g8(♘), ♔b7; 5 ♔e5, ♘g7; 6 ♘f6, ♔c7; 7 ♗h4, ♔c8; 8 ♗g5, ♔c7; 9 ♗h6+.

DIAGRAM 118

J. E. PECKOVER

TIDSKRIFT FÖR SCHACK

1962

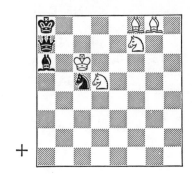

+

Despite the contrast in the settings, the austere positional strangulation in the previous diagram is the leading factor also here; this time as the offspring of a crude but mighty combinational prelude.

Composers often vary the style and model of their works, to adapt them to varied tastes.

1 N—N6 ch	Q×N ch	3 K×B N×B	
2 K×Q	N—Q2 ch		

Again, a miniature of minor pieces but with the kings so far removed that effective control seems out of the question. It is the hallmark of an artistic study that it defies established theory and proves the unlikely to be true in the face of insuperable odds.

4 N—K5!!	K—N1	7 K—Q6	K—K1
5 K—N6	K—B1	8 B—B7 ch	K—Q1
6 K—B6	K—Q1	9 B—R5!	N—R2

If 9 ... K—B1; 10 K—K7, N—R2; 11 N—B7 and 12 B—N6+.

10 N—B7 ch	K—K1	12 N—K6 ch!!	
11 N—N5 dis. ch	K—B1		

An astonishing reversal of the "natural" course. If 12 N×N ch, K—N2; 13 N—N5, K—R3 with a draw.

12 ...	K—N1	14 B—B7 wins	
13 K—K7	K—R1		

Alg.: 1 ♘b6† ♕:b6†; 2 ♔:b6, ♘d7†; 3 ♔:a6, ♘:f8; 4 ♘e5, ♔b8; 5 ♔b6, ♔c8; 6 ♔c6, ♔d8; 7 ♔d6, ♔e8; 8 ♗f7†, ♔d8; 9 ♗h5, ♘h7; 10 ♘f7†, ♔e8; 11 ♘g5†, ♔f8; 12 ♘e6†, ♔g8; 13 ♔e7, ♔h8; 14 ♗f7+.

DIAGRAM 119

C. H. HATHAWAY

LASKER'S CHESS MAGAZINE

JUNE, 1908

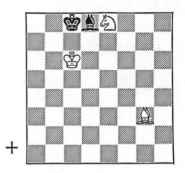

+

Already a "modern", concisely structured, "realistic" miniature. A sharp point is brought out with minimal material. Normally, two pieces versus one do not suffice to win.

1 B—K5 B—K2		3 N—B6 B—R6
2 B—B7 B—B1 (or N5)		4 N—Q5 wins

If 1 ... B—R5; 2 N—Q6 ch, K—Q1; 3 B—Q4!+.
If 1 ... B—R4; 2 N—Q6 ch, and 3 N—N7+.

Hathaway's presentation is an improved version of a faulty endgame by Jan Kotrč (*Deutsche Schachzeitung*, December 1896, example 738).

Diagram 118 has been frequently reproduced with the identical solution, but in variously changed settings, e.g. *American Chess Bulletin*, August 1912, p. 185; or in R. Rey Ardid, *Finales de Ajedrez* (1945), Vol. II, p. 189. Keidanz quotes the same position, referring to some more elementary forerunners of Cook's, not included in this volume.

Alg.: 1 ♗e5, ♗e7; 2 ♗c7, ♗f8; 3 ♘f6, ♗a3; 4 ♘d5+.

DIAGRAM 120

S. ALMGREN

CHESS REVIEW

1937

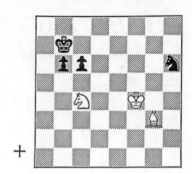

+

One of a series of up-to-date positional studies. With material so reduced and rather balanced, a win looks unlikely—but Sven Almgren proves otherwise.

    1 K—K5! N—B2 ch!

Best. White wins more easily after either line 1 ... N—N1?; 2 K—K6, P—N4; 3 N—K3, P—N5; 4 K—B7, P—N6; 5 B—K5, N—R3 ch; 6 K—N7, N—B4 ch; 7 N×N, P—B4; 8 N—K3 and 9 N—Q1!+. Or 1 ... N—N5 ch?; 2 K—B5, N—R3 ch; 3 K—N6, N—N5; 4 K—N5!+

2 K—B6	P—N4	5 N—B5	N—N2
3 N—K3	N—Q1	6 K—K8!	N—any
4 K—K7	K—B1	7 N—Q6 ch!	

winning Black's knight by discovered check, and the game. Black survives after 1 K—N5?, N—N1!; 2 B—Q6, K—B1 and K—Q1=; or 1 N—Q6 ch?, K—B2; 2 K—N5, N—N1 and ... K—Q2=.

Alg.: 1 ♔e5, ♘f7†; 2 ♔f6, b5; 3 ♘e3, ♘d8; 4 ♔e7, ♔c8; 5 ♘f5, ♘b7; 6 ♔e8, ♘∞; 7 ♘d6†+.

DIAGRAM 120 (A)

E. B. COOK

From: H. Keidanz,

THE CHESS COMPOSITIONS OF E. B. COOK

NEW YORK, 1927

+

The win with bishop and knight against bishop was systematically explored in J. Kling and B. Horwitz *Chess Studies* (London, 1851) but it did not deter composers from searching for other, unique, set-ups which may require a specific maneuver at a precise moment.

        1 N—N6

The key-move which wins against both Black's defenses.

(A) 1 ...   B—Q7   3 N—B4 B—N5(or R4)
    2 N—Q5 B—K8(or R4)   4 N—Q3
    White threatens 5 N—B1 mate, and if 4 ... B—Q7; 5 K × B wins.

(B) 1 ...   B—K6   4 N—Q3 B—Q7
    2 N—R4 B—Q7   5 K × B wins
    3 N—B5 B—any

Alg.: (A) 1 ♘b6, ♝d2; 2 ♘d5, ♝e1; 3 ♘f4, ♝b4; 4 ♘d3+.
      (B) 1 ♘b6, ♝e3; 2 ♘a4, ♝d2; 3 ♘c5, ♝∞; 4 ♘d3, ♝d2; 5 ♔:d2 +.

DIAGRAM 121

S. ALMGREN

CHESS REVIEW

1937

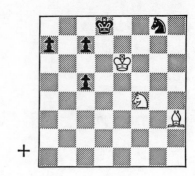

+

A paraphrase of the strategy shown in diagram 120. The full exploration of all facets of a given topic is very instructive for students of practical play.

1 K—B7	N—K2	2 K—B8

aiming at 3 N—K6 ch, K—Q2; 4 N—N5 dis. ch, K—Q3; 5 N—B7 ch+.

2 ...	N—B3	4 N × P/5 dis. ch K—N1
3 N—K6 ch K—B1		5 N—Q7 ch K—N2
		6 B—N2 wins

If 5 ... K—B1; 6 N—K5, dis. ch+.

Of no avail is 3 ... K—Q2; 4 N—N5 dis. ch, K—Q3; 5 N—B7 ch, K—Q4; 6 B—N2 ch, K—Q5; 7 B × N, P—B5; 8 K—K7, P—B6; 9 B—R4, K—Q6; 10 N—K5 ch, K—Q7 (10 ... K—Q5; 11 N—B3 ch and N—K1—B2+); 11 N—B4 ch, K—any; 12 N—R3 and wins.

In here, if 9 ... K—B5; 10 N—K5 ch, K—N5; 11 B—Q1, K—R6; 12 N—Q3, P—B4; 13 N × P, K—N7; 14 N—Q3 ch, K—N8; 15 N—K1, K—B8; 16 B—R4 and 17 N—B2+.

Alg.: 1 ♔f7, ♘e7; 2 ♔f8, ♘c6; 3 ♘e6†, ♚c8; 4 ♘:c5†, ♚b8; 5 ♘d7† ♚b7; 6 ♗g2+.

DIAGRAM 122

S. ALMGREN

CHESS REVIEW

1941

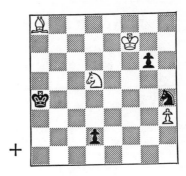

Featuring minor-piece strategy in a complex variety of forms. The impressive main line, with the final forks, runs:

1 N—K3 K—N6	4 B—B2 ch! K×B
2 B—K4 N—B4!?*	5 N—K3 ch wins
3 N×N! P—Q8(Q)	

Or 4 ... Q×B; 5 N—Q4 ch+. "Simply" splendid.

---

* A belated question arises, however, as to a win after 2 ... K—B6; 3 B x P, K—Q5; 4 N—Q1, K—K4; 5 B—R5; K—B5; 6 B—N4 ch, K—N6; 7 N—B3, K—B7.

Alg.: 1 ♘e3, ♚b3; 2 ♗e4, ♘f5; 3 ♘:f5, d1(♕); 4 ♗c2†, ♚:c2; 5 ♘e3†+.

DIAGRAM 123

S. ALMGREN

CHESS REVIEW

1941

$+$

Black's wide-ranging bishop seems free to move between the long or short diagonals so as to prevent White's pawn from queening. White dislodges the piece partly by control of the protective squares, partly by well-timed temporizing. Every move counts.

　1 N—B4

Taking control of Black's direct access square N7, the indirect access squares Q7 and K6, and the square K4, thus making the defence 1 ... B—B5 useless, and if 1 ... B—N4; 2 K—N7 wins.

1 ...	B—R3	3 K—N8	B—R3
2 K—R7	B—B1	4 N—K5!	

threatens to dominate all access squares by 5 N—N4! and if then 5 ... B—B8; 6 K—B7, B—N7; 7 N—B6 wins. The same procedure applies even if Black delays by 4 ... P—B5; 5 N×P, K—N4; 6 N—K5+. Upon 4 ... K—N4; 5 N—N4, P—B5; White seems to waste precious time in promoting his pawn, but Black's apparent lead is an illusion, e.g. 6 N×B, P—B6; 7 N—B5!, K—B5 (if 7 ... P—B7; 8 N—Q4 ch); 8 N—K3 ch, K—Q6; 9 N—Q5, K—B5 (9 ... P—B7; 10 N—N4 ch); 10 N × P wins.

4 ...	K—R2	5 K—R8!	

Now the scene shifts to tempo play. Premature is 5 N—N4 at once, e.g. 5 ... P—B5!; 6 N×B, P—B6 with a draw.

| 5 ... | B–B1 | 6 K—R7! K—R3 (or N2) |

If 6 ... K—R1?; 7 N—Q7, P—B5; 8 N×B, P—B6; 9 P—N7, P—B7; 10 P—N8(Q), P—B8(Q); 11 N—Q7, dis. ch winning the queen or mating in three.

7 N—Q7	P—B5!	10 N—B5 ch K—any
8 N×B	P—B6	11 N—Q3 wins
9 N—K6	P—B7	

Alg.: 1 ♘c4, ♗h6; 2 ♔h7, ♗f8; 3 ♔g8, ♗h6; 4 ♘e5, ♔a7; 5 ♔h8, ♗f8; 6 ♔h7, ♔a6(b7); 7 ♘d7, c4; 8 ♘:f8, c3; 9 ♘e6, c2; 10 ♘c5†, ♔∞; 11 ♘d3+.

DIAGRAM 124

OSCAR WEINBERGER

BRITISH CHESS MAGAZINE

JUNE, 1961

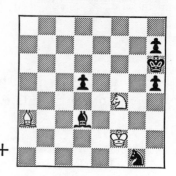

+

A virtuoso who has sprung a number of unique inventions on the world or chess art—and was awarded quite a few "Oscars" for them. Dealing with a similar precept, this diagram is not so tight as Almgren's No. 123 but it has a more combinative flair.

    1 B—B8 ch! K—N4

If 1 K×N, B any=. If N×B, N—R6 ch; 2 K—N3, N—N4=.

2 N×B	N—R6 ch	4 N—B1 P—Q5
3 K—N3	N—N8	

If 4 ... K—B4; 5 K—N2, K—K5; 6 K×N, P—Q5; 7 B—R6, P—Q6; 8 N—N3, K—any; 9 N—Q2+.

5 B—B5	P—Q6	7 B—K3 ch wins
6 B×N	P—Q7	

The music of chess.

Alg.: 1 ♗f8†, ♚g5; 2 ♘:d3, ♘h3†; 3 ♚g3, ♘g1; 4 ♘c1, d4; 5 ♗c5, d3; 6 ♗:g1, d2; 7 ♗e3†+.

DIAGRAM 125

S. ALMGREN

CHESS REVIEW

1941

=

Black is an aggressively placed exchange up and strategically poised for a win.

Upon 1 P—N7, R—Q1!; 2 N—B8, P×P; 3 P—N8(Q), P—N8(Q) Black wins by simple tactics.

1 P—N4 ch! P×P		3 K—N8	B—B5 ch
2 P—N7	B—Q6 ch		

3 K—N7?, R—QN7 easily wins for Black.

4 K—R7	B—N1 ch	5 K—N7!

If 5 K×B?, R—Q1 ch; and 6 ... R—QN1+.

5 ...	R—QN7	7 P—N8(Q) R×Q
6 N—N5!	R×N	

with a "pure" stalemate! A beautiful conclusion.

Alg.: 1 g4†, f:g4; 2 b7, ♗d3†; 3 ♔g8, ♗c4†; 4 ♔h7, ♗g8†; 5 ♔g7, ♖b2; 6 ♘b5; ♖:b5; 7 b8(♕), ♖:b8⊜.

Types, Styles and Classification of Endgame Study

There have been many attempts to categorize studies—by content or style, by historical development or type, by structure or technique, but the undertaking has remained for the most part in the realm of semantics, beyond satisfactory definition.

André Chéron, for example, merely draws a line between didactic endings (of utilitarian purpose) and artistic endgames constructed for beauty. But this distinction oversimplifies, under the subjective captions, a great multiplicity of composition types.

Historically, endgame studies have found their inspiration in two sources. One, the didactic, derives from the analytical or theoretical endings contrived by the old masters of chess of more than two centuries ago (see diagrams 67 and 109) and links up directly with the modern positional study.

The other source was the schematic treatment borrowed from problem composition. Cook's diagram 4 or Loyd's diagrams 17 and 19 are of this class. As a next step, an ornamental, decorative species was added, with romantic overtones—such as diagram 28 (Petrov), or diagram 29 (Cook). To our taste, they have a touch of the stereotype.

Meanwhile, the positional study established itself as a natural habitat for the artistic endgame. In its more elementary forms it has also been called "classic", a rather chronological term and somewhat meaningless as a functional description. The term "natural" or "realistic" has become more acceptable for studies with a surprising turn capping a linear development (diagrams 13, 100, 120, etc.) and "artistic" for more complex textures (diagrams 81, 112, etc.).

However, striking a balance between the decorative-schematic specimen and the tightly structured, but more game-like positional study, the "combinational" style interposed itself, e.g. diagrams 126 and 127. This trend, in turn, builds bridges to the "neo-Romantic" and "thematic" studies also widely explored throughout against a varied backgound, as in diagrams 24 and 25.

These stylistic norms are satisfactory for the overall enjoyment of a strong player and reader, but with the accumulation of sources, outlets, and composing activity, the breakdown by appearance is in many respects inadequate. The discriminating connoisseur welcomes the chance for wide comparison of compositions of different types; the methodical composer, or the tourney judge, needs a "memory bank" that recalls antici-pations or various interpretations of a given theme containing varying material (diagrams 140 and 141 are a proper case in point).

These demands call for more exact classifications that interlock the kind of material, strategy, tactical means and effect, and meaningful clarification of themes—a task which is in progress but as yet unresolved. Bondarenko, Fritz, Harmon, Kasparian, Korolkov, Troitsky and others achieved a degree of codification which was summarized by A. J. Roycroft.*

* see Bibliography.

DIAGRAM 126

W. KORN

BRITISH CHESS MAGAZINE

1944

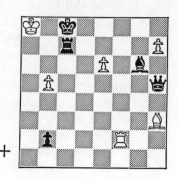

+

A case of deflections and sacrificial combinations against a lot of odds.

1 P—R8(Q) ch	Q×Q	3 P—K7 dis. ch	Q—B4
2 R—B8 ch	Q×R	4 B×Q ch	R—Q2!

If 4 P—K8(Q) ch, B×Q; 5 B×Q ch, B—Q2; 6 B—N1, R—B6+.

5 P—N6!	P—N8(Q)	7 B×B	drawn
6 B×Q!	R×P		

Alg.: 1 h8(♕)†, ♕:h8; 2 ♖f8†, ♕:f8; 3 e7†, ♕f5; 4 ♗:f5†, ♖d7; 5 b6, b1 (♕); 6 ♗:b1, ♖:e7; 7 ♗:g6=.

DIAGRAM 127

W. KORN

MANCHESTER GUARDIAN

MAY 11, 1950

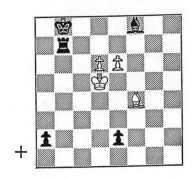

+

The value here rests more with lines that should *not* be played during this series of multiple coronation of queens.

If 1 P—Q7 dis. ch, K—R2; 2 B—K3 ch (2 P—Q8(Q), P—K8(Q)=), K—R3; 3 Q—Q8(Q), P—K8(Q); 4 Q—R8 ch, K—N4; 5 Q×R ch, K—R5; 6 Q—B6 ch, K—N6=.

  1 P—K7! P—K8(Q)!

If 1 ... R—N4 ch; 2 K—B6, P—K8(Q); 3 P × B(Q) ch! K—R2; 4 Q—K7 ch wins. But 3 P—K8(Q) ch? Q × Q; 4 P—Q7 dis. ch, K—R2; 5 P × Q(Q), P—R8(Q); 6 B—K3 ch, B—B4! draws.

  2 P—K8(Q) ch!!

If 2 P×B(Q) ch, K—R7=.

2 ...	Q×Q	4 P×Q(Q)	P—R8(Q)
3 P—Q7 dis. ch	K—R2	5 B—K3 ch	wins

Alg.: 1 e7, e1(♛); 2 e8(♛)†, ♛:e8; 3 d7†, ♚a7; 4 d:e8(♛), a1(♛); 5 ♗e3†+.

DIAGRAM 128

J. KLING§

CHESS EUCLID

LONDON, 1849

"White mates without moving his king".

Normally, in a position as given, White mates within five moves, starting with 1 Q—Q2 and 2 K—Q5, etc.

The composer's condition "without moving his king" transforms the task into a formalistic ending. The solution has lengthy sidelines, but the course is clear, e.g.

1 Q—R6 ch	K—N7	6 Q—K6	K—Q6
2 Q—R4	K—N8	7 Q—K1	K—Q5
3 Q—R3	K—B7	8 Q—K2	K—B6
4 Q—N4	K—K6	9 Q—Q1	etc.
5 Q—B5	K—Q5		

Black's king is gradually driven to his QR4 square and mated there. This early detail is enlarged into a broader fresco in the following diagrams.

Alg.: 1 ♕h6†, ♔g2; 2 ♕h4, ♔g1; 3 ♕h3, ♔f2; 4 ♕g4, ♔e3; 5 ♕f5, ♔d4; 6 ♕e6, ♔d3; 7 ♕e1, ♔d4; 8 ♕e2, ♔c3; 9 ♕d1 etc.+.

DIAGRAM 129

S. LOYD

AMERICAN CHESS JOURNAL

MARCH, 1878

From Story "The Diamond
Castle"

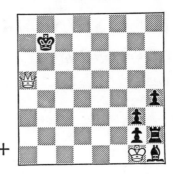

+

Loyd picked up the idea in diagram 128 and re-structured it
into a straight and "unconditional" ending.

1 Q—QB5	K—N1	3 Q—N5	K—R1
2 Q—B6	K—R2	4 Q—N6!	R—R6

As Black's king has been de-activated, the rook must move and
becomes vulnerable.

5 Q—Q8 ch	K—R2	7 Q×R
6 Q—Q7 ch	K—R1	

Now the queen captures the pawns on R4 and N3, then again
forces the black king into any corner; White's king moves to
R2, forcing the knight's pawn to move, and Black may then
resign.

Alg.: 1 ♕c5, ♔b8; 2 ♕c6, ♔a7; 3 ♕b5, ♔a8; 4 ♕b6, ♖h3; 5 ♕d8†,
♔a7; 6 ♕d7†, ♔a8; 7 ♕:h3 ∞; 8 ♕:h4, ∞; 9 ♕:g3, ∞; 10
♔h2+.

DIAGRAM 130

W. A. SHINKMAN

PITTSBURGH POST

1923

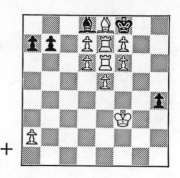

+

Shinkman excelled in these paradoxical "shut-ins". He molded Kling's matrix into yet another shape.

Black threatens 1 ... P—N4, with rapid promotion. By preventing Black from queening too early, White gains the time needed to invent a saving clause.

1 P—R4!	P—N3	6 K—R6	P—N6
2 K—N4	P—R3	7 K—R7	P—N7
3 K×P	P—N4	8 K—R8!	P—N8(R or
4 P×P	P×P		B or N)
5 K—R5!	P—N5	9 K—R7	draw

If 8 ... P—N8(Q or B) stalemate, and that is the crux. Only a black queen could have forced the win, as she could drive the king back on to KR8 (h8) by cutting off his retreats, finally mating by Q—R6. But the untimely stalemate prevents Black from using this device and he has no other waiting move to fall back on.

Tricky configurations of this kind also permit another mental exercise; how to reconstruct a real game, ending up with this position.

Alg.: 1 a4, b6; 2 ♔g4, a6; 3 ♔:h4, b5; 4 a:b5, a:b5; 5 ♔h5, b4; 6 ♔h6, b3; 7 ♔h7, b2; 8 ♔h8, b1 (♖ or ♗ or ♘); 9 ♔h7=.

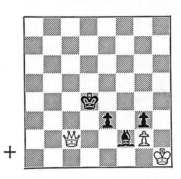

DIAGRAM 131

I. A. HOROWITZ

CHESS REVIEW

1943

+

Subsequent to Kling's diagram 128 and Loyd's and Shinkman's diagrams 129 and 130, two more novelettes were created by I. Horowitz in 1943, and even more artistically by the Roumanian P. Joita in *Revista de Şah* in 1954—both with a modern positional face. In Horowitz's piece, reproduced here, the now familiar plan is to secure first the release of White's king by driving Black's king into any corner, e.g.

1 Q—B5	K—B5		7 Q—B3	K—R7
2 Q—K4 ch	K—B6		8 Q—N4	K—R8
3 Q—Q5	K—B7		9 Q—N3	P—K7
4 Q—Q4	K—B8		10 Q—B3 ch	K—N8
5 Q—Q3	K—N7		11 Q—Q3 ch	
6 Q—B4	K—N8			

Winning the king's pawn.

The same process of stalemating the king forces the bishop to move to K8 (otherwise White wins the knight's pawn), and be captured likewise by a series of checks.

Alg.: 1 ♕f5, ♚c4; 2 ♕e4†, ♚c3; 3 ♕d5, ♚c2; 4 ♕d4, ♚c1; 5 ♕d3, ♚b2; 6 ♕c4, ♚b1; 7 ♕c3, ♚a2; 8 ♕b4, ♚a1; 9 ♕b3, e2; 10 ♕c3†, ♚b1; 11 ♕d3†+.

DIAGRAM 132

E. B. COOK

INTERNATIONAL CHESS
MAGAZINE

1886

=

In wide open space, White's rook succeeds with a perpetual sacrificial merry-go-round—avoiding any capture by the queen, which would lift the stalemate.

1 R—R7 ch K—N1	8 R—R5 ch K—Q5
2 B—N3! Q×B	9 R—R4 ch K—K4
3 R—R8 ch K—N2	10 R—R5 ch K—B5
4 R—R7 ch K—N3	11 R—R4 ch K—N4
5 R—R6 ch K—N4	12 R—R5 ch K—R5
6 R—R5 ch K—N5	13 R×P ch K—N5
7 R—R4 ch K—B4	14 R—N5 ch drawn

A masterly specimen of great simplicity.

Alg.: 1 ♖a7†, ♚b8; 2 ♗g3, ♛:g3; 3 ♖a8†, ♚b7; 4 ♖a7†, ♚b6; 5 ♖a6†, ♚b5; 6 ♖a5†, ♚b4; 7 ♖a4†, ♚c5; 8 ♖a5†, ♚d4; 9 ♖a4†, ♚e5; 10 ♖a5†, ♚f4; 11 ♖a4†, ♚g5; 12 ♖a5†, ♚h4; 13 ♖:h5†, ♚g4; 14 ♖g5†=.

R. BRIEGER

SCHACH-ECHO

1960

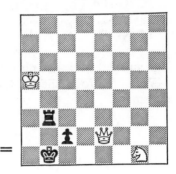

DIAGRAM 133

In this later adaptation of the same basic thought as in diagram 132 White, reversing the roles, succeeds in breaking the deadlock. In addition, the study contains some subtle tries.

1 K—R4   R—K6!   3 Q—B5!
2 Q—N5 ch K—R8

If 3 Q—B1 ch, K—N7; 4 N—K2, R—K5 ch!; 5 K—N5, R×N; 6 Q×R, K—R8!

3 ... K—N7   4 Q—N4 ch

If 4 Q—Q4 ch, K—N8; 5 Q—N6 ch?, K—R7; 6 Q × R, P—B8(Q); 7 Q × Q ⊜.

4 ... K—R7

If 4 ... K—R8; 5 Q—Q2!, K—N8; 6 N—K2, R —K5 ch; (if 6 ... R×N; 7 Q×R, P—B8(Q); 8 K—N3 wins); 7 K—R3, R×N; 8 Q×R, P—B8(Q); 9 K—N3+.

5 Q—B4 ch K—R8*   8 K—B4   R—N5 ch
6 Q×P   R—R6 ch   9 K—Q3   R—N6 ch
7 K—N4   R—N6 ch   10 K—Q4   R—N5 ch

* The position following Black's fifth move is the version reproduced in R. Brieger's booklet (example No. 54).

11	K—K3	R—N6 ch	15 K—N4	R—B5 ch
12	K—B4	R—N5 ch	16 K—N5	R—N5 ch
13	K—N3	R—N6 ch	17 K—B6	R—B5 ch
14	N—B3!	R×N ch	18 K—K5!	wins

The suicidal rook has no more useful checks.

When the rook checks, the queen captures and dissolves the stalemate.

Alg.: 1 ♔a4, ♖e3; 2 ♕b5†, ♔a1; 3 ♕c5!, ♔b2; 4 ♕b4†, ♔a2; 5 ♕c4†, ♔a1; 6 ♕:c2, ♖a3†; 7 ♔b4, ♖b3†; 8 ♔c4, ♖b4†; 9 ♔d3, ♖b3†; 10 ♔d4, ♖b4†; 11 ♔e3, ♖b3†; 12 ♔f4, ♖b4†; 13 ♔g3, ♖b3†; 14 ♘f3!, ♖:f3†; 15 ♔g4, ♖f4†; 16 ♔g5, ♖g4†; 17 ♔f6, ♖f4†; 18 ♔e5+.

DIAGRAM 134

W. KORN

BRITISH CHESS MAGAZINE

1940

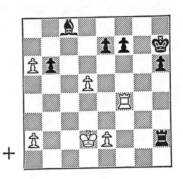

+

A combinational prelude to sophisticated theoretical lines. The plain 1 R×P ch, ends in failure. 1 ... K—N3; 2 P—R7, K×R; 3 P—R8(Q), B—N5!; 4 Q—B6, R×P ch; 5 K—Q3, R×P with a book draw, or 4 Q—N7, R×P ch; 5 K—Q3, R—K8!; 6 Q—B6, R—KB8; 7 Q×P, R—B3=, or 6 Q×P, R—KB8; 7 Q×P, R—B3; 8 Q—R7 ch, K—B1; 9 P—R4, B—Q2; 10 P—R5, B—N4 ch; 11 K—Q4, B—R3= and Black's fortress remains impenetrable. Hence:

1 P—R7	B—N2	6 R×B	R—QR1
2 P—Q6!	R—R4!	7 R×P ch	K—any
3 P×P	R—K4	8 R—N7 and White
4 R×P ch	K—N3		wins easily
5 P—K8(Q) R×Q			

But this study is more remarkable for its false leads or "tries" or simply for what White may *not* do, e.g. (1 P—R7, B—N2); 2 R×P ch, K—N3; 3 P—Q6, K×R; 4 P—Q7, B—B6!! (refer to sub-diagram 134 (A) with a draw after either—

(*a*) 5 K—Q3, B×P ch; 6 K—K3, B—B6; 7 P—Q8(Q), R×P; 8 Q×R, or 7 K×B=. Or

(*b*) 5 K—K3, R×P ch; 6 K—Q3, R—K3=; or 6 K×B, R—Q7; 7 P—R8(Q), R×P; and 8 ... R—Q3=. Or

(*c*) 5 P—R8(Q), B×Q: 6 P—Q8(Q), B—B6; 7 Q×NP, R×P ch; 8 K—Q3, R—K3 and 9 ... R—KB3=.

175

Altogether the subject revolves around the theoretical draw of rook and pawn versus queen.

A tempting move that fails is designated a "try".

Alg.: 1 a7, ♗b7; 2 d6, ♖h5; 3 d:e7, ♖e5; 4 ♖:f7†, ♔g6; 5 e8(♕), ♖:e8; 6 ♖:b7, ♖a8; 7 ♖:b6†, ♔ any; 8 ♖b7+.

W. KORN

DIAGRAM 134 (A)

=

Diagram No. 134 may be viewed as a conglomerate of an overture, simple main play, and a remarkable try which, if ignored, may lose its full impact.

Therefore, composers may isolate such a typical try and draw attention to it as an independent segment in the way shown here.

The colors are reversed, with the danger of a loss becoming a demand for a draw.

   1 B—B6!!

If 1 R—R4, P—K8(N) ch; and 2 ... N×B wins for Black.

   1 ... K—K3!

Easier to defend are:

(A) 1 ... P—K8(Q); 2 R×P ch, and 3 R—Q3=; or
(B) 1 ... K—Q3; 2 R×P ch, K×B! (2 ... K—K3; 3 R—Q3,
    P—K8(Q); 4 R—QB3=); 3 R—K7, P—R8(Q); 4 R×KP,
    and 5 R—K3=; or
(C) 1 ... P—R8(Q); 2 B×Q, P—K8(Q); 3 B—B6, Q×P;
    4 R×P ch, K—K3; 5 R—Q3, Q—N3 (5 ... Q—B2;
    6 R—QB3); 6 K—B3, Q—B3 ch; 7 K—N3=.

   2 B×P ch! K—Q3   3 B—B6!!

Returning to the crucial square. Black cannot win after
(A) 3 ... P—K8(Q); 4 R×P, Q×P (or 4 ... K×B; 5 R×P,
  Q×NP; 6 R—K2, Q×P; 7 R—K3=); 5 B—K4, Q—K4;
  6 P—Q3=.
(B) 3 ... K×B; 4 R×P (4 R—K7, P—R8(Q); 5 R×KP, and
  6 R—K3=), 4 ... P—K8(Q); 5 R×P, Q×P; 6 R—K2 =.
In reverse, White overcomes the same kind of defense in
position 134(a):
W. Korn, *British Chess Magazine* 1942 (amended). White to
move and win.

White: K on KR5; Ps on QR7, K7, KR7.
Black: K on Q3; R on KR1; P on Q2.

1 K—N6   R—K1

If 1 ... R—R1; 2 K—B7 +. If 1 ... K×P; 2 K—N7, R—R1;
3 P—R8(Q), R×P; 4 Q—B8ch +.

2 P—QR8(Q)

Not 2 K—B7, R×Pch; 3 K—B8, R×P; 4 K—N8, R—K2;
5 P—R8(Q), R—K3=.

| 2 ... | R×Q | 4 P—K8(Q) | R×P ch |
| 3 K—B7 | R—R1 | 5 K—N6 | R—R6(or R8) |

If 5 ... R—R5; 6 K—B5, R—QB5; 7 Q—N8ch, R—B2;
8 K—B6+.

6 Q—K4!   K—B2   7 K—B7 wins.

Alg.: 1 ♗c6, ♔e6; 2 ♗:d7†, ♔d6; 3 ♗c6=.

J. E. PECKOVER

SZACHY

JULY, 1958

DIAGRAM 135

=

3rd Prize

Reintroducing one of the most inventive Anglo-American composers.

| 1 B—N3 | R—QN8 | 2 B—B2! | N—Q4 |

If 2 ... N—B4; 3 K—K2, R—N7; 4 K × P, N—Q5; 5 K—B3, or 5 B—K3=; and if 3 ... N—Q5 ch; 4 K × P, N—B6 ch; 5 K—B3=; or 4 ... R—KN8; 5 B—K3=.

If 2 B × N? R × B ch; 3 K—K2, R—K6 ch!!+

| 3 K—K2 | P—Q8(Q) ch | 5 K—Q2 | N × B |
| 4 B × Q | N—B6 ch | 6 K—B2 | R—N4 |

If 6 ... R—R8; 7 B—B1, N—B7; 8 K—N2=; or 6 ... R—R8; 7 B—B1, N—B6; 8 B—N2=.

| 7 B—B1! | R—Q4 | 9 B—K3 ch | K—N4 |
| 8 B—Q2! | N—N7 | 10 K × N | draw |

A captivating fight ending in a book draw—with only a few unfavorable exceptions, these rook versus bishop endings are drawn. A similar composition by the Russian V. A. Bron won an Olympic 1st Prize, but one year after Peckover's effort was shown.

Alg.: 1 ♗b3, ♖b1; 2 ♗c2, ♘d5; 3 ♔e2, d1(♕)†; 4 ♗:d1, ♘c3†; 5 ♔d2, ♘:d1; 6 ♔c2, ♖b5; 7 ♗c1, ♖d5; 8 ♗d2, ♘b2; 9 ♗e3†, ♔b5; 10 ♔:b2=.

DIAGRAM 136

J. E. PECKOVER

PROBLEM (YUGOSLAVIA)

SEPTEMBER, 1966

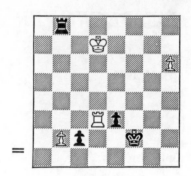

=

Peckover has been going strong for many decades. He began to gain great prominence in the 1950s.

1 R—B3	R×P	3 P—R7	P—K7
2 R×P ch	R×R	4 P—R8(Q)	R—Q7 ch

If 4 ... P—K8(Q); 5 Q—R2 ch, winning the rook back. Now Black appears to remain a rook ahead, but:

5 K—B7	P—K8(Q)	8 Q—K4 ch! K—Q8
6 Q—R4 ch!	K—B8	9 Q—N1 ch! with per-
7 Q—R1 ch!	K—K7	petual check

Slipping in and out of windows has been in vogue since Cook's diagram 137, but our contemporary has blended sophistication with humor.

Alg.: 1 ♖c3, ♖:b2; 2 ♖:c2†, ♖:c2; 3 h7, e2; 4 h8(♛), ♖d2†; 5 ♔c7, e1(♛); 6 ♕h4†, ♔f1; 7 ♕h1†, ♔e2; 8 ♕e4†, ♔d1; 9 ♕b1†=.

DIAGRAM 137

E. B. COOK

From: H. Keidanz,

THE CHESS COMPOSITIONS OF E. B. COOK

NEW YORK, 1927

=

In diagram 136 the king was trying to hide behind his body-guards. In the present situation it is the bodyguards stepping in front. White seems unable to stop Black from queening. But he has a surprising combination in reserve which starts off with a subtle waiting move.

| 1 Q—B4 ch K—R8 | 3 K—B5!! |
| 2 Q—R4 ch Q—R7 | |

A stall, which invites 3 ... Q × Q, with an amazing stalemate in the center of an almost bare board.

3 ... P—N8(Q)	6 Q—R4 ch Q/7—R7
4 Q—Q4 ch Q/8—N7	7 Q—Q4 ch etc.
5 Q—Q1 ch Q/R—N8	

and White draws against two black queens by perpetual check on QR4, Q4 or Q1 respectively. The black player has a game-like alternative in 3 ... P—N8(N) but after 4 Q × Q ch, K × Q; 5 K—B6, White wins after a prolonged ending.

Alg.: 1 ♕c4†, ♔a1; 2 ♕a4†, ♕a2; 3 ♔c5, b1(♕); 4 ♕d4†, ♕b2; 5 ♕d1†, ♕a b1†; 6 ♕a4†, ♕b2 a2; 7 ♕d4†=.

DIAGRAM 138

E. B. COOK

From: H. Keidanz,

THE CHESS COMPOSITIONS
OF E. B. COOK

NEW YORK, 1927

+

To quote Keidanz, "the motif consists of two heterogeneous parts, one a problem-like combination in six moves, winning the black queen . . ."

1 R—K2 ch R—K6

If the king moves, White mates soon.

2 R×R ch Q×R   5 Q—N6 ch K—B6
3 Q—K6 ch K—Q5!   6 Q×Q
4 B—B2   Q×B

". . . the other a game-like finish to which several other methods of winning are applicable. After 6 Q×Q, Black continues best with P—N7. White then wins in the quickest way as follows: 7 Q—B5 ch, K—Q7 (7 . . . K—N6; 8 Q—Q5 ch, and 9 Q—R2+); 8 Q—N4 ch, K—B7; 9 Q—B4 ch, K—N8; 10 Q—N3, etc., wins easily."

The main sequence contains the harmonious echo 3 . . . K—B5; 4 B—Q2, Q × B; 5 Q—R6 ch, K—any; 6 Q × Q, but leaves Black with an obviously more desperate ending.

Alg.: 1 ♖e2†, ♖e3; 2 ♖:e3†, ♕:e3; 3 ♕e6†, ♚d4; 4 ♗f2, ♕:f2;
    5 ♕b6†, ♚c3; 6 ♕:f2+.

DIAGRAM 139

W. KORN

BRITISH CHESS MAGAZINE

1945

=

A "natural" with two variations.

1 K—R6 K—B1	4 P—B5 P×P
2 K—R7 R—Q2 ch	5 P—R6 R×P
3 K—R8 R—KN2	6 P—R7 stalemate

The other variant runs 1 ... R—Q1; 2 P—N7, K—B2; 3 K—R7, R—KN1; 4 P—R6, R—any; 5 P—B5, P×P; 6 P—N8(Q) ch, R×Q=.

The style of this—and other compositions by the same author—is typical of the Bohemian (or Czech) school, which ranks purity and economy of execution and of the mates above loose thematic freedom.

Alg.: 1 ♔h6, ♔f8; 2 ♔h7, ♖d7†; 3 ♔h8, ♖g7; 4 c5, b:c5; 5 h6, ♖:g6; 6 h7(=).

DIAGRAM 140

W. KORN

BOHEMIA

1933

1st Prize

$+$

An artistic rendering of a positional study, with a clear-cut economical finale.

1	P—R6 P—R6!	3	P—R7 R×P/6
2	P×P R—QR5		

The low-key overture has served to deflect Black's rook from the fifth to the sixth rank. The importance of that detour becomes plain as play proceeds. At this moment, both white pawns are threatened with capture, voiding a win. Therefore, White first protects the other pawn as well.

4	N—Q8! R—N6 ch	7	K—B7 R—QR6
5	N—N7 R—QR6	8	K—N7 R—N6 ch
6	N—Q6! R—N6 ch	9	N—N5!!

Now it transpires why Black's rook was initially forced on to the sixth rank. In consequence of White's oblique zigzag N—Q8—N7—Q6—N5, the rook can no longer go back to QR6 to deter the rook's pawn from queening, as the knight controls the square; but the knight is *en prise!*

9	... R×N ch	11	P—B8(Q) ch K×Q
10	K—R6! R—N8	12	P—R8(Q) ch wins

Each piece, having had its say, disappears in the wings, until the sole winning force of queen against rook remains for the last bow.

The solution also contains a substantially important try, (1 P—R6), R×P; 2 P—R7, K—B3; 3 N—Q8!!, R×P; 4 K×R, K—K4; 5 K—R6, K—K5; 6 K—R5, K—Q6; 7 K×P, securing the pawn and win; whereas 3 P—R8(Q), R—B1 ch; 4 K—N7, R×Q; 5 K×R, K—K3; 6 N—Q4 ch, K—Q4; 7 N—B2, K—B5; 8 N—R1, K—Q6; 9 K—R7, K—Q7; 10 K—R6, K—B8 recalls the maneuvers in diagrams 100 and 101 but does not win here as White lost valuable ground as compared to the line with 3 N—Q8!

How the same final episode can be staged with different actors is shown in diagram 141.

Alg.: 1 a6, a3; 2 b:a3, ♖a4; 3 a7, ♖:a3; 4 ♘d8, ♖b3†; 5 ♘b7, ♖a3; 6 ♘d6, ♖b3†; 7 ♔c7, ♖a3; 8 ♔b7, ♖b3†; 9 ♘b5, ♖:b5†; 10 ♔a6, ♖b1; 11 f8(♕)†, ♔:f8; 12 a8(♕)†+.

DIAGRAM 140 (A)

C. S. HOWELL*

From: C. S. Tattersall,

A THOUSAND ENDGAMES

1911

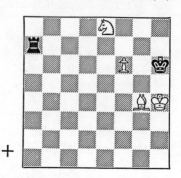

+

Another ultimate expression of an idea by minimum means, on another plane, and with a different mode of execution. But the tactic of cutting off the rook from the square where to administer the last saving check, recalls the one used in the previous diagram.

   1 B—R5 R—R8

White wins after 1 ...R —R5 ch; 2 K—N3, K×B; 3 P—B7, R—R6 ch; 4 K—B4, R—R5 ch; 5 K—B5, R—R4 ch; 6 K—K6, R—R3 ch; 7 K—Q7! R—R2 ch; 8 N—B7! wins.

2 P—B7 R—KB8	5 N—K6! K×B
3 N—B7! R—R8 ch	6 N—B4 ch wins
4 K—N3 R—KB8	

If 5 ... R—B3; 6 K—R4 wins.

---

  * C. S. Howell of New York, 1881–1936—see also diagram No. 194.

Alg.: 1 ♗h5, ♖a1; 2 f7, ♖f1; 3 ♘c7, ♖h1†; 4 ♔g3, ♖f1; 5 ♘e6, ♔:h5; 6 ♘f4†+.

DIAGRAM 141

R. BRIEGER

1973*

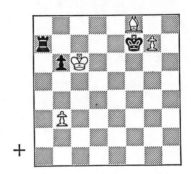

+

Just a pragmatical ending—but what a conclusion! The first try, 1 K×P?, R—R1; 2 K—N7, R—R4; 3 P—N4, R—N4 ch; 4 K—B6, R×P; 5 B×R, K×P only draws.

   1 P—N4 R—R1   2 P—N5

Not 2 K×P?, R—N1 ch; 3 K—B5, R—B1 ch; 4 K—Q6, R—N1; 5 K—B5, R—B1 ch draw. The pawn is not able to advance.

2 ...	R—N1	9 K—N8	R—QN8
3 K—B7	R—K1	10 P—N7	R—QB8
4 K×P	R—N1 ch	11 K—R7	R—R8 ch
5 K—B6	R—B1 ch	12 K—N6	R—N8 ch
6 K—N7	R—B8	13 K—B7	R—B8 ch
7 P—N6	R—QN8	14 B—B5!	R×B ch
8 K—B7	R—B8 ch		

If 14 ... R—QN8; 15 B—N6, R—B8 ch; 16 K—Q6, R—Q8 ch; 17 K—B5, R—B8 ch; 18 K—Q4, R—Q8 ch; 19 K—B3, R—B8 ch; 20 K—Q2±.

* R. Brieger, op. cit., example No. 39.

Progressing from an entirely different conception, White now winds up in the same manner as in the preceding diagram 140.

15 K—N6	R—B8	17 P—N8(Q) ch wins
16 P—KN8(Q)	K × Q	

Alg.: 1 b4, ♖a8; 2 b5, ♖b8 ; 3 ♔c7, ♖e8; 4 ♔:b6, ♖b8†; 5 ♔c6, ♖c8†; 6 ♔b7, ♖c1; 7 b6, ♖b1; 8 ♔c7, ♖c1†; 9 ♔b8, ♖b1; 10 b7, ♖c1; 11 ♔a7, ♖a1†; 12 ♔b6, ♖b1†; 13 ♔c7, ♖c1†; 14 ♗c5, ♖:c5†; 15 ♔b6, ♖c1; 16 g8 (♕)†, ♔:g8; 17 b8(♕)†+.

DIAGRAM 142

C.G. REICHHELM

DEUTSCHE
SCHACHZEITUNG

1901

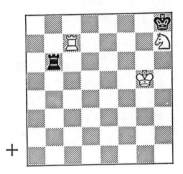

$+$

To go back for a moment to the good old days, the above setting served as a blueprint on how to tackle similar phases of rook versus knight.

    1 K—B5

1 N—B6!? threatens mate but also clinches the stalemate or dissolves the mate, e.g. 1 ... R—N2!=; or 1 ... R—N4 ch; 2 K—N6, R—N4 ch; 3 K—R6, R—N3 ch=.

    If 1 K—R5, R—N1; 2 N—B6, R—N2!; 3 R × R stalemate (or 3 R—any, K—N2=), and if 2 K—N6, R—N1 ch; 3 K—R6, R—N8 draw.

    1 ...   R—KR3

If 1 ... K—N1; 2 N—B6 ch, K—B1; 3 N—Q7 ch+ and if 1 ... R—N4 ch; 2 K—N6, R—N3 ch (or 3 ... R—N1).

| 2 N—B6 R—R8 | 4 K—B7 R—QB8 |
| 3 K—K6 R—K8 ch | 5 R—K7 |

The control point.

    5 ...   R—K8?!   6 N—K4!! K—R2

The only riposte to prevent an "ambush" by 7 R—K8 ch, K—R2; 8 N—B6 ch, winning the rook.

If 6 ... R—KN8; 7 R—K8 ch, K—R2; 8 N—B6 ch+.

   7 R—K5! K—R3   8 R—K6 ch!

White discards the camouflage with 8 ... K—R2, 9 N—N5 ch, or 8 ... K—R4; 9 N—N3 ch, and 10 R×R, winning.

If 7 ... R—KR8; 8 R—KN5!, R—B8 ch; 9 N—B6 ch, or 8 ... K—R8; 9 R—N8 ch +.

An ambush is a device in which a key piece (the white rook) attacks indirectly (in the above case, by threatening discovered check).

Alg.: 1 ♔f5, ♖h6; 2 ♘f6, ♖h1; 3 ♔e6, ♖e1†; 4 ♔f7, ♖c1; 5 ♖e7, ♖e1; 6 ♘e4, ♔h7; 7 ♖e5, ♔h6; 8 ♖e6†+.

DIAGRAM 143

C. G. REICHHELM

WIENER
SCHACHZEITUNG

1887

+

Another duel of rook versus knight, but with a different complexion.

> 1 P—R7 N—B6   2 P—R8 (R!)

If White queens, it is stalemate. If 2 K×N, K—N8=. The following moves are all forced.

2 ...	N—N8	6 K—B2	N—Q7
3 R—R1	P—B6	7 R—Q4	N—N8
4 R—R4	N—R6 ch	8 K—N3 wins	
5 K×P	N—N8 ch		

A finely balanced see-saw of repeated stalemate defense and its avoidance.

Alg.: 1 h7, ♘c3; 2 h8(♖), ♘b1; 3 ♖h1, c3; 4 ♖h4, ♘a3†; 5 ♔:c3, ♘b1†; 6 ♔c2, ♘d2; 7 ♖d4, ♘b1; 8 ♔b3+.

Contemporary Composition

The classics who invented artistic firmaments, and the recent moderns, who expanded them into a galaxy, have also exhausted many or even most of the conventional themes and the means of portraying them.

The present-day composer thus often concentrates on combining several known prototypes, or on reapplying them by the use of different material, to enrich a given strategy with a wealth of tactical finesses and to strengthen and refine Black's defense mechanism so as to make it even harder for White to succeed, as shown in the pair of diagrams 160 and 161. This, moreover, improves skill and the instructive aspect that is ever present in composing and solving. Among the landscapes that follow, many exquisite illustrations may be found of this type, e.g. Weinberger's diagram 147, Brieger's No. 190, or for instance, the rhythmical libretto shown in diagrams 144–145, the multi-faceted twins in diagram 165 and 165A; or the treatment of maximum/minimum force foreshadowed in the bizarre diagram 37, later on advanced further in the "grotesque" experimentations, deliberately so construed by the Soviet artist Gurvich (but their inclusion would exceed the scope of this compendium). These modernistic transactions are also dubbed "paradoxical" as distinct from "typical" anatomy. A parallel may be found in the development of problems (two-, three-, four-, or multi-movers) away from the "orthodox" and into the "heterodox" or "fairy chess" field.

DIAGRAM 144

W. KORN

CHESS REVIEW

DECEMBER, 1967

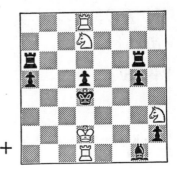

"The Rhythmical Echo Pair"
(The Right Hand)

$+$

This and the next diagram open a novel vista of unorthodox "motional" symmetry. White wins "dualistically" in all variations.

1 N×B P×N(Q)   2 R×Q

(A) 2 ... R/R—K3; 3 R—QR1, R—QB3; 4 R—R4 ch, R—B5; 5 R×R ch, K×R; 6 N—K5 ch, or 5 ... P×R; 6 N—B8 dis. ch+.

(B) 2 ... R/N—K3; 3 R—N4 ch, R—K5; 4 R×R ch, with an echo-like win as in (A).

(C) 2 ... P—N5; 3 R—QR1 and (*a*) 3 ... R/R—QB3, etc., as in (A). Or (*b*) 3 ... R/N—QB3; 4 R—KB1!+ as in (B). Or (*c*) 3 ... P—R5 with convolutions continuing with 4 R—QN1 or R—KB1, and proceeding as before.

Alg.: 1 ♘:g1, h:g1(♕); 2 ♖:g1, ♖ae6; 3 ♖a1, ♖c6; 4 ♖a4†, ♖c4; 5 ♖ :c4†, ♔:c4; 6 ♘e5†+. Or 2 ... ♖ge6; 3 ♖g4†, ♖e4; 4 ♖:e4, +. Or 2 ... g4; 3 ♖a1, ♖gc6; 4 ♖f1!+.

DIAGRAM 144 (A)

W. KORN

CHESS REVIEW

DECEMBER, 1967

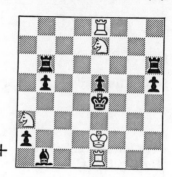

"The Rhythmical Echo Pair"
(The Left Hand)

Corresponding with the foregoing diagram 144 as a matter of harmony. Again the opening moves run

    1 N×B P×N(Q)   2 R×Q

with a repetition of the whole process by (A) 2 ... R/R—KB3; or (B) 2 ... R/N—KB3; or (C) 1 ... P—R5; etc.

As a further step, in twin diagram 144(A), Black's bishop and advanced pawn, and White's knight on the rook's file, may all be removed, allowing the symmetrical first key moves of either 1 R—QN1 or 1 R—KR1, with White to start and continue the rhythm from any part of the chain.

Diagram 144 and its companion 144(A) were designed for the New Year and, the lower corner constellations aside, the contours of the Cross, the Cross of Lorraine, the Star of David, and even the Crescent, are encompassed within the square's masonry of the universe.

Alg.: 1 ♘:b1, a:b1(♕); 2 ♖:b1, as in diagram 144 but in reverse.

DIAGRAM 145

A. J. ROYCROFT[§]

E. G.

MARCH, 1969

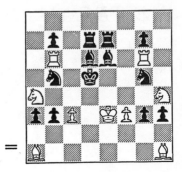

=

Another most attractive experiment in symmetry and parity. Black threatens 1 ... B—B4 dis. ch; 2 K—Q2, B—B5 ch; 3 K—Q1, B—B7; and 1 R×B?, R×R ch; 2 K—Q3, R—K8+. Therefore:

 1 K—Q3!

With the threat 2 P—B4 mate. Black counters with

 1 ... K—K4!

If 1 ... R—QB2?; 2 P—B4 ch, R×P; 3 R×KN ch, B—B4 ch; 4 R×B/4 ch, K—K3; 5 R—K5 ch, K—Q2 (or B2); 6 R×R ch, K×R; 7 K×R+ or 4 ... B—K4; 5 P—B4 dis. ch, P—N7; 6 B×B+.

 2 K—K3 K—Q4!=

with a permanent pendulum.

Alg.: 1 ♔d3, ♚e5; 2 ♔e3, ♚d5=.

DIAGRAM 146

J. E. PECKOVER

SZACHY

1957

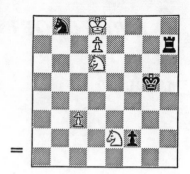

=

A taste of Peckover's streamlined craftsmanship. The various maneuvers, dominations, and threatening forks tell their own story

1 N—K4 ch	K—N5
2 N×P ch	K—B6
3 N—R3!	K×N
4 K—B7!	N×P
5 N—N5	R—R4
6 N—K6!	R—R2
7 N—N5	R—N2

8 N—K6!	R—B2
9 N—N5	R—B4
10 N—K6!	R—B2
11 N—N5	R—K2
12 K—Q6	R—K4
13 N—K6!=	

Delightful.

Alg.: 1 ♘e4†, ♔g4; 2 ♘:f2†, ♔f3; 3 ♘h3, ♔:e2; 4 ♔c7, ♘:d7; 5 ♘g5, ♖h5; 6 ♘e6, ♖h7; 7 ♘g5, ♖g7; 8 ♘e6, ♖f7; 9 ♘g5, ♖f5; 10 ♘e6, ♖f7; 11 ♘g5, ♖e7; 12 ♔d6, ♖e5; 13 ♘e6!=.

DIAGRAM 147

O. WEINBERGER

E. G.

JULY, 1967

=

A piece full of tactical possibilities, ingenious defenses and refuted sidelines.

1 R—B8 ch	K—K2	4 R×Q	N—N6 ch
2 R—K8 ch!	K—Q2	5 K—K5!	N×B
3 P—B8(N) ch!	Q × N	6 N—N7!	B × N!

If 6 ... P—Q8(Q); 7 R—Q8 ch, wins.

7 R—B1	B—B6!	9 R—Q3 ch Q×R
8 R×B	P—Q8 (Q)	stalemate

Alg.: 1 ♖c8†, ♔e7; 2 ♖e8†, ♔d7; 3 f8(♘)†, ♕:f8; 4 ♖:f8, ♘g3†;
5 ♔e5, ♘:h5; 6 ♘b7, ♗:b7; 7 ♖f1, ♗f3; 8 ♖:f3, d1(♕);
9 ♖d3†, ♕:d3 (=).

J. E. PECKOVER

PROBLEM (YUGOSLAVIA)

JANUARY, 1962

DIAGRAM 148

=

Practically one pawn draws against rook and knight!

1	B—B3	R—K2	
2	K—N6	K—N1	
3	P—B7 ch	R×P	
4	B—N7	N×B	
5	P—R7 ch!!	K—R1	
6	K×R	draw	

Sheer wizardry.

Alg.: 1 ♗f3, ♖e7; 2 ♔b6, ♔b8; 3 c7†, ♖:c7; 4 ♗b7, ♘:b7; 5 a7†, ♔a8; 6 ♔:c7=.

198

DIAGRAM 149

J. E. PECKOVER

SZACHY

1957

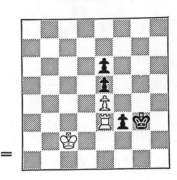

=

1st Prize

Peckover—professionally a commercial artist—turns into a real chess portraitist.

1 R—Q3! K—N7		3 K—Q3
2 R—Q2 ch P—B7		

Regrouping for more effective defense.

3 ... K—N8		5 K—K3!! K—N7
4 R—Q1 ch P—B8 (Q) ch		

If 5 ... Q×R stalemate.

6 R×Q K×R		8 K—K3 draw!
7 K—B3 K—K8		

Delicious!

Alg.: 1 ♖d3, ♔g2; 2 ♖d2†, f2; 3 ♔d3, ♔g1; 4 ♖d1†, f1(♕)†; 5 ♔e3, ♔g2; 6 ♖:f1, ♔:f1; 7 ♔f3, ♔e1; 8 ♔e3=.

J. E. PECKOVER

PROBLEM

1960

1st Prize, 1958–9 tourney

Award Published in No. 69

DIAGRAM 150

=

Black's primary threat is ... B—Q3.

1 K—Q8 R—Q3 ch	3 K—Q7 R—KR3!
2 K—K7 R—QB3	4 B—B6! B—N8!

Each move a hammerblow. If 4 ... R×B; 5 P—B8(Q), B—K3 ch; 6 K—K7=.

5 K—K6 R—R4!	6 B—N5!

Repeating the same tactical maneuver as before on move four. If 6 ... R×B; 7 P—B8(Q), B—B4 ch; 8 K—B6=.

6 ... R—R1	8 B—N5 draw by
7 B—Q8 R—R4	repetition of moves

Again, an American's first prize had to be won in foreign lands, a laudable feat against strong competition—but in the absence of a domestic forum.

Alg.: 1 ♔d8, ♖d6†; 2 ♔e7, ♖c6; 3 ♔d7, ♖h6; 4 ♗f6, ♗b1; 5 ♔e6, ♖h5; 6 ♗g5, ♖h8; 7 ♗d8, ♖h5; 8 ♗g5=.

DIAGRAM 151

J. E. PECKOVER

SHAKHMATNAYA MOSKVA
(Chess in Moscow)

1964

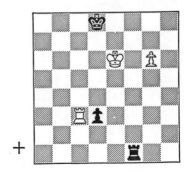

$+$

A rook ending—one of the exacting chapters in the theory of the endgame as well as one of the most difficult phases of practical play.

When one of the chess giants, Grandmaster A. Rubinstein, arrived at an ostensibly even rook and pawn ending, his opponents were gripped by fear of a potential loss—Rubinstein was reckoned to be rook endings personified. For a composer, the analytical task is no less fearsome.

1 P—N7!

Very convincing looks the sober 1 R × P ch!?, K—K1; 2 P—N7, R—KN8; 3 K—B6, R—B8 ch; 4 K—N6, R—N8 ch; 5 K—R7, R—R8 ch; 6 K—N8, K—K2; 7 R—K3 ch, K—Q3; 8 R—K4 with a clear book win—except for the surprising 2 ... R—B3 ch! (instead of 2 ... R—KN8?); 3 K—K5 (3 K × R is stalemate), R—KN3 with an immediate draw.

| 1 ...   R—K8 ch | 3 K—N8 R—B6 |
| 2 K—B7 R—B8 ch | |

If 3 ... R—Q8; 4 R—B4 and now (*a*) 4 ... K—K2; 5 R—K4 ch! K—Q3; 6 R—KN4, K—K4; 7 K—B7, P—Q7; 8 P—N8(Q), R—B8 ch; 9 K—K7, P—Q8(Q); 10 Q—K6 mate; or (*b*) 4 ... P—Q7; 5 R—KR4(KB4), K—K2 (the king must move away from the file, else 5 ... R—any; 6 R—Q4 ch wins the pawn); 6 R—R2 and White wins—just by a hair's breadth.

4 K—R7 R—R6 ch	6 K—B6 R—B6 ch
5 K—N6 R—N6 ch	7 K—K5 R—K6 ch

If 7 ... R—N6?; 8 R×P ch! wins.

8 K—B4 R—K1	10 K—B5 wins
9 R×P ch K—B2	

Alg.: 1 g7, ♖e1†; 2 ♔f7, ♖f1†; 3 ♔g8, ♖f3; 4 ♔h7, ♖h3†; 5 ♔g6, ♖g3†; 6 ♔f6, ♖f3†; 7 ♔e5, ♖e3†; 8 ♔f4, ♖e8; 9 ♖:d3†+.

J. E. PECKOVER

SZACHY

1958

DIAGRAM 152

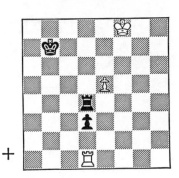

1st–2nd Prize, *Ex Aequo**

$+$

Laconic and poignant in motif and of firm texture.

1 P—K6 K—B2	3 K—K8! R—Q5
2 P—K7 R—B5 ch	

No better is 3 ... R—B6; 4 R—B1 ch, K—Q3; 5 K—Q8, R—K6; 6 R—B3! (but not 6 R—Q1, K—B4; 7 K—Q7, K—B5=), 6 ... P—Q7; 7 R×R, P—Q8(Q); 8 P—K8(Q) wins.

4 K—B7

Not 4 R—KB1, P—Q7; 5 K—B7, R—B5 ch!; 6 R×R, P—Q8(Q); 7 P—K8(Q), Q—R4 ch; 8 K—B8, Q—R3 ch, or 8 K—K7, Q—K4 ch, both winning the rook with equality.

4 ...	R—B5 ch	8 K—K4	R—B7
5 K—K6	R—K5 ch	9 K×P	K—Q2
6 K—B6	R—B5 ch	10 K—K3 dis. ch wins	
7 K—K5!	R—B6		

* *ex aequo*—side by side—with an equally excellent composition by the famous G. M. Kasparian.

Alg.: 1 e6, ♚c7; 2 e7, ♜f4†; 3 ♔e8! ♜d4; 4 ♔f7, ♜f4†; 5 ♔e6, ♜e4†; 6 ♔f6, ♜f4†; 7 ♔e5, ♜f3; 8 ♔e4, ♜f2; 9 ♔:d3, ♚d7; 10 ♔e3†+.

DIAGRAM 153

J. E. PECKOVER

TIDSKRIFT FÖR SCHACK

1966

=

On the surface, this is just another theoretical ending—but the point is in the two corresponding "echoes" that result from the alternative pawn moves.

    1 P—N5!

Black has two choices, and both subject White to a tenuous defense.

    The natural course is

1 ...	R×P	4 K—N8	K—K2
2 P—N6	K—Q2	5 K—R7	K—B3
3 P—N7	R—B4 ch	6 P—N8(N) ch!	draws

Black's more sophisticated try for a win is

1 ...	R—KN5	4 K—K8	K—Q3
2 P—K6	R×P	5 K—Q8	R—QR4
3 P—K7	R—B5 ch	6 P—K8(N) ch	draws

As defined in diagram 50, but in other words, an echo is a

parallel repetition of a thematic pattern in two different variations. They may also occur as sequential maneuvers, but need
not be confused with a simple rhythmical chain of moves.

Alg.: 1 g5 (A) 1 ... ♖:e5; 2 g6, ♔d7; 3 g7, ♖f5†, 4 ♔g8, ♔e7; 5 ♔h7,
      ♔f6; 6 g8(♘)†=.
      (B) 1 ... ♖g4, 2 e6, ♖:g5; 3 e7, ♖f5†; 4 ♔e8, ♔d6; 5 ♔d8,
      ♖a5; 6 e8(♘)†.

DIAGRAM 153 (A)

J. E. PECKOVER

SZACHY

1960

2nd Hon. Mention   =

Another struggle of a rook against queening pawns, but with a particular Peckover twist, and a crowning point.

   1 K—Q5!! K—N6

Threatens 2 ... P—QN8(Q); 3 R—N8 ch, K—B7; 4 R×Q, K×R and 5 ... P—N8(?)+.

   2 R—N3 ch K—R5   3 R—N4 ch K—R4

After 3 R—N8? P—QN8(Q); 4 R—R8 ch, K—N6; 5 R—N8 ch, K—B7; 6 R×Q, K×R and 7 ... P—N8(Q) Black wins. But after the text, the pawns are in real danger of falling if Black attempts to promote them.

   4 R—N8 K—N4!   5 R—N7! K—N3

Tempo play. 5 ... P—QN8(Q) still loses for Black, therefore Black's king tries to outflank.

   6 R—N6 ch K—B2   8 K—Q6! K—B1!
   7 R—N7 ch K—Q1

If 8 ... K—K1; 9 R—K7 ch! and 10 R—K1 even wins for White—a turn which is Peckover's particular contribution to the facets of this theme.

9	K—B6	K—N1	12	R—N8	K—R4
10	R—N8 ch	K—R2	13	K—B5!	K—R5
11	R—N7 ch	K—R3	14	R—N4 ch! draw	

(A draw results also from 14 K—B4, K—R4 (not 14 ... K—R6; 15 R—R8 mate); 15 K—B5, K—R3; 16 K—B6, K—R2; 17 R—N7 ch, K—N1; 18 R—N8 ch, etc. —W.K.)

Alg.: 1 ♔d5, ♚b3; 2 ♖g3†, ♚a4; 3 ♖g4†, ♚a5; 4 ♖g8, ♚b5; 5 ♖g7, ♚b6; 6 ♖g6†, ♚c7; 7 ♖g7†, ♚d8; 8 ♔d6, ♚c8; 9 ♔c6, ♚b8; 10 ♖g8†, ♚a7; 11 ♖g7†, ♚a6; 12 ♖g8, ♚a5; 13 ♔c5, ♚a4; 14 ♖g4†=.

R. BRIEGER

NEW STATESMAN

1967–8

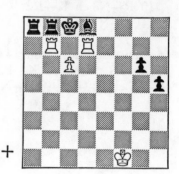

DIAGRAM 154

+

2nd Hon. Mention, Study Tourney

The judges'* comment: "Some polish may be said to be lacking, but the set-up on the knight's, bishop's and queen's files is attractively bewildering."

   1 P—B7 R—R8 ch

If 1 ... B—R5; 2 P×R(Q) ch, R×Q; 3 R/N—B7‡.

   2 K—N2! R—R7 ch

If 2 K—K2?, R—K8 ch; 3 K—Q3 (3 K×R, B—R5 ch+), R—Q8 ch; 4 K—K4, R—Q5 ch; 5 K—B3, R—Q6 ch; 6 K—K2, R—Q7 ch; 7 R×R, B×P=.

   3 K—B3 R—R6 ch   7 K—B7 R—B5 ch
   4 K—K4 R—R5 ch   8 K×P! R—N5 ch
   5 K—Q5 R—Q5 ch   9 K—R7 R—N2 ch
   6 K—K6 R—K5 ch

* W. Korn and A. J. Roycroft.

If 9 K×P?, R—R5 ch; 10 K—N6, R—N5 ch; 11 K—B5, R—B5 ch; 12 K×R, B—N4 ch; 13 K×B, R×R=.

10 R×R! wins

Alg.: 1 c7, ♖a1†; 2 ♔g2, ♖a2†; 3 ♔f3, ♖a3†; 4 ♔e4, ♖a4†; 5 ♔d5, ♖d4†; 6 ♔e6, ♖e4†; 7 ♔f7, ♖f4†; 8 ♔:g6, ♖g4†; 9 ♔h7, ♖g7†; 10 ♖:g7+.

DIAGRAM 155

R. BRIEGER

NEW STATESMAN

1967–8

3rd Hon. Mention, Study Tourney

+

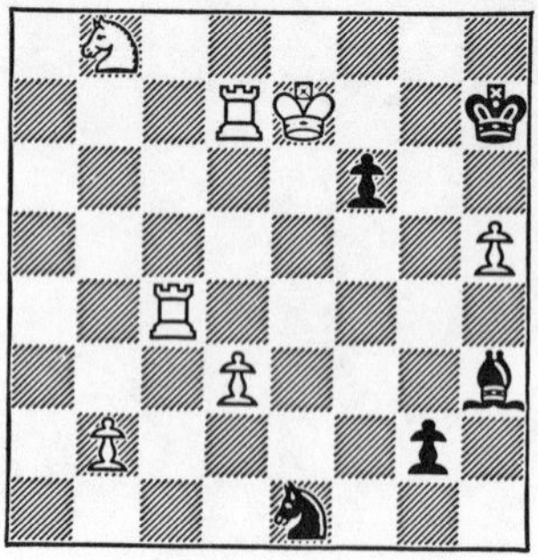

The judges'* evaluation that accompanied this award: "With a lively introduction, excelsior knight-promotion and a (familiar) two-knights mate, not a dull moment."

1 K—B8 dis. ch	B×R	4 N×P ch	K—R1!
2 N×B	P—N8(Q)	5 N×Q	N×P
3 R—KN4!	Q×R		

The simple but forceful introduction is over. The next and main phase is a knight chase, which drives up White's pawn—or, vice versa, tries in vain to prevent the pawn's inexorable advance. The theme of starting a white pawn on its own square, and making it give mate after promotion to knight, dates back to Loyd's days and is termed an "Excelsior".

6 P—N3 N—B8!

If 6 ... N—N5, 7 K—K7, N—Q6; 8 K—Q6+.

7 P—N4	N—R7	10 P—N7	N—B4
8 P—N5	N—B6	11 P—N8(N)!	N—K3 ch
9 P—N6	N—R5		

* W. Korn and A. J. Roycroft.

If 11 ... K—R2; 12 K—B7, N—K5; 13 N—Q7, N—N4 ch;
14 K—B8, N—K3 ch; 15 K—K7, N—B5; 16 N—B8 ch+.

12 K—B7	N—N2	15 N—K5	N—any
13 N—Q7	N×P	16 N/5—N6 mate	
14 N—B8	N—B3		

Alg.: 1 ♔f8†, ♗:d7; 2 ♘:d7, g1(♕); 3 ♖g4, ♕:g4; 4 ♘:f6†, ♔h8;
5 ♘:g4, ♘:d3; 6 b3, ♘c1; 7 b4, ♘a2; 8 b5, ♘c3; 9 b6, ♘a4;
10 b7, ♘c5; 11 b8(♘), ♘e6†; 12 ♔f7, ♘g7; 13 ♘d7, ♘:h5;
14 ♘f8, ♘f6, 15 ♘e5, ∞; 16 ♘g6#.

DIAGRAM 156

J. E. PECKOVER

SZACHY

1957 (AMENDED)

+

Variations on a well-known theme—but the finish is out of the ordinary and the whole opus is not easy to resolve.

First examine the try 1 N—B3, R×P!; 2 B—Q2, N—N3; 3 R—QN1 (threatening 4 R—N4+), N—Q4; 4 R—N3 (threat: 5 N—Q4), R—QN3; 5 R—R3 ch, K—N4=.

1 R—K4 R×R   2 N×R

If 2 P—Q7?, R—K7 ch; 3 K—N1, R—K8 ch; 4 K—R2, R—K7 ch; 5 K—N1, R—K8 ch; 6 K—N2, N—N3; 7 P—Q8(Q), P—Q7; 8 Q×N (8 Q×P?, N—B5 ch= or 8 Q—Q4 ch, K—N4=), R—N8 ch; 9 K×R, P—Q8(Q) ch; 10 K—R2, Q—Q4 ch; 11 K—R1, Q—Q8 ch; 12 Q—N1, Q—Q5 ch and, with exact play, Black maintains perpetual check—or wins the bishop, drawing the game.

2 ... N×P

If 2 ... P—Q7; 3 P—Q7!, P—Q8(Q); 4 N—B3 ch+.

3 N×N P—Q7!   4 N—K4! P—Q8(N!)

If 4 B×P, stalemate! Black in turn underpromotes the pawn, hoping to salvage his trapped knight.

5 B—Q2!	K—N4	9 N—N4!	K—B4
6 K—N3	K—B3	10 N—R6 ch!	K—any
7 K—B2	K—Q4!	11 K×N	wins
8 N—B6 ch	K—K3		

Originally, the black knight was situated on K1, but was later moved by the composer to QB1, to eliminate a dual.

Alg.: 1 ♖e4, ♖:e4; 2 ♘:e4, ♘:d6; 3 ♘:d6, d2; 4 ♘e4, d1(♘); 5 ♗d2, ♔b5; 6 ♔b3, ♔c6; 7 ♔c2, ♔d5; 8 ♘f6†, ♔e6; 9 ♘g4, ♔f5; 10 ♘h6†, ♔ ∞; 11 ♘:d1+.

DIAGRAM 157

J. E. PECKOVER

SZACHY

1957

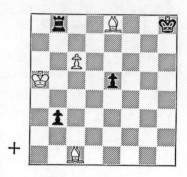

+

| 1 B—N6 P—N7 | 3 B×Q   R×B |
| 2 B—N5 P—N8(Q) | |

The end of the tactical prelude. The main plot unfolds.

| 4 P—B7   R—R8 ch | 6 K—N7 R—KB1! |
| 5 K—N6   R—R1 | 7 B—K7 R—KN1 |

White gradually limits the rook's influence. If 7 B—Q8, R—B2=.

| 8 B—Q8 R—N2 | 9 B—B6 wins |

Alg.: 1 ♗g6, b2; 2 ♗g5, b1 (♕); 3 ♗:b1, ♖:b1; 4 c7, ♖a1†; 5 ♔b6, ♖a8; 6 ♔b7, ♖f8; 7 ♗e7, ♖g8; 8 ♗d8, ♖g7; 9 ♗f6+.

DIAGRAM 158

J. E. PECKOVER

PROBLEM

1961

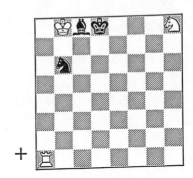

$+$

With minimal force, an aura of both exactness and flair is conveyed in a natural flow.

1 R—Q1 ch N—Q2 ch

If 1 ... B—Q7; 2 N—N6!, N—B5! (if 2 ... K—K1; 3 K—B7, B—N5; 4 R—K1 ch, K—B2; 5 N—K5 ch+); 3 R—Q4, N—R4; 4 N—K5, K—K1!; 5 K—B7! (5 R×B, N—B3 ch=), B—B4; 6 R—QR4!, N—N6; 7 K—Q6, K—B1 (7 ... B—B1; 8 R—R8, K—Q1; 9 N—B6 ch+); 8 R—KB4+.
White's king is hemmed in—although not for long.

2 K—R7   K—B2
3 R—B1 ch K—Q1

4 N—B7 ch

If Black had played 2 ... K—K2, then 3 R—QB1, K—Q1 would have led to the same position. Now Black's bishop is hemmed in.

4 ... K—K2

5 N—N5! K—Q1

If 5 ... K—B3; 6 N—R7 ch, K—N2; 7 R×B, K×N; 8 R—B7+.

6 N—K6 ch K—K2

7 N—Q4! K—Q1

8 N—B6 ch K—K1

9 R—K1 ch K—any

10 N—K7! wins

Black's bishop is doomed.

Alg.: 1 ♖d1†, ♞d7†; ♚a7, ♚c7; 3 ♖c1†, ♚d8; 4 ♞f7†, ♚e2; 5 ♞g5, ♚d8; 6 ♞e6†, ♚e7; 7 ♞d4, ♚d8; 8 ♞c6†, ♚e1; 9 ♖e1†, ♚∞; 10 ♞e7+.

R. BRIEGER

MAGYAR SAKKÉLET

1970

Commendation

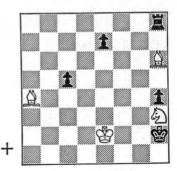

DIAGRAM 159

+

1 B—B4 ch K×N   2 K—B3 R—Q1

To prevent 3 B—Q7#.

3 B—N5 R—Q8   5 B—Q3 P—K3
4 B—B4 R—K8   6 B—B4!

Black is in a perplexing squeeze. If the rook moves along the file it is lost and otherwise mate in two follows, e.g. 6 ...
R—KN8; 7 B×P ch, R—N5; 8 B×R#.

Alg.: 1 ♗f4†, ♔:h3; 2 ♔f3, ♖d8; 3 ♗b5, ♖d1; 4 ♗c4, ♖e1; 5 ♗d3, e6; 6 ♗c4+.

"Originals"— Improvement versus Anticipation

The next two diagrams, 160 and 161, confront the eternal dilemma of defining an anticipation and an improvement.

Common to both studies is the genre of the smothered mate (the "choke"), which in this particular shape was presented in a first prize winner in 1950. Formally, the adaptation published in 1969 was no longer an elemental first. Moreover, even in 1950 it was no original, as documented in diagram 162.

While a purist may therefore also call diagram 161 anticipated and not an original in the very strict sense, it yet holds its own. Brieger, another individualistic artist, performs in a chess concerto in the manner in which his own inner ear would orchestrate it. He conducts the variation on a theme by Bron, or rather Branton, in a more variegated and complex vein.

The borderline between refinement and improvement, or plain anticipation, can become a very delicate and agonizing matter in judging the comparative values of a composition. Mostly the balance between a composer's original settings on the one hand and improvements on the other hand, may decide the merits of a composer's total output.

To be too dogmatic in calling any improvement an anticipation would simply carry the term back to the ancient inventors of any first experimental matrix, make technical advance unjustly appear to be sterile copy, and frustrate genuine improvisation. Another issue, rather of finesse, arises when a composer recasts, or improves upon an earlier idea of his own. It may even pose a vexing question for an endgame tourney judge. Diagrams 171 and 172 deal with such a point.

DIAGRAM 160

V. A. BRON§

SHAKHMATY v SSSR

1950

1st Prize (awarded in 1952)

+

1 P—R5! N×P ch

If 1 ... K—N2; 2 P—R6 ch, K—R2; 3 K—B6, N—R5; 4 N—K2, B—B3; 5 N—B4, B—K1; 6 B—B2! and Black has run out of moves and loses the pawn.

2 K—B6 N—K5 ch!

2 ... K—R3; 3 P×P, B—B3; 4 P—N7, N—R2 ch; 5 B×N, K×B; 6 K—B7, B—K1 ch; 7 K—B8 leads to a simple win for White.

3 N×N P×P   4 N—N5 ch K—R1

In mate ends 4 ... K—N1; 5 B—R2 ch, K—B1; 6 B—B7, etc.

5 B—R2! B—N2

5 ... P—R5; 6 K—B7, P—R6; 7 K—B8, P—R7; 8 N—B7 ch with mate in two.

6 K—B7 B—R3 (or B1)	9 B—R7 B×B
7 K—B8 B—Q6 (or B4)	10 N—B7 mate
8 B—N8 B—N3	

Compact precision. The echoing replicas to Black's 6th and 7th moves added some flavor. This technical refinement over an earlier version has pedagogical points.

Alg.: 1 h5, ♞:g5†; 2 ♔f6, ♞e4†; 3 ♞:e4, g:h5; 4 ♞g5†, ♔h8; 5 ♗a2, ♗b7; 6 ♔f7, ♗a6; 7 ♔f8, ♗d3; 8 ♗g8, ♗g6; 9 ♗h7, ♗:h7; 10 ♞f7#.

DIAGRAM 161

R. BRIEGER

TIDSKRIFT FÖR SCHACK

1969

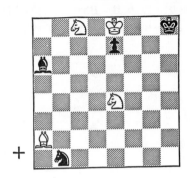

+

| 1 K—B8 B×N* | 2 N—N5! |

Not 2 B—N8?, B—N5!; 3 N—N5, B—R4=.

| 2 ... B—B4 | 4 B—R7 B—K1! |
| 3 B—N8 B—N3 | |

Postponing the final phase 4 ... B—R4; 5 B×N, etc., as shown below. If 5 K×B, N—Q7; 6 K—B8, N—B6=.

| 5 B×N B—R4 | 6 B—B2 |

or 6 B—K4, P—K4; 7 B—Q3, P—K5; 8 B×P, B—N3=.

| 6 ... P—K4 | 7 B—K4! wins |

Clever, but unproductive, is Black's try (1 K—B8), N—B6; 2 B—N8!, B—B5 (if 2 ... N×N; 3 N×P, and 4 N—N6 mate; or 2 ... B×N; 3 N—N5, B—K3; 4 B×B wins; or

---

* This position, without the overture of the first move, is a later version as published by the composer in 1973 (R. Brieger, op. cit., Example No. 28). It reduces the task to a simpler formula as behooves a basic booklet, and omits the try.

2 ... B×N; 3 N—N5, B—K3; 4 B×B, followed by 5 N—B7 ch and 6 B—B5 mate); 3 N×P, B×B; 4 N—N5, B—B2; 5 K×B, and 6 N—N6 mate.

Alg.: 1 ♔f8, ♗:c8; 2 ♘g5, ♗f5; 3 ♗g8, ♗g6; 4 ♗h7, ♗e8; 5 ♗:b1, ♗h5; 6 ♗c2, e5; 7 ♗e4 +.

DIAGRAM 162

A. H. BRANTON

BRITISH CHESS MAGAZINE

1949

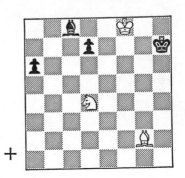

+

An early product of great promise by the shy and personable Texan, now domiciled in Northern California.

1 B—K4 ch K—R1

If 1 ... K—R3; 2 N—B5 ch, K—N4; 3 N—Q6, K—B5; B—N1, etc. +

2 N—B3 P—Q4!

3 N—N5 and 4 N—B7 mate threatened. Now Black intends 3 ... B—N5 and 4 ... B—R4 with a draw.

3 B—N6! B—K3!		5 B—R7! B—K3!	
4 N—N5 B—N1		6 B—N1!	

If 6 B—B2, B—N1; 7 B—N3, P—R4; 8 B—R2, P—R5=.

6 ...	B—N1	10 B—N3 P—R7	
7 B—R2 P—R4		11 B×P P—Q5	
8 B—N3 P—R5		12 B×B P—Q6	
9 B—R2 P—R6		13 N—B7 mate	

Alg.: 1 ♗e4†, ♚h8; 2 ♘f3, d5; 3 ♗g6, ♗e6; 4 ♘g5, ♗g8; 5 ♗h7, ♗e6; 6 ♗b1, ♗g8; 7 ♗a2, a5; 8 ♗b3, a4; 9 ♗a2, a3; 10 ♗b3, a2; 11 ♗: a2; d4; 12 ♗:g8, d3; 13 ♘f7 #.

DIAGRAM 163

C. RAINA§

REBUS

1932

+

To sum up the origins, here is the sensible and plain, but crude matrix.

Black's knight and pawn are actually ineffectual.

1 P—Q6 B×P

If 1 ... B—Q1; 2 N—N6 ch, K—N1; 3 B—K5 wins.

2 B—R7	B—B2	5 B—K5	P—R6
3 B—N8	B—Q1	6 B—R2	wins
4 B×N	P—R5		

Now Black's bishop must move, allowing the mate.

Alg.: 1 d6, ♗:d6; 2 ♗a7, ♗c7; 3 ♗b8, ♗d8; 4 ♗:g3, h4; 5 ♗e5, h3; 6 ♗h2+.

P. BENKO

MAGYAR SAKKÉLET

1970

DIAGRAM 164

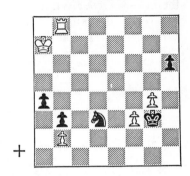

+

A baffling configuration, containing, as will be seen, a bagful of intricate concepts. Black is about to win by ... N×P or ... K×BP; followed by ... K×NP; in either case establishing a passed pawn on each wing. Therefore, White's king must somehow get near the action, to defend an otherwise lost cause. But if 1 K—R6?, N×P!; 2 K—R5, P—R6!; 3 K—N4, P—R7; 4 R—QR8, N—R5!! (freeing the NP's line); 5 R×N, P—N7+. The key is an eye-opener.

    1 K—N6!! P—R6!   2 P×P

Obvious. The focal constellation now on the board is in composer's jargon called a "direct battery"—two pieces on the same line as the crucial spot that is aimed at. When the front piece moves, the gun behind comes into action. Here the rook is the gun aiming at the protection of Black's ultimate queening square QN8.

For example, if 2 ... P—N7; 3 K—B6 (the front piece moves away!), K×P; 4 P—R4, K×P; 5 P—R5 and White wins easily.

    2 ... N—N5!!

A magnificent tactical stroke. 3 P×N would spike White's own battery, with 3 ... P—N7 winning for Black. Likewise, the move introduces an added nuance known as the "star-flight" theme—wherever White's king moves aside to clear the line for the rook, the knight checks and captures the rook! Thus, White shifts his strategy:

    3 R—Q8! P—N7   4 R—Q1 N—R7!

Threatens 4 ... N—B8.

    5 R—QN1 N—B6!   6 R—KR1

If 6 R × P, N—R5 ch and 6 ... N × R.

Now follows a bit of a run-around.

    6 ...   K—N7   8 R—KR1 K—K7!
    7 R—K1 K—B7   9 R—R2 ch

If 9 R—KN1, N—Q8!; 10 R—N2 ch, K × P; 11 R × P, N × R+
Thus White must once more look for another stratagem.

    9 ... K × P   10 R—R1 P—N8(Q) ch

If 10 ... K × P; 11 K—B5!, P—N8(Q); 12 R × Q, N × R;
13 P—R4, N—Q7; 14 K—N4! N—K5; 15 P—R5, N—Q3;
16 P—R6, N—B1; 17 K—B5, P—R4; 18 K—B6, P—R5;
19 K—B7!, N—R2; 20 K—N6!, N—B8 ch; 21 K—B7!=.

    11 R × Q N × R   15 K—B5! K—K5
    12 P—R4 N—Q7   16 K—B4! N—B3
    13 K—N5 N—N6   17 K—B5! N—R4
    14 K—N4! N—Q5

The foregoing moves were a fight for equilibrium—to stop White's passed pawn and to keep Black from gaining one. If 17 ... N—N1; 18 P—R5!, K—K4; 19 K—N6!, K—Q3; 20 K—N7, N—Q2; 21 K—B8!, N—B4; 22 K—Q8!, N—Q6; 23 P—R6!=

    18 K—N5 N—N6   20 K—B3!!
    19 K—N4 N—Q7!

Strangely, the only move holding the game together. If 20 P—R5?, K—Q4!; 21 K—N5, K—Q3!; 22 P—R6, K—B2;

SUB–DIAGRAM 164 (A)

POSITION AFTER WHITE'S

20 K—B3

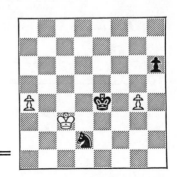

=

23 K—B5, N—K5 ch; 24 K—Q4, N—B3!; 25 K—K5, N×P ch; 26 K—B5, P—R4; 27 K—N5, N—B3!+. If 20 K—B5, K—K4; 21 K—B6, N—N6; 22 K—N5, K—Q4; 23 K—N6, K—Q3 wins again.

20 ... N—B6		24 P—R7! K—N2
21 K—B4 K—K4!		25 K—Q5! N—R7
22 P—R5! K—Q3		26 P—N5!!
23 P—R6 K—B3		

Utilizing a device that dates back to Ponziani (see diagram 203).

If passively 26 K—K4?, N×P; 27 K—B5, P—R4; 28 K—N5, N—B3! and White is finally lost.

26 ... P×P		29 K—B4 K—N3
27 K—K4 K×P		30 K—N3 draw
28 K—B5 P—N5		

A complete grammar of transformations.

Alg.: 1 ♔b6, a3; 2 b:a3, ♘b4; 3 ♖d8, b2; 4 ♖d1, ♘a2; 5 ♖b1, ♘c3;
6 ♖h1, ♔g2; 7 ♖e1, ♔f2; 8 ♖h1, ♔e2; 9 ♖h2†, ♔:f3; 10 ♖h1,
b1(♕)†; 11 ♖:b1, ♘:b1; 12 a4, ♘d2; 13 ♔b5, ♘b3; 14 ♔b4,
♘d4; 15 ♔c5, ♔e4; 16 ♔c4, ♘c6; 17 ♔c5, ♘a5; 18 ♔b5, ♘b3;
19 ♔b4, ♘d2; 20 ♔c3, ♘f3; 21 ♔c4, ♔e5; 22 a5, ♔d6; 23 a6,
♔c6; 24 a7, ♔b7; 25 ♔d5, ♘h2; 26 g5, h:g5; 27 ♔e4, ♔:a7;
28 ♔f5, g4; 29 ♔f4, ♔b6; 30 ♔g3=.

DIAGRAM 165

P. BENKO

MAGYAR SAKKÉLET
TOURNEY

1967–68

2nd Prize

Position I

=

A set of studies, termed "twins". It consists of two settings only slightly dissimilar, but with solutions greatly apart. The other fraternal twin, Position II, is depicted in diagram 165(A).

1 K—B1 P—B7   2 B—B7 R—N7

2 B—K5?, R—R4; 3 B—Q6, R—KB4+. Or 2 B—Q6?, R—R3; 3 B—B5, K—N6; 4 B×P ch, K—B6+.

3 B—Q6 R—B7   5 B—B4 R—K7!
4 B—K5 R—Q7   6 B—N8 R—K1

6 K×R?, K—N7+. Or 6 B—Q6, R—N7; 7 B—K5, R—N4; 8 B—Q4, K—N6+. Or 6 B—B7?, R—R7; 7 B—N3, K—N5; 8 B×P, K—B6+.

7 B—N3 K—N5   9 K—N2 draw
8 K×P R—B1 ch

7 B—R7?, K—N6; 8 B×P ch, K—B6+.

The many tributary lines of this complex endgame are detailed as a full page of unabridged dialogue, in A. Chéron's monumental *Lehr- und Handbuch der Endspiele*, Vol. IV (Berlin, 1970).

P. BENKO

DIAGRAM 165 (A)

Position II

Same as in diagram 165, but with White's king moved to KN1 (g1) and Black's rook to QN7 (b2).

1 B—Q6 R—Q7	3 K—B1 P—B7
2 B—B4 R—N7 ch	4 K—K2 draw

If 4 ... K—N5; 5 B—B7, P—B8(Q) ch; 6 K×Q, K—B6; 7 K—K1=.

Pál Benko, like Rossolimo, is a visible exponent of globe-trotting chess. Born in Paris of Hungarian parentage and an American national, he is at home wherever chess is in serious demand. His foremost hobby is the construction of helpmates and chess acronyms, but he is adept in all other branches of the art. He is an International Grandmaster.

Alg.: Position I. 1 ♔f1, f2; 2 ♗c7, ♖b2; 3 ♗d6, ♖c2; 4 ♗e5, ♖d2; 5 ♗f4, ♖e2; 6 ♗b8, ♖e8; 7 ♗g3, ♔g4; 8 ♔:f2, ♖f8†; 9 ♔g2=.
Position II. 1 ♗d6, ♖d2; 2 ♗f4, ♖g2†; 3 ♔f1, f2; 4 ♔e2=.

DIAGRAM 166

M. MARBLE

THE CHESS AMATEUR

1914

White to play—what result?

Position I

One of the earliest still embryonic occurrences of twins, hatched in the United States.

Twins must represent specific unique positions that are valid only in their artistic context, but not generally applicable. Otherwise almost any comparative endings analyses might be viewed as twins, or up to sextuplets!

In the given setting, the pawns can be stopped, for example:

    1 N—K4 P—R5!

Insufficient is 1 ... P—N5; 2 K—B4!=

    2 K—B3 K—R4   3 N—Q2 P—N5 ch

If 3 ... P—B4; 4 N—N1, P—N5 ch; 5 K—B4, P—R6; 6 K—N3, K—N4; 7 N—Q2, K—N3; 8 K—B4, P—R7; 9 N—N3=.

    4 K—B4!   P—R6   6 N—B5 ch
    5 N—N3 ch K—R5   with perpetual check.

Alg.: 1 ♘e4, a4; 2 ♔c3, ♔a5; 3 ♘d2, b4†; 4 ♔c4, a3; 5 ♘b3†, ♔a4; 6 ♘c5†=.

M. MARBLE

DIAGRAM 166 (A)

What result?

Position II

As in diagram 166, but White's and Black's pieces and pawns all moved one rank lower, towards White's side of the board.

Black's gain of a whole rank makes all the difference. Some pawn must go through, e.g.:

1 N—K3 P—R6		4 N—K3 P—N6 ch
2 K—B2 K—R5		5 K—B3 P—R7
3 N—Q1 P—B5		6 K—N2 P—B6 ch

and Black will win.

Because the exact role and definition of "twins" allows much leeway, they are in disfavor and often excluded from competitions. They nevertheless offer much to experiment with, even in orthodox endgame study composition.

Alg.: 1 ♞e3, a3; 2 ♔c2, ♚a4; 3 ♞d1, c4; 4 ♞e3, b3†; 5 ♔c3, a2; 6 ♔b2, c3†+.

DIAGRAM 167

J. BUCHWALD

CHESS LIFE & REVIEW

1968

Twin =

Position I

1 P—Q4   Q×QP   3 B—B3 ch Q×B
2 P—R8(Q) Q×Q   Stalemate

Buchwald, a problemist of stature, performed equally well when stimulated by a required exercise in the domain of endgame study.

The twins are identical except for White's minor pieces.

The results differ.

Alg.: 1 d4, ♛:d4; 2 h8(♛), ♛:h8; 3 ♗c3†, ♛:c3⊜.

DIAGRAM 167 (A)

J. BUCHWALD

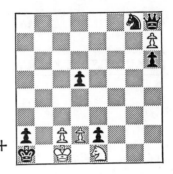

Twin +

Position II

1 P—B3 Q×RP
2 P—Q3 Q×P
3 N×Q any

4 N—K1 any
5 N—B2 mate

Alg.: c3, ♕:h7; 2 d3, ♕:d3; 3 ♘:d3, ∞; 4 ♘e1, ∞; 5 ♘c2♯.

DIAGRAM 168

O. WEINBERGER

F.I.D.E.
OLYMPIC STUDY TOURNEY

1960

2nd Hon. Mention

$+$

A native *Zugzwang* of the purest brew.

    1 P—B7 B—Q3   2 K—N2 K×P

Making Black's king lose ground, and gaining time and space for White.

    3 K—B3 K—N6   4 K—K4! K—B5!

If 4 ... P—N3?; 5 K—Q5, B—R6; 6 K—K6, K—B5; 7 K—B6, K—Q4; 8 K×P, K—K3; 9 K—N7, K—B4; 10 P—N6, K—N4; 11 K—R7+. If 4 K—N4?, P—N3 draws.

    5 K—B5 K—Q4   8 K—N8 K—K2
    6 K—N6 B—B1   9 P—N6!!
    7 K—R7 K—K3

Black's king must abandon the bishop.

Alg.: 1 f7, ♝d6; 2 ♔g2, ♚:a2; 3 ♔f3, ♚b3; 4 ♔e4, ♚c4; 5 ♔f5, ♚d5; 6 ♔g6, ♝f8; 7 ♔h7, ♚e6; 8 ♔g8, ♚e7; 9 g6+.

DIAGRAM 169

A. H. BRANTON

BRITISH CHESS MAGAZINE

1949

+

One of the American composer's boyhood pieces. It already shows consummate skill.

As a start, White's king moves sidewise to threaten mate. If he selects:

1 K—B7, N—B5!; 2 B—B3 ch, N—N7; 3 R×N (if 3 B×N ch, K—N8; 4 B—K4 dis. ch, K×P; 5 B×R, P—R8(Q)=; or 5 R—R7, K—N8=), B—K7; 4 B—K4, B—Q6; 5 B×B, K×R; 6 B×R, K×P; 7 B—K4, K—K6; 8 B—Q5, K—Q5; 9 K—K6, K—B4!, Black draws. How, then, does White win?

1 K—R6!	N—B5	6 B—B6	B—N4
2 B—B3 ch	N—N7	7 B—N7	B—R3
3 R×N	B—K7	8 B—R8!!	R×P
4 B—K4!	B—Q6	9 R—N7 dis. ch!	B—N2
5 B—Q5!	B—B5	10 R×B	wins

If 10 B×B ch, R×B; 11 R×R, K—N7; 12 R—N1, K×P=. A pandora of cross-pinnings, un-pinnings, and an "Indian" theme (B—R8), beautiful to behold.

Alg.: 1 ♔h6, ♘f4; 2 ♗f3†, ♘g2; 3 ♖:g2, ♗e2; 4 ♗e4, ♗d3; 5 ♗d5, ♗c4; 6 ♗c6, ♗b5; 7 ♗b7, ♗a6; 8 ♗a8, ♖:b2; 9 ♖g7†, ♗b7; 10 ♖:b7+.

DIAGRAM 170

A. H. BRANTON

BRITISH CHESS MAGAZINE

1950

=

A year later, Branton created an impressive positional study with two accompanying variations.

    1 R—B6 ch K—R4!

1 ... K—B2; 2 K—B5, P—R6; 3 B—B6, P—R7; 4 R—B7 ch, K—any; 5 K—Q6 and 6 R—B8‡.

    2 K—B5 P—R6   3 B—R5! P—R7

3 B—B6?, P—R7; 4 B—N7, K—R5; 5 B—Q5, P—R4; 6 R×P, B×R; 7 B×B, K—N6‡.

    4 R×P   P—R8(Q)!   6 P—N4 ch K—R5
    5 R—R3 ch! P×R   7 B—Q1 ch Q×B

Stalemate! Black walls himself in but White stalemates himself. The interlocking mechanism deserves attention.

Alg.: 1 ♖f6†, ♔a5; 2 ♔c5, h3; 3 ♗h5, h2; 4 ♖:f3, h1(♕); 5 ♖a3†, b:a3; 6 b4†, ♔a4; 7 ♗d1†, ♕:d1 =.

DIAGRAM 171

A. H. BRANTON

SZACHY

1965

1st Hon. Mention

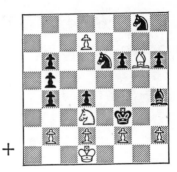

$+$

A tense tempo play of rare attraction—and devotion.

1 B—R5 ch K—K5

If 1 ... K—N7; 2 N—B4 ch, N×N; 3 P—Q8(Q)+.

2 P—B3 ch K×N

On a sure but narrow path, White wins after 2 ... K—Q4; 3 B—B7, P—B4; 4 N—B4 ch, K—Q3; 5 N×N, K×P; 5 B×N.

3 P—N3 P—B4

The initial development of forces has delivered all actors to their proper stations. Crush hour is at hand.

4 P—Q8(Q)	B×Q	8 P—R4	P—B5
5 B—K8	N—B2	9 B—R3!	any
6 B—Q7	N—K2	10 B—B1 mate	
7 P—R3	P—R4		

Inadvertently, in the end position the contours of a cross may be discerned.

Alg.: 1 ♗h5†, ♔e4; 2 f3†, ♔:d3; 3 b3, f5; 4 d8(♕), ♗:d8; 5 ♗e8, ♘c7; 6 ♗d7, ♘e7; 7 h3, h5; 8 h4, f4; 9 ♗h3, ∞; 10 ♗f1#.

DIAGRAM 172

A. H. BRANTON

*CALIFORNIA CHESS
REPORTER*

1953

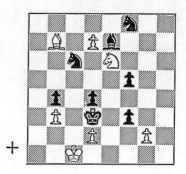

+

The previous diagram was positionally more proficient, but this forerunner has the vigorous freshness of youth. The knight interferences on two of White's bishop diagonals and their clearance are very problem-like.

1 P—Q8(Q) B×Q

If 1 ... N×Q? (baring the diagonal!); 2 N—B4 with a pure mate.

2 K—Q1!

Moving in with the threat 3 N—B5 mate—another pure mate on the other wing.

2 ... N×N

If 2 ... K—K5; 3 B×N ch, K—K4; 4 N×B wins.

3 P×P	N—B2	5 B—Q7!!	P—B5
4 B—B8	N—K2		

Again, a neo-symbolic construction of a perfect cross. Now Black's king is crucified: 6 B—R3 and mate to follow.

Alg.: 1 d8(♛), ♗:d8; 2 ♚d1, ♘:e6; 3 g:f3, ♘c7; 4 ♗c8, ♘e7; 5 ♗d7, f4; 6 ♗h3+.

DIAGRAM 173

S. ALMGREN

CALIFORNIA CHESS
REPORTER

1963

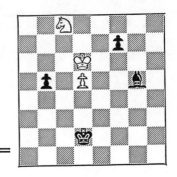

=

After a long leave of absence, another miniature of Almgren's master touch.

    1 K—B5 P—B4   2 N—Q6 B—K2

If 2 ... P—N5!?; 3 K—B4!, P—N6; 4 K×P, P—B5; 5 N—K4, draws easily.

    3 K—Q4 P—B5

If 3 ... B×N stalemate, forming the symbol of a cross.

    4 N—B5! P—N5   6 N×B
    5 P—Q6! B×P

Another, squarish, cross—or plus—sign.
    Black may continue 6 ... P—B6; 7 N—B4 ch, K—K7; 8 N—Q6!, P—B7; 9 N—K4= or create an echo by 6 ... P—N6; 7 N—K4 ch, K—B7; 8 N—Q6, P—N7; 9 N—B4=.

But a question remains about 2 K × P, P—B5; 3 N—Q6, which may also draw.

Alg.: 1 ♔c5, f5; 2 ♘d6, ♗e7; 3 ♔d4, f4; 4 ♘f5, b4; 5 d6, ♗:d6; 6 ♘:d6, f3; 7 ♘c4†, ♔e2; 8 ♘d6, f2; 9 ♘e4=.

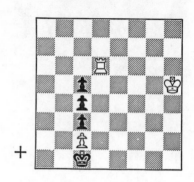

DIAGRAM 174

O. WEINBERGER

BRITISH CHESS MAGAZINE

1960

+

A very subtle give and take.

 1 K—N4 K×P   2 K—B3 K—B8

If 2 ... K—N7; 3 R—N6 ch, K—any; 4 K—K2 wins.

 3 K—K2

If 3 R—QN6, K—Q7; 4 R—Q6 ch, K—K8 draw.

 3 ... P—B7

Or 3 ... K—B7; 4 R—QN6, K—B8; 5 R—N5, K—B7; 6 R×P, K—N6; 7 K—Q1 and White wins.

 4 R—QN6 P—B6

Black threatens ... P—B5, provoking either a stalemate or a perpetual check.

 5 R—N3! P—B5   7 K—Q2 wins
 6 R×P   K—N7

Almost another cross—almost a trend.

Alg.: 1 ♔g4, ♚:c2; 2 ♔f3, ♚c1; 3 ♔e2, c2; 4 ♖b6, c3; 5 ♖b3, c4; 6 ♖:c3, ♚b2; 7 ♔d2+.

DIAGRAM 175

O. WEINBERGER

J. ZABINSKI* MEMORIAL
TOURNEY–SZACHY

1960

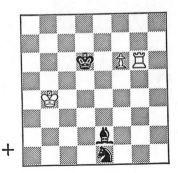

5th Commendation

+

A very graceful demonstration . . . .

1 P—B7 dis. ch	K—K2	3 R—K8 ch	K×P
2 R—K6 ch	K—B1	4 R×B	N—Q6 ch

. . . resulting in a rook versus knight ending where the latter is neatly pinned.

5 K—B4	N—B5	6 R—KB2 wins

---

* Polish composer (1860–1928). Dia. 153(A) was also in his honor.

Alg.: 1 f7†, ♚e7; 2 ♖e6†, ♚f8; 3 ♖e8†, ♚:f7; 4 ♖:e2, ♞d3†; 5 ♚c4, ♞f4; 6 ♖f2+.

DIAGRAM 176

A. H. BRANTON

CANADIAN CHESS CHAT

1966

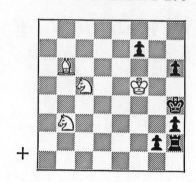

+

A thoroughly tricky and cunning execution, with wily tries, and a total surprise at the finish.

1 B—Q8 ch K—N6

If 1 ... K—R4; 2 N—Q3, and 3 N—B4, mate.

2 B—B7 ch K—B6!

There is no escape in 2 ... K—B7; 3 N—K4 ch! K—B6; 4 N—Q4 ch! K—K6; 5 B×R, K×N; 6 K—B4+.

3 N—Q4 ch!

3 N—Q2 ch, K—K7; 4 B×R, K×N; 5 K—B4 (5 N—K4 ch, K—K7; 6 K—B4, P—N8(Q); 7 B×Q, K—B8=), K—K7; 6 N—K4, P—N8(Q); 7 B×Q, K—B8=.

3 ... K—B7

If 3 ... K—K6; 4 B×R, K×N; 5 B—N1 ch+.

4 N—K4 ch K—B8   7 N—K4 ch K—R5
5 N—Q2 ch K—B7   8 N—B3 ch K—R4
6 B—N3 ch!! K×B   9 N—N3 mate

A wholly unexpected change of scenery, with Black's men blocking off the king's flight from the pursuing knights.

To draw another parallel with the story of diagrams 72–4, the sideline (1 B—Q8 ch, K—N6; 2 B—B7 ch) 2 ... K—B7; 3 N—K4 ch, K—B6 seemingly leads to a draw after 4 B × R, P—N8(Q); 5 B × Q, K—N7, but 6 N—B2, P—R7; 7 B × P, K × B; 8 N—N4 ch, K—N6; 9 N × P wins with two knights against pawn.

Alg.: 1 ♗d8†, ♔g3; 2 ♗c7†, ♔f3; 3 ♘d4†, ♔f2; 4 ♘e4†, ♔f1; 5 ♘d2†, ♔f2; 6 ♗g3†, ♔:g3; 7 ♘e4†, ♔h4; 8 ♘f3†, ♔h5, 9 ♘g3‡.

DIAGRAM 177

A. H. BRANTON

NEW STATESMAN

1966-7

=

2nd Prize, Study Tourney

White elegantly prevents Black's pawn from queening.

1 N—Q3 ch K—Q5	3 K—Q2 N—B5 ch	
2 B×P B—B6 ch		

If 3 K×B, K×N; 4 B—K5, N—B5; 5 B—R1 (5 B—B6, N—N7; followed by ... K—B7 and ... P—R7—R8(Q) wins), N—N7; and ... K—B7—N8 wins.

4 K—B2 B—Q8 ch	6 B—B1! K—B6
5 K—N1! K×N	

If 6 ... B—N6; 7 B×P! N×B ch; 8 K—N2 winning one of Black's pieces. Just the same:

7 B×P!! N×B ch	8 K—B1!

Wherever the bishop moves, White has stalemated himself!

Alg.: 1 ♘d3†, ♚d4; 2 ♗:f4, ♝f3†; 3 ♚d2, ♞c4†; 4 ♚c2, ♝d1†; 5 ♚b1, ♚:d3; 6 ♗c1, ♚c3; 7 ♗:a3, ♞:a3; 8 ♚c1=.

A. H. BRANTON

TIDSKRIFT FÖR SCHACK

1966–7

DIAGRAM 178

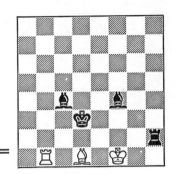

1st Prize, Study Tourney   =

Analysis of the components reveals that Black is only one minor piece ahead, so that, normally, White should be able to draw. But as is obvious to any practical chess strategist, White's king on the edge is being strangled by several attacks that threaten direct mates or loss of material by discovered checks. In the situation on the board, White is without checks to defend himself adequately, as Black's pieces control all such squares. If Black were to move, he winds up with 1 ... K—K6 dis. ch; 2 K—N1 (2 K—K1, B—N6‡), B—Q4; 3 B—B3, K×B; 4 R—B1 ch, K—K7; 5 R×B, R—N7 ch+.

1 K—N1!	B—Q4	5 R—N3 ch	K—K5
2 B—B3!	B×B	6 R—N4 ch	K—K4
3 R—N3 ch	K—K5	7 R×B!	R—N7 ch!
4 R—N4 ch	K—K6		

If 7 ... R—R8 ch; 8 K—B2, K×R=.

8 K—R1	R—B7 dis. ch	11 K—R2	R—N7 ch
9 K—N1	R—N7 ch	12 K—R1	draw
10 K—R1	R—N6 dis. ch		

White's rook is untouchable because of stalemate.

Alg.: 1 ♔g1, ♗d5; 2 ♗f3, ♗:f3; 3 ♖b3†, ♔e4; 4 ♖b4†, ♔e3; 5 ♖b3†, ♔e4; 6 ♖b4†, ♔e5; 7 ♖:f4, ♖g2†; 8 ♔h1, ♖f2†; 9 ♔g1, ♖g2†; 10 ♔h1, ♖g3†; 11 ♔h2, ♖g2†; 12 ♔h1=.

DIAGRAM 179

A. H. BRANTON

E. G.

1973

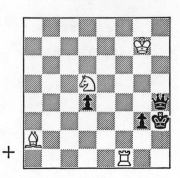

Dedicated to J. E. Peckover

+

1 R—R1 ch

1 N—B4 ch leads nowhere after 1 ... K—R7.

    1 ... K—N5   2 N—B6 ch

If 2 R×Q ch? K×R; 3 N—B4, P—Q6; 4 B—Q5, P—Q7; 5 B—B3, P—N7; 6 N×P ch, K—N6 =.

    2 ... K—N4   3 N—R7 ch

Likewise, 3 R×Q, K×R; 4 B—Q5, P—Q6; 5 N—K4, P—N7 =; or 5 B—B3, P—Q7; 6 N—any, P—N7 =.

But an extremely close try is 3 B—Q5, Q×R! (The only defense. If 3 ... P—N7; 4 B×P, Q—N6 (B7); 5 N—K4 ch wins); 4 B×Q, K—B5; 5 N—Q5 ch, K—K4; 6 N—N4, K—B5; 7 N—Q5 ch (7 N—B2, P—Q6!), K—K4; 8 K—N6, P—Q6; 9 N—K3, K—Q5; 10 N—Q1 (10 N—B5 ch, K—B6; 11 N×P, P—Q7; 12 B—B3, K—B7; 13 N—B1, P—Q8(N)! =), P—Q7; 11 K—B5, K—Q6; 12 K—B4, K—B7; 13 N—K3 ch, K—B8; 14 B—B3, P—N7 =.

    3 ... K—R4!   4 B—B7 ch! K—N5

Not 4 B—Q5? Q×R; 5 B×Q, K—N5; 6 B—N2, K—B5; 7 N—B6, K—K6 etc.

 5 B—K6 ch K—R4   6 R—K1 Q—B5

To prevent 7 R—K5 ch. If 6 ... Q—K2 ch; 7 B—B7 ch and 8
R × Q wins. If 6 ... Q—Q1 (orQ—R7); 7 R—K5 ch, K—R5;
8 R—K4 ch, K—R4; 9 B—B7 mate.

 7 N—B6 ch K—N4

7 ... K—R5; 8 R—R1 ch, K—N4; 9 R—R5 mate.

 8 N—K4 ch K—R4   10 N×P ch K—N4
 9 R—R1 ch Q—R5   11 R×Q   wins

At last, after a tenacious dog fight.

Alg.: 1 ♖h1†, ♔g4; 2 ♘f6†, ♔g5; 3 ♘h7†, ♔h5; 4 ♗f7†, ♔g4; 5 ♗e6†,
   ♔h5; 6 ♖e1, ♕f4; 7 ♘f6†, ♔g5; 8 ♘e4†, ♔h5; 9 ♖h1†, ♕h4:
   10 ♘:g3†, ♔g5; 11 ♖:h4+.

DIAGRAM 180

O. WEINBERGER

*J. ZABINSKI MEMORIAL
TOURNEY–SZACHY*

1960

4th Hon. Mention

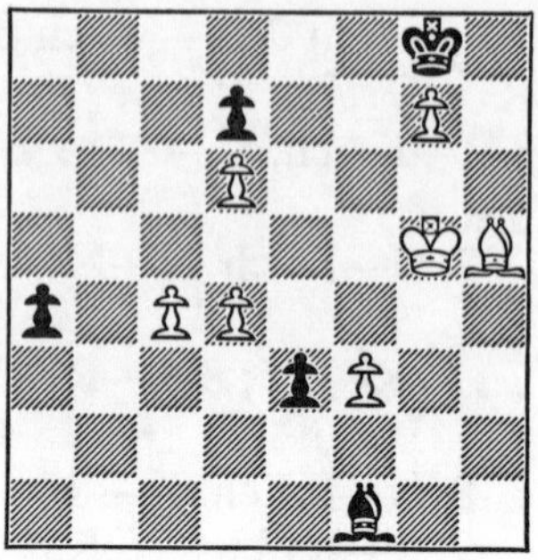

$+$

By the modest means of an advanced pawn and a bishop, White inconspicuously weaves a mating net against Black's much superior force and an advanced rook's or king's pawn.

    1 K—R6 B—Q6!

If 1 ... P—K7; 2 B—N6, P—K8(Q); 3 B—R7 ch, K—B2; 4 P—N8(Q) ch, K—B3; 5 Q—N6#.

    2 P—B4?!

Is White out to postpone defeat by 2 ... P—K7; 3 B×P? In fact, his move is a ruse, and a mate is to come.

2 ... P—K7	3 B—B3! B×P

If 3 ... P—K8(Q); 4 B—Q5 ch, Q—K3 ch; 5 B×Q ch, P×B; 6 P—Q7+.

4 B—K4! K—B2	6 B—N6 ch K—B3
5 P—Q5 P—K8(Q)	7 P—N8(N) mate

Alg.: 1 ♔h6, ♗d3; 2 f4, e2; 3 ♗f3, ♗:c4; 4 ♗e4, ♔f7; 5 d5, e1(♕); 6 ♗g6†, ♔f6; g8(♘)#.

DIAGRAM 181

O. WEINBERGER

PROBLEM

SEPTEMBER, 1962

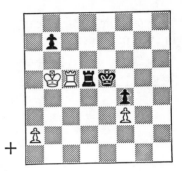

+

A modern comeback of orthodox pawn-tempo play. After a prologue, a dialogue ensues between a queen and an advanced bishop's pawn.

If 1 K—N6, K—Q3!; 2 R×R ch, K×R; 3 K×P, K—Q5; 4 P—R4, K—K6 =.

1 K—B4 R×R ch		4 K—B5 P—N5
2 K×R P—N3 ch!		5 K×P
3 K—B4 P—N4 ch		

White's king wisely delayed taking the pawn.

After 4 K×P, K—Q5; 5 P—R4, K—K6; 6 P—R5, K×P; 7 P—R6, K—K7; 8 P—R7, P—B6; 9 P—R8(Q), P—B7 the position would have been a book draw. But as played, the White king is one important rank nearer.

5 ... K—Q5		9 P—R7 P—B6
6 P—R4 K—K6		10 P—R8(Q) P—B7
7 P—R5 K×P		11 Q—R2 ch K—K8
8 P—R6 K—K7		

If 11 ... K—B8; 12 Q—N8!, K—K8; 13 Q—KN3, K—K7; 14 Q—N2, K—K8; 15 K—B3! K—K7 (15 ... P—B8(Q); 16 Q—Q2); 16 K—B2, K—K8; 17 Q—N3, K—B8; 18 K—Q3, K—K8; 19 K—K3+.

12 K—B3! P—B8(Q)   13 Q—Q2 mate

The next diagram, of earlier vintage, contains the same motif in even purer essence.

Alg.: 1 ♔c4, ♖:c5†; 2 ♔:c5, b6†; 3 ♔c4, b5†; 4 ♔c5, b4; 5 ♔:b4, ♚d4; 6 a4, ♚e3; 7 a5, ♚:f3; 8 a6, ♚e2; 9 a7, f3; 10 a8(♕), f2; 11 ♕a2†, ♚e1; 12 ♔f3, f1(♕); 13 ♕d2#.

DIAGRAM 182

W. KORN

CHESS

1943

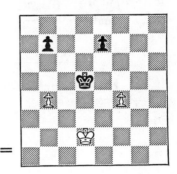

=

King-and-pawns *tempo* and opposition play, with an exhaustive alternative of queen versus bishop's pawn on the seventh rank.

1 K—Q3 P—N4

If 1 ... P—N3; 2 P—N5! K—B4 (or 2 ... P—K4; 3 P×P, K×P; 4 K—K3, K—Q4; 5 K—Q3, K—B4; 6 K—B3, K×P; 7 K—N3+, or 2 ... P—K3; 3 K—K3, P—K4; 4 P—B5+); 3 K—K4, K×P; 4 K—Q5=.

2 K—K3 K—B5   4 K—Q5!
3 K—K4 K×P

Instead of the direct route 4 K—K5 and 5 K—K6, White's king with an expert's instinct marches forward in an oblique pattern, because Black is thus deprived of the choice 4 ... K—B4 or 4 ... K—B5 whatever they are worth.

And indeed, 4 K—K5? would be a careless give-away, as shown in sub-diagram 182(A).

4 ... K—B6   5 K—K6

If 5 P—B5?, K—Q6; 6 K—K6, K—K5; 7 K×P, K×P; 8 K—Q6, P—N5+.

5 ... K—Q5

If 5 ... P—N5?; 6 K×P, P—N6; 7 P—B5, P—N7; 8 P—B6, P—N8(Q); 9 P—B7 with a book draw. Black's king is too far away to matter.

    6 K×P K—K5   7 K—K6!! draw

If 7 ... K×P; 8 K—Q5 catches Black's pawn. If 7 ... P—N5; 8 P—B5 =.

Alg.: 1 ♔d3, b5; 2 ♔e3, ♚c4; 3 ♔e4, ♚:b4; 4 ♔d5, ♚c3; 5 ♔e6, ♚d4; 6 ♔:e7, ♚e4; 7 ♔e6=.

SUB-DIAGRAM 182 (A)

With colors reversed

Position after Black's
...K/Q4—Q5? (instead of
...K/Q4—K5!=)

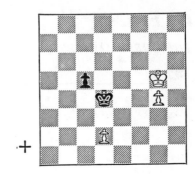

In diagram 182, if White plays 4 K—K4, he loses. The crucial juncture is reproduced here with colors reversed, thus exemplifying the try in the shape of "White to win."

1 K—B4	K—Q6	4 P—N7	P—B6
2 P—N5	P—B5	5 P—N8(Q)	P—B7
3 P—N6	K×P		

One of the exceptional cases has arisen when Black's bishop's pawn on the seventh fails to secure a draw because Black's king is on the wrong side of his pawn and White's king is in favorable vicinity. The basics were first shown by Lolli in 1763! The *modus operandi* is as in Weinberger's piece No. 181 but, as the queen operates on the other wing, more protracted pressure needs to be applied here.

6 Q—R2!	K—Q8	10 Q—Q4 ch	K—B8
7 K—B3	K—Q7	11 Q—QN4	K—Q8
8 Q—N2	K—Q8	12 Q—K1 mate	
9 K—B2	K—Q7		

Diagrams 181, 182 and 182(A) form a useful course in endgame theory.

Alg.: 1 ♔f4, ♚d3; 2 g5, c4; 3 g6, ♚:d2; 4 g7, c3; 5 g8(♕), c2; 6 ♕a2, ♚d1; 7 ♔f3, ♚d2; 8 ♕b2, ♚d1; 9 ♔f2, ♚d2; 10 ♕d4†, ♚c1; 11 ♕b4, ♚d1; 12 ♕e1 ⧣.

DIAGRAM 183

O. FRINK

THE CHESS AMATEUR

1927

An endgame analysis

+

A study that would have made history, had the "greats" acknowledged it. As late as in 1922, J. Berger* assessed the position a draw because White's king seemed unable to get near enough. But Prof. Orrin Frink found the way:

    1 K—B5!! P—B7   2 Q—K8 ch K—Q7

2 ... K—B8; 3 K—N4, K—N8; 4 K—N3 mates in three.

3 Q—N5!	K—K8	7 Q—K3 ch	K—B8
4 Q—N1 ch	K—K7	8 K—N4	K—N7
5 Q—K4 ch!	K—Q7	9 Q—K2	K—N8
6 Q—B3	K—K8	10 K—N3	wins

This analysis is a valuable supplement to the theory of the endgame, but it is not exactly a study, because White's first two moves can be interchanged.

A. Chéron in 1952 also corrected Berger's statement, but apparently did not recall Frink's findings. Later on, Chéron amplified the endgame position by quoting a study containing elements of the same, new idea (see diagram 184).

* J. Berger, op. cit., No. 175.

Alg.: 1 ♔f5, f2; 2 ♕e8†, ♔d2; 3 ♕b5, ♔e1; 4 ♕b1†, ♔e2; 5 ♕e4†, ♔d2; 6 ♕f3, ♔e1; 7 ♕e3†, ♔f1; 8 ♔g4, ♔g2; 9 ♕e2, ♔g1; 10 ♔g3+.

DIAGRAM 184

H.D.GRIGORYEV§

USSR, 1932

(As quoted in A. Chéron's "Lehr-
und Handbuch der Endspiele",
1964, Vol. II, Dia. 702)

+

1 K—B5!	K—K6	7 P—R8(Q)	P—B2
2 K—K5	P—B3!	8 Q—Q5 ch	K—K7
3 P—R4	K—Q6	9 Q—R2	K—Q7
4 P—R5	P—B4	10 K—Q4	K—Q8
5 P—R6	P—B5	11 K—K3	P—B8(Q) ch
6 P—R7	P—B6	12 K—Q3! wins	

A very interesting sequel to diagram 183, but O. Frink himself
had already supplied an American first, which remained dormant
(see diagram 185).

Alg.: 1 ♔f5, ♚e3; 2 ♔e5, c6; 3 a4, ♚d3; 4 a5, c5; 5 a6, c4; 6 a7, c3;
7 a8(♕), c7; 8 ♕d5†, ♚e2; 9 ♕a2, ♚d2; 10 ♔d4, ♚d1; 11 ♔e3,
c1(♕)†; 12 ♔d3+.

DIAGRAM 185

O. FRINK

THE CHESS AMATEUR

1927

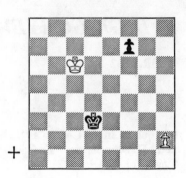

+

The sole difference between this and the previous diagram is the addition there of another introductory move. Grigoryev himself, a towering personality in this field of pawn endings, probably used the above position as an example, added to many of his own comparisons of available maneuvers.

To quote all sidelines as well:

  1 K—Q5 P—B3!!

The amazing, best, defence. If 1 ... K—K6; 2 K—K5, P—B3 ch (or 2 ... K—B6); 3 K—B5 wins (note here that, if White's pawn were at R3, 3 ... K—N6 would draw). After Black's 1 ... P—B3 the win becomes more intricate.

  2 P—R4 K—K6!   3 P—R5 P—B4

Upon 3 K—K6 follows 3 ... K—B5; 4 K × P, K—N5 =.

  4 P—R6 P—B5   6 P—R8(Q) P—B7
  5 P—R7 P—B6   7 Q—K5 ch!

Until Frink's analysis was published, the conventional strategy here, e.g. 7 Q—R3 ch, K—K7; 8 Q—N2, K—K8; 9 Q—N3, K—K7; 10 Q—K5 ch, K—Q8!; 11 Q—R5 ch, K—K8!; 12 Q—R4, K—K7; 13 Q—R2, K—B6! only proved a draw with

256

the best defence. If Black slips with 7 ... K—Q7; 8 Q—R2, K—K8 (8 ... K—K6; 9 Q—N2+); 9 K—K4!, P—B8(Q); 10 K—K3 wins in the same manner as in the second sub-variation below.

7 ... K—Q6!?

If 7 ... K—B6; 8 Q—K4 ch, K—N6; 9 Q—R1 wins. At every move and in every sideline one critical tempo decides the out-come.

If 7 ... K—Q7; 8 Q—R2, K—K7; 9 K—K4, K—K8; 10 K—Q3, P—B8(Q) ch; 11 K—K3 wins.

8 Q—N2!! P—B8(Q)   9 Q—N5 ch wins

Alg.: 1 ♔d5, f6; 2 h4, ♚e3; 3 h5, f5; 4 h6, f4; 5 h7, f3; 6 h8(♕), f2; 7 ♕e5†, ♚d3; 8 ♕b2, f1(♕); 9 ♕b5†+.

DIAGRAM 186

M. H. KLEIMAN

CHESS REVIEW

1968

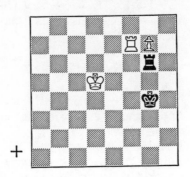

+

After squaring a circle, White's rook and king reach their goal.

1 R—B1 K—R6

If 1 ... R×P?; 2 R—N1 ch+.

2 R—R1 ch K—N7	4 K—K5 K—N5
3 R—R7 K—B6	5 R—R1! K—B6

If 5 ... K—N4; 6 P—N8(Q), R×Q; 7 R—N1 ch+.

6 R—B1 ch K—N7   7 R—B7 wins

If 7 ... K—N6; 8 K—B5, R—N5; 9 K—B6 etc.

One of a number of dainties by a Brooklyn/Floridian composer, although anticipated—see remarks to diagram 187, where the guiding strategy in this piece was missed 42 years earlier.

Alg.: 1 ♖f1, ♚h3; 2 ♖h1†, ♚g2; 3 ♖h7, ♚f3; 4 ♔e5, ♚g4; 5 ♖h1, ♚f3; 6 ♖f1†, ♚g2; 7 ♖f7+.

I. KASHDAN and I. A. HOROWITZ vs. H. STEINER and O. FRINK

DIAGRAM 187

CONSULTATION GAME, MANHATTAN CHESS CLUB

January, 1926
(quoted from *The Chess Amateur,* **July, 1926)**

Black's king is near the enemy's pawns and White's king can be cut off.

The game was called a draw after G. Maróczy, analyzing the position, was also unable to demonstrate a win after 1 R—B7 ch, K—N4; 2 P—N7, R—R1; 3 K—K6, K—R3; 4 R—B8, R—R3 ch; 5 K—B7, R—R2 ch etc. But Kashdan's postmortem turned up an elegant formula of a win.

1 R—B7 ch	K—N4	4 K—B6	R—R3 ch
2 K—K7!	K × P	5 K—B5	R—R4 ch
3 P—N7	R—R2 ch		

Amusing is 5 ... R—KN3?; 6 P—N8(Q), R×Q; 7 R—R7 mate.

    6 K—B4 R—R5 ch

Upon 6 ... R—KN4; follows 7 R—B5!

    7 K—B3 R—R6 ch

If 7 ... R—KN5; 8 R—B5 ch, K—R5; 9 R—B4.

8 K—N2!	R—R7 ch	11 K—B3	R—R6 ch
9 R—B2	R—R1	12 K—K4	wins
10 R—B8	R—R7 ch		

White's king marches over to QN7 and Black has no remedy left.

But to fill out the story of composition and practical play, the same position is also "book," based on a game by Labourdonnais, dissected by Karstedt and by Kling and given in J. Berger*.

Berger's sober solution runs:

1 R—B7 ch, K—N4; 2 P—N7, R—R1; 3 K—K6, R—KN1; 4 R—K7, K—R3 (4 ... K×P; 5 K—B7+); 5 K—B6, R—QR1 (5 ... K—R2; 6 P—R6, K×P; 7 R—K1, K—R4; 8 K—B7+); 6 K—B7, K—R2; 7 P—R6, R—QN1; 8 R—K8, R—N2 ch; 9 K—B8 wins.

The two winning alternatives in this endgame, as against the unilateral solution in diagram 186, explain why composition is the more monolithic and valuable phase of chess art.

But A. J. Roycroft noted that even diagram 186 is only a coincidence. With wings reversed, the analogous winning process was shown by H. D. Grigoryev in *Shakhmaty v SSSR* 1938 (position 187a):

White: K on K4; R on QN7; P on QN6.
Black: K on QR6; R on KR3.

White wins by 1 R—R7 ch, K—N5; 2 P—N7, R—QN3 (forced); 3 K—Q4! (3 K—Q5? K—N4=), R—Q3 ch; 4 K—K5, R—QN3.

The position as reached now is identical with Kleiman's with the one exception that White's rook stands on the rook's instead of the bishop's file, thus prolonging the struggle:

5 R—R1!! K—B6; 6 R—B1 ch, K—N7; 7 R—B7, K—N6; 8 K—Q5, K—N5 (or 8 ... K—R5; 9 K—B5, K—R4; 10 P—N8(Q), R×Q; 11 R—R7⧣); 9 R—B1, K—R6; 10 R—R1 ch, K—N7; 11 R—R7 +.

If at once 3 R—R1? K—B4 =.

* Op. cit., p. 288, para. (A).

Alg.: 1 ♖f7†, ♔g5; 2 ♔e7, ♔:h5; 3 g7, ♖a7†; 4 ♔f6, ♖a6†; 5 ♔f5, ♖a5†; 6 ♔f4, ♖a4†; 7 ♔f3, ♖a3†; 8 ♔g2, ♖a2†; 9 ♖ f2, ♖a8; 10 ♖f8, ♖a2†; 11 ♔f3, ♖a3†; 12 ♔e4, etc.+.

N. ROSSOLIMO

KASSELER POST

1950

DIAGRAM 188

+

Another pretty duel between two rooks, with quite a few thematic points, composed by a roving Greek-Russian-French-Spanish journalist and radio commentator—now an American national.

    1 P—R7 R—KR3

The white pawn's advance is totally arrested, with White's rook stuck in front to protect him, and 2 ... P—N4, etc., might draw easily.

    2 K—N5!

Now threatens 3 R—R8 ch, queening the pawn—a familiar stratagem in rook and pawn endings.

2 ...	K—N6	5 K—K5	K—K6
3 K—B5	K—B6	6 K—B5	K—B6
4 K—Q5	K—Q6	7 R—KB8!!	

Presaging 8 P—R8(Q), a move which, as before, can—and of course must—be countered by ... R×P. But simultaneously, White has set up a direct battery with fatal effect. (Compare diagram 164.)

7 ...	R×P	11 K—N5	K—R6
8 K—N6 dis. ch	K—N6	12 R—R8 ch	K—N6
9 K×R	P—N4	13 R—R4 wins	
10 K—N6!	P—N5		

To add spice, a solitary advanced pawn protected by the king, with Black's rook and king well behind, mostly holds the draw; but here Black catches up.

Alg.: 1 h7, ♖h6; 2 ♔b5, ♔b3; 3 ♔c5, ♔c3; 4 ♔d5, ♔d3; 5 ♔e5, ♔e3; 6 ♔f5, ♔f3; 7 ♖f8, ♖:h7; 8 ♔g6†, ♔g3; 9 ♔:h7, g5; 10 ♔g6, g4; 11 ♔g5, ♔h3; 12 ♖h8†, ♔g3; 13 ♖h4+.

R. BRIEGER

HUNGARIAN CHESS FED.
TOURNEY

1966–7

DIAGRAM 189

+

3rd Commendation

White creates a straitjacket, with Black struggling till the needle hits him in the right spot.

    1 N—B3

With the direct threat 2 R—R3#, which Black can prevent only by a shuttle that keeps the critical square QR3 under surveillance. Besides, Black's knight must stay (otherwise R—N5 #). Tempo play is the motto of the day.

1 ...	Q—R8 ch		5 B—N2	Q—QB8
2 B—K4	Q—QB8		6 B—K4	Q—QR8
3 B—N2	Q—QR1		7 B—B6	Q—QB8
4 B—B6	P—N6			

If 7 ... P—Q4; 8 B×P, Q×N; 9 R×Q, N×B; 10 R—B5 ch+.

8 R×N	K×R	10 N×Q	wins
9 N—R2 ch	K—B5		

e.g. 10 ... P—Q4; 11 N—K2, P—N7; 12 K—N6, P—Q5; 13 B×P, P—Q6; 14 N—N3, P—Q7; 15 B—B3+.

Alg.: 1 ♘c3, ♛h1†; 2 ♗e4, ♛c1; 3 ♗g2, ♛a1; 4 ♗c6, g3; 5 ♗g2, ♛c1. 6 ♗e4, ♛a1; 7 ♗c6, ♛c1; 8 ♖:b4, ♚:b4; 9 ♘a2†, ♚c4; 10 ♘:c1+;

DIAGRAM 190

R. BRIEGER

AJEDREZ (ARGENTINA)

1970–1

5th Prize

+

The composer utilizes the same rook and knight stronghold as in diagram 189, but expands the theme into a wider projection.

1 N—B3 N—Q7!

If 1 ... Q—R1 ch; 2 N/6—K4, N—Q7; 3 R×N+.

2 R—B2	Q—R1 ch	4 N×P	Q—R1 ch
3 N/6—Q5	Q—R8	5 N/7—Q5	Q—R8

If 5 ... Q—R6; 6 R×N, Q×N; 7 N×Q, K×R; 8 N—Q5, K—Q6; 9 K×P, K—K5; 10 N—K7, K—K4; 11 K—N4+.

6 K×P K—B8		7 N—K3 ch

If 7 R×N, Q—K8 ch; 8 K-any, Q×R+.

7 ...	K—K8	10 N—B6	Q—R1 ch
8 K—N2	Q—R1 ch	11 N/6—K4	Q×N ch
9 N/K3—Q5	Q—R8		

The queen has run out of waiting moves, as 11 ... Q—R8(R6); 12 R×N ends it all.

12 N×Q	N×N	14 K—K3 K—Q8
13 K—B3	N×P ch	

264

From here on the struggle becomes one of rook against knight, which is normally won for the rook if the knight is cut off from his king.

If 14 ... K—B8; 15 R—KR2, K—N8; 16 R—R5, N—B2; 17 R×P, N—Q3; 18 R—R5, N—B5 ch; 19 K—Q3, N—N7 ch; 20 K—K2, N—B5; 21 R—Q5+.

15 R—B6	N—B2		21 R—B6 ch	K—N5
16 R—B5	P—R3		22 R—B6	N—Q1
17 R—B5	N—N4		23 R—Q6	N—B2
18 R—B6	K—B7		24 R—Q7	N—R3
19 R×P	K—B6		25 R—KN7 wins	
20 K—B4	N—B2			

Alg.: 1 ♘c3, ♘d2!; 2 ♖c2, ♕a8†; 3 ♘fd5, ♕a1; 4 ♘:e7, ♕a8†; 5 ♘ed5, ♕a1; 6 ♔:g3, ♔f1; 7 ♘e3†, ♔e1; 8 ♔g2, ♕a8†; 9 ♘ed5, ♕a1; 10 ♘f6, ♕a8†; 11 ♘fe4, ♕:e4; 12 ♘:e4, ♘:e4; 13 ♔f3, ♘:g5; 14 ♔e3, ♔d1; 15 ♖c6, ♘f7; 16 ♖c5, h6; 17 ♖f5, ♘g5; 18 ♖f6, ♔c2; 19 ♖:h6, ♔c3; 20 ♔f4, ♘f7; 21 ♖c6†, ♔b4; 22 ♖f6, ♘d8; 23 ♖d6, ♘f7; 24 ♖d7, ♘h6; 25 ♖g7+.

DIAGRAM 191

W. KORN

BRITISH CHESS MAGAZINE

1941

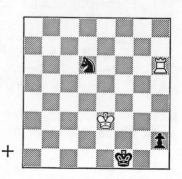

+

A struggle of rook against knight generally peters out in a draw. With Black's king "on the edge" and with precise play, White extracts a win by "corralling" the horse.

    1 R×P N—B4 ch

If 1 ... K—N8; 2 R—R5, N—B5 ch; 3 K—Q3, N—N7 ch; 4 K—K2! N—B5; 5 R—QB5, N—Q3; 6 K—B3+.

    2 K—K4 K—N1   3 R—R7!! N—Q3 ch

If 3 ... N—N6 ch; 4 K—B3, N—B8; 5 R—N7 ch, and 6 K—B2+. Or 4 ... N—R1; 5 R—QR7, K—R7; 6 R—R2 ch, K—R6; 7 R—KN2+. Or 4 ... N —B4; 5 R—Q7, N—R5 ch; 6 K—N3, N—B4 ch; 7 K—N4, N—K6 ch; 8 K—B3, N—B4; 9 R—Q5, N—R5 ch; 10 K—N3+.

    4 K—B4! N—B5   8 R—R2 ch K—K8
    5 R—Q7   K—B7   9 K—K3   N—B6
    6 R—Q4   N—R6   10 R—R1 ch N—Q8 ch
    7 R—R4   N—N4   11 K—Q3   wins

Alg.: 1 ♖:h2, ♘f5†; 2 ♔e4, ♔g1; 3 ♖h7, ♘d6†; 4 ♔f4, ♘c4; 5 ♖d7, ♔f2; 6 ♖d4, ♘a3; 7 ♖a4, ♘b5; 8 ♖a2†, ♔e1; 9 ♔e3, ♘c3; 10 ♖a1†, ♘d1†; 11 ♔d3+.

DIAGRAM 192

E. B. COOK

From: H. Keidanz,

THE CHESS COMPOSITIONS OF E. B. COOK

NEW YORK, 1927

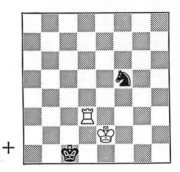

+

White's king cunningly retreats from the scene to return with a vengeance. White first chases the knight.

1 K—B3 K—B7	2 K—K4 N—N2

If 2 ... N—K2; 3 R—Q7, N—N3; 4 R—N7, N—B1 (or R5); 5 K—B5 (or B4) and the knight is lost by next move.

If 2 ... N—R3 (or R5); 3 R—KN3, N—B2; 4 K—Q5 and 5 R—N7 wins.

3 R—Q6 K—N6!	6 R—KN8 N—R4
4 K—K5 K—N5	7 R—N5 wins
5 R—Q8 K—B4	

Upon 1 ... N—R5 ch; 2 K—N3, N—N3; 3 R—K3, K—Q7; 4 R—K6, N—B1; 5 R—KB6, N—R2; 6 R—B5, K—K6; 7 K—N4, K—K5!; 8 R—B7 wins.

Alg.: 1 ♔f3, ♚c2; 2 ♔e4, ♞g7; 3 ♖d6, ♚b3; 4 ♔e5, ♚b4; 5 ♖d8, ♚c5; 6 ♖g8, ♞h5; 7 ♖g5+.

DIAGRAM 193

O. FRINK

THE CHESS AMATEUR

1927

=

1 N—B1! P—R8(Q)	3 N×Q R—R2 ch
2 N—N3 ch K—N4	4 K—N8 K—B3!

If 4 ... K—N3; 5 P—R8(N) ch! K—B3; 6 N—B2 =.

    5 P—R8(Q) ch K—N3

If 5 P—R8(N), R—N2 ch; 6 K—B8, R—KR2+.

6 K—B8 R—R1 ch	8 N—B2! K—B4
7 K—K7 R×Q	9 N—Q3 drawn

Fruitless are 8 ... R—R7; 9 N—N4 or 8 ... R—R5; 9 K—K6 =
or 8 ... R—QB1; 9 N—N4, K—N4; 10 K—Q7 =.

Right at the beginning, 1 N—B5? K—N4 would win for
Black. To quote the magazine, "some Frinkish perplexities,
resulting in another rook versus knight encounter."

Alg.: 1 ♘f1, h1(♕); 2 ♘g3†, ♔g5; 3 ♘:h1, ♖a7†; 4 ♔g8, ♔f6;
    5 h8(♕)†, ♔g6; 6 ♔f8, ♖a8†; 7 ♔e7, ♖:h8; 8 ♘f2!, ♔f5;
    9 ♘d3=.

268

DIAGRAM 194

C. S. HOWELL

THE CHESS AMATEUR

1926

(Amended by W. Korn)

+

   1 R—B1!*

1 K × N or 1 R × N, P—R8(Q) ultimately ends in a draw.

   1 ... N—K7

Black embarks on a heroic uphill fight.

   If 1 ... N—B3 ch!?2 K—B6, N—N5; 3 K—K6 (not 3 P—N6, N—Q4 ch; 4 K—B7, N—K6; 5 R—QR1—5 P—N7, N × R = —N—B4; 6 K—B6, N—R3 =), N—Q6; 4 K—B5! (4 P—N6, N—B5 ch! 5 R × N, P—R8(Q)=), N—N5; 5 P—N6, N—Q4; 6 P—N7, N—K2 ch; 7 K—K6, N—N1; 8 R—KR1, N—R3; 9 R × N, P—R8(Q); 10 P—N8(Q), Q—R3 ch; 11 K—K5+.

In here, if 8 ... K—N7; 9 K—B7, N—R3 ch; 10 R × N, P—R8(Q); 11 P—N8(Q) and White shelters at KR8 square, winning.

   2 P—N6 N—N6   4 P—N8(Q) ch
   3 P—N7! N × R

With Black's king on square QR6 the game would now be a draw.

  * This was Howell's original set-up, with the legend "Black to move cannot draw against White's best moves."

4 ... K—N7   5 Q—N8 ch

forcing Black's king into the corner, and winning because the knight makes stalemate impossible.

Faulty is 5 Q—N2 ch, N—Q7; 6 Q—N7 ch, N—N6 =.

Alg.: 1 ♖f1, ♘e2; 2 g6, ♘g3; 3 g7, ♘:f1; 4 g8(♕)†, ♔b2; 5 ♕b8†+.

Composition as formal exercise

In their vast majority, endgame studies originate from motifs freely chosen by the composer. But in some instances, as in "theme tournaments", composers are confronted with a prescribed theme, which all entries must comply with.

Such a stipulation is a legacy from problem composition, which basically revolves around set themes and rigorously classifies problems by themes.

A connoisseur of studies, with their informal flow, often disdains a construction that does not reflect an actual game even remotely. In studies, themes often occur just incidentally, or are combined, or may overlap. Therefore, the prior requirement to comply with a set theme is rarely a condition in study tourneys—though it may be.

The composer must readjust his mind. He does not marshall his resources for the purpose of technical and artistic perfection of a conception of his own choosing, but is instead commissioned to create an artistically and technically perfect—and unique—prototype of an imposed subject. Given the title of a thesis selected for and accepted by him and others, he has to fill the empty frame with the most telling content. And he has to beat a deadline for completion and submission.

Such formal exercise is a stiff challenge to one's ability to analyze the task, ferret out predecessors, learn from their technique, avoid copying them, and then synthesize all possibilities into one's own finished product. Diagrams 195 and 196 are fitting examples of this aspect of composition, with the make-up marking them as endgames. Diagram 197 is a masterpiece.

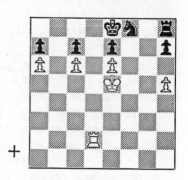

DIAGRAM 195

J. BUCHWALD

2nd INTERNATIONAL
FRIENDSHIP TEAM
TOURNEY

1966–7

+

An outstanding American problemist takes a hand at a pre-scribed task. The catharsis erupts with the second move:

1 R—QN2 N—N3 ch	2 K—B5 K—B1!?

The point is, Black cannot play the natural saving move 2 ... O—O ch. The requirement of the tournament was that appropriate retro-analysis should prove that neither castling nor even *en passant* capture was possible.

In the position arrived at here, Black cannot castle, because his rook or king must have moved at least twice before. Immediately prior to White's 1 R—QN2, Black's knight could not have moved as he would have had to come from square Q2 or KN3, in each case checking the white king on K4, who would thus have had to move. Therefore, either Black's king had moved from Q1 to K1, out of check by White's rook on Q2, or Black's rook had moved from N1 to R1 and thus 2 ... O—O is no longer permissible.

3 P—R6 K—N1	5 R—N7 wins
4 R—N8 ch N—B1	

Luckily, 2 P × N does not win as well, else the study would be "cooked". If 2 K—B5, N—R5 ch; 3 K—N4, K—B1; 4 K × N, K—N2; 5 R—N7 wins.

Alg.: 1 ♖b2, ♘g6†; 2 ♔f5, ♚f8; 3 h6, ♚g8; 4 ♖b8†, ♘f8; 5 ♖b7+.

DIAGRAM 196

E. M. HASSBERG
and J. BUCHWALD

*2nd INTERNATIONAL
FRIENDSHIP TEAM TOURNEY*

1966–7

+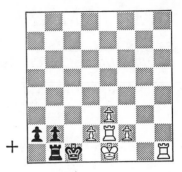

1 P—Q3

If 1 P—Q4?, P—R8(Q); 2 R—Q2, Q—R3 =. Or 2 O—O, R—K2=.

1 ... P—R8(Q)

If 1 ... P—R8(B)—planning for stalemate—2 K—B1! K—Q1; 3 P—B3+.

2 R—Q2 Q—R1   3 P—K4 wins

The same stipulation applied here as in diagram 195. Thus the plausible 2 O—O mate, is not permissible because White's king must have moved, otherwise White's rook on K2 could not have placed itself on this square; both neighboring pawns are still on their original squares and the frontal pawn is only one step away.

The result of the competition was published in 1970 by the Dutch Association of Problemists.

Alg.: 1 d3, a1(♕); 2 ♖d2, ♕a8; 3 e4+.

DIAGRAM 197

H. M. LOMMER[§]

SPANISH CHESS
PROBLEMISTS ASSOCIATION

THEMATIC TOURNEY, 1963

+

The mode of this study was dictated by the tourney promoters' pre-stated requirement to create a matrix of "annihilation of two knights, coupled with pawn promotions".

One might almost say that problemists cannot help using a cryptic jargon, even for study composition—but the formidable Harold Lommer (an occasional visitor to the U.S.A.) undertook to resolve the stated task masterfully.

    1 N/5—N3 ch

The win fails after 1 N×N ch, K—N8; 2 N—R3 ch, K—B8; 3 P—K4, N—B6; 4 P—K5, N—Q4 ch; 5 K—B5, N—B5 with a draw.

    1 ... K—N8   2 N—N5!

A glance back at Loyd's diagram 19 shows the identical position, with the board reversed and with an additional pair of pawns on each side. They serve Lommer's purpose of complying with the tourney requirement of promotion; and with deep insight into its potential, he picked the Loyd matrix for the formula.

2 ...	P—R4	6 P—K6	P—R6
3 P×P e.p.	P×P	7 P—K7	P—R7
4 P—K4	P—R4	8 P—K8(Q)	P—R8(Q)
5 P—K5	P—R5	9 Q—N6	Q—QR1

9 Q—N6 threatened 10 N—R3 mate and 9 ... Q—QR1 was the only available defense.

10 K—B7!

So far all forced and forcing. The text is a strong *Zugzwang* move, continuing control over Black's queen. Black's reply is also mandatory, because of 10 ... Q—R5; 11 Q—Q3!, Q—R6 (or R8); 12 Q—Q1 ch, and 13 N—B3 mate.

| 10 ... | Q—KB1 | 12 Q×N ch | N—B8 |
| 11 Q—N1 ch | N—K8 | | |

The postulated promotions occurred on move 8. On moves 12 and 13 the knights annihilate themselves.

13 Q—K4 ch N—Q6

If 13 ... K—R7; 14 Q—R4 ch, Q—R6; 15 N—B3 mate, or 14 ... K—N8; 15 N—Q2 mate.

14 Q×N ch K—R7   15 N—Q2!

Another Zugzwang on a wide open board. The threat is 16 Q—N3 ch, K—R8; 17 Q—R4 ch and mate.

| 15 ... | Q—K2 ch | 17 K—R5 |
| 16 K—N6 | Q—K3 ch | |

The end of the exercise. Yet, it has all the characteristics of a real natural study.

Alg.: 1 ♘ab3†, ♔b1; 2 ♘b5, h5; 3 g:h5 e.p., g:h6; 4 e4, h5; 5 e5, h4; 6 e6, h3; 7 e7, h2; 8 e8(♕), h1(♕); 9 ♕g6, ♕a8; 10 ♔c7, ♕f8; 11 ♕g1†, ♘e1; 12 ♕:e1†, ♘c1; 13 ♕e4†, ♘d3; 14 ♕:d3†, ♔a2; 15 ♘d2, ♕e7†; 16 ♔b6, ♕e6†; 17 ♔a5.

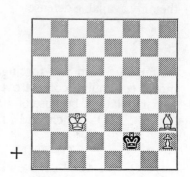

DIAGRAM 198

O. FRINK

PITTSBURGH POST*

1923

+

This modest looking miniature concerns the book draw of a sole rook's pawn supported by a bishop of a color different from the queening square R8. The opposing king occupying his square R1 or N2 cannot be normally dislodged—only stalemated.

A good number of studies revolve around possible exceptions. The task at hand here is how, if at all, Black's king can be prevented from reaching his square KR1.

1 B—Q7!!	K—K6	4 P—R6	K—B3
2 P—R4	K—K5	5 B—K8!! wins	
3 P—R5	K—K4		

Black's king is cut off from access to the queening square.

---

* Apparently reproduced from *The Chess Amateur.*

Alg.: 1 ♗d7, ♔e3; 2 h4, ♔e4; 3 h5, ♔e5; 4 h6, ♔f6; 5 ♗e8+.

A. EFRON

L'ITALIA SCACCHISTICA

1962

DIAGRAM 199

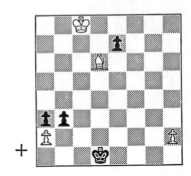

+

A somewhat more combinational construction with the ultimate aim of cutting off White from reaching the passed pawn. Here White's king becomes the obstructor.

　1 B×RP P×P

Primitive is 1 ... K—B7; 2 P×P, P—K4; 3 B—Q6, P—K5; 4 P—N4, P—K6; 5 P—N5, P—K7; 6 B—N3+.

　2 B—N2　K—B7　　　5 K—K6　K—B6
　3 B—K5　K—Q6　　　6 K—B5! wins
　4 K—Q7　K—K5

Continued 6 ... P—K3 ch; 7 K—N5, K—K5; 8 B—R1+.

Alg.: 1 ♗:a3, b:a2; 2 ♗b2, ♔c2; 3 ♗e5, ♔d3; 4 ♔d7, ♔e4; 5 ♔e6, ♔f3; 6 ♔f5+.

G. GRECO§

TRATTATO . . . DEGLI
SCACCHI

1619

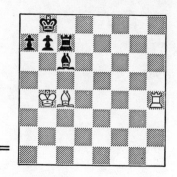

DIAGRAM 200

=

In an actual game White might not hesitate to resign. Not so Greco! By a combinational brainwave, he reaches the book draw pointed out in diagram 198.

| 1 R—R8 ch R—B1 | 3 B—R6!! |
| 2 R×R ch K×R | |

3 ... K—B2; 4 B×P, B×B; 5 K—R3, or 3 ... P×B; 4 K—R3, and the King retreats to square QR1 with an inevitable draw.

Alg.: 1 ♖h8†, ♖c8; 2 ♖:c8, ♔:c8; 3 ♗a6=.

DIAGRAM 200 (A)

V. A. KOROL'KOV§ and J. E. PECKOVER

SHAKHMATY v SSSR

1966

4th Hon. Mention =

Apparently Peckover sent his study to Korol'kov for submission to the Russian periodical, and Korol'kov added some *nuance*. Thus a tandem resulted with a prizeworthy outcome.

1 K—K2 B—N5	3 K—B4 B—N3
2 K—Q3 B × P	

If 3 ... B—B7; 4 P—R4, K—K2; 5 K—N5, K—Q2 (5 ... K—K3; 6 P—R5, K × P; 7 P—R6, P × P; 8 K × P=); 6 P—R5, K—B2; 7 P—R6, P—N3; 8 P—R7, K—N2; 9 P—K6, B—R5; 10 P—R8(Q) ch and 11 K × P=.

4 K—N5 B—Q1	6 K—R6!
5 P—R4 P—N3!	

Initiating a tense tempo play. Instructive for understanding the maneuvers is 6 K—B6? K—K2; 7 K—N7, K—Q2; 8 K—N8, K—B3; 9 K—B8, B—R5!; 10 P—K6, K—Q3; 11 K—N7, B—Q1!; 12 K—B8, K—K2! and Black wins.

6 ... K—K2	7 K—R7 K—K3

7 ... K—Q2; 8 K—N7, K—K3; 9 K—B8, K—K2; 10 P—K6, K—K1; 11 K—N7, K—B1; 12 K—N8, K—K2; 13 K—B8=.

8 K—N8 K × P	11 K—B6 K—Q5
9 K—B8 B—K2!	12 K—N5 K—any
10 K—B7 B—B4	13 P—R5 draw

Alg.: 1 ♔e2, ♗b4; 2 ♔d3, ♗:c5; 3 ♔c4, ♗b6; 4 ♔b5, ♗d8; 5 a4, b6; 6 ♔a6, ♚e7; 7 ♔a7, ♚e6; 8 ♔b8, ♚:e5; 9 ♔c8, ♗e7; 10 ♔c7, ♗c5; 11 ♔c6, ♚d4; 12 ♔b5, ♚∞; 13 a5=.

DIAGRAM 201

R. J. FISCHER—
M. TAIMANOV

2nd MATCH GAME

VANCOUVER, 1971

What result?

Black's missing the possibility of a draw against the rook's pawn and (wrong!) bishop, played a fateful role at a crucial moment.

Black, hanging on to his knight, played 81... K—K5? and fell victim to a distinct squeeze after 82 B—B8!! K—B5; 83 P—R4, N—B6; 84 P—R5, N—N4; 85 B—B5, N—B6; 86 P—R6, N—N4; 87 K—N6, N—B6; 88 P—R7, N—K4 ch; 89 K—B6, with a win for Fischer.

Black should have played:

| 81 ... | N—Q6! | 83 K—B5 K—Q3! |
| 82 P—R4 N—B5 | | |

Black marches his king to the corner square and draws, using the knight to distract White's king.

| 84 K—B6, N—Q4 ch | 85 K—B7, N—B5= |

Alg.: 81 ..., ♘d3; 82 h4, ♘f4; 83 ♔f5, ♔d6; 84 ♔f6, ♘d5†; 85 ♔f7, 5 ♘f4=.

DIAGRAM 202

A. EFRON

SCHACH-ECHO

1957

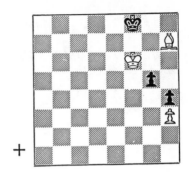

+

The same poser as in diagram 198, but a different profile. White must capture both black pawns so as to be left with one passed pawn—but without allowing Black any chance to draw against a *rook's* pawn! Having said that, the solution is only half a guess away. Anyhow, it should be noted first that 1 B—B5, K—K1! 2 K—K6, K—Q1; 3 K—Q6, K—K1; 4 B—K6, K—B1; 5 K—Q7, P—N5!; 6 P × P, K—N2 draws, as the bishop must guard against the black pawn's advance, while Black captures White's pawn. Thus:

1 B—N6! K—N1	2 B—R5 K—R2

If 2 ... K—B1; 3 B—B7 immobilizing Black's king and thus forcing 3 ... P—N5; 4 P×P—the rook's pawn has become a knight's pawn!— 4 ... P—R6; 5 P—N5, P—R7; 6 P—N6, P—R8(Q); 7 P—N7‡.
If 2 ... K—R1; 3 K—B7, K—R2; 4 B—N6 ch+.

3 B—B7! K—R3	4 B—N6

If 3 ... K—R1; 4 K—N6, P—N5; 5 P×P, P—R6; 6 B—Q5+.

4 ... P—N5	6 P—N5 mate
5 P×P P—R6	

Quite illuminating, and to be compared to the precursor shown in diagram 203.

Alg.: 1 ♗g6, ♚g8; 2 ♗h5, ♚h7; 3 ♗f7, ♚h6; 4 ♗g6, g4; 5 h:g4, h3; 6 g5‡.

DIAGRAM 203

D. L. PONZIANI§

IL GIUOCO INCOMPARABILE
DEGLI SCACCHI

1769

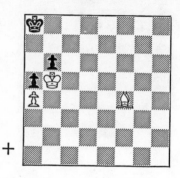

+

The conversion of the rook's pawn loosely sketched in the eighteenth century, yet a "first".

   1 K—R6!

Immobilizing Black's king and forming a mating net.

1 ...	P—N4	3 P—N6	P—R6
2 P×P!	P—R5	4 P—N7	mate

This is the schema utilized in diagram 202, and a fitting complement to Loyd's diagram 17.

Alg.: 1 ♔a6, b5; a:b5, a4; 3 b6, a3; 4 b7♯.

M. R. VUKCEVICH

THE PROBLEMIST

1971

DIAGRAM 204

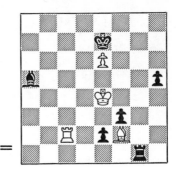

1st Commendation

=

A truly climactic scene wherein the rook's pawn and bishop of wrong color are again the spoilers.

White's show turns into a fiasco after 1 K×P, P—K8(Q); 2 B×Q, B×B; 3 R—KR2, R—N4 and Black wins.

  1 B—R4 ch! K×P

If ... K—Q3; 2 K×P!, P—K8(Q); 3 B×Q, B×B; 4 R—KR2, R—N4 (4 ... P—R5; 5 R—R1 =); 5 R—K2 =.

  2 K×P P—K8(Q)   3 B×Q B×B!

If 3 ... R×B; 4 R—K2 ch, R×R; 5 K×R =.

  4 R—KR2

If 4 R—KN2?, R—B8 ch; 5 K—K2, R—KR8 wins.

  4 ... P—R5

If 4 ... R—N4; 5 R—K2 ch, R—K4; 6 R×R ch=.

  5 R—KR1 R×R   6 K—N2 draw

Alg.: 1 ♗h4†, ♔:e6; 2 ♔:f3, e1(♕), 3 ♗:e1, ♗:e1; 4 ♖h2, h4; 5 ♖h1, ♖:h1; 6 ♔g2=.

DIAGRAM 205

M. R. VUKCEVICH

THE PROBLEMIST

AWARDED 1972

2nd Prize, Study Tourney 1970–1 =

White is faced with Black's suffocating threats 1 ... N—B6 ch; and if 2 K—R1, R—R7 mate; and if, e.g., 1 Q—R3, N—B6 ch; 2 K—B1, B—R3 mate.

White uses desperate bravado, and after his first move it is difficult for Black to find a win.

   1 N—B6 ch K × B

If 1 ... K—B1! 2 Q—B5 ch!, K × B; 3 Q—R7 ch!, K—B3 (any other K move loses the rook); 4 Q—Q4 ch, K—B4; 5 N—K7 ch, K—N4; 6 Q—N1 ch, with at least a draw.
If 1 ... K—B3; 2 Q—B1, will win, and if 1 ... K—Q3; 2 Q—R3 ch, K × N; 3 Q—R6 ch, K—B2; 4 Q—R7 ch, K—Q3; 5 Q—N8 ch, N—B2; 6 Q—Q8 ch, K—B6; 7 B—K8 ch, draw.

2 N—Q8 ch	K—N1		6 N—B8 ch	K—R1
3 Q—N5	K—R2		7 N—N6 ch	K—N1
4 N × P	N—B6 ch		8 N—B4 dis. ch	B × Q
5 K—B1	B—R3		Stalemate	

Prof. Milan Vukcevich, an expert in metallurgy, established early fame as a problemist but produces here another selective *œuvre* in the area of studies.

Alg.: 1 ♘c6†, ♔:f7; 2 ♘d8†, ♔g8; 3 ♕g5, ♔h7; 4 ♘:e6, ♘c3†; 5 ♔c1, ♗h6; 6 ♘f8†, ♔h8; 7 ♘g6†, ♔g8; 8 ♘f4†, ♗:g5(=).

DIAGRAM 206

A. H. BRANTON

CALIFORNIA CHESS
REPORTER

1953

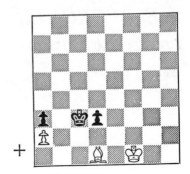

+

Said to be the composer's favorite miniature, full of pitfalls for so little material.

Just as a trial run: If 1 K—B2, P—Q7; 2 K—K3, K—N7; 3 B—N3, P—Q8(Q)=.

 1 B—N3 K—N7!

If 1 ... K—Q7; 2 K—B2, K—B6; 3 K—K1+.

 2 K—K1!

If 2 K—B2, P—Q7!

 2 ... K—B8 3 K—B2!! K—N7

Another novel triangulation ensues after 3 ... K—Q7; 4 K—B1, K—K6 (4 ... K—B8; 5 K—K1+); 5 K—K1, P—Q7 ch; 6 K—Q1, K—Q6; 7 B—N8! K—B6; 8 B—B7, K—Q6; 9 B—N3+.

 4 K—K3 K—B6 5 K—K4! wins

If 5 ... P—Q7; 6 K—K3 wins as Black must give up the QP without compensation; and if 5 ... K—Q7; 6 B—B4+.

Alg.: 1 ♗b3, ♚b2; 2 ♔e1, ♚c1; 3 ♔f2, ♚b2; 4 ♔e3, ♚c3; 5 ♔e4+.

DIAGRAM 206 (A)

J. E. PECKOVER

L'ITALIA SCACCHISTICA

1961

+

Irritatingly simple and confoundingly successful.

1 B—B6? P—N6; 2 K—R3, K—Q6!, Black's key-move to draw.

1 B—B1 K—Q6		3 K—B2 K—K8	
2 K—N3 K—K7		4 B—N2 K—K7	

The starting moves are self-evident. But if now 4 ... P—N6 ch; 5 K—B3, K—Q8; 6 B—R3, K—K7; 7 B—B1, K—Q1; 8 K—N2+.

5 B—R1! P—K6!

Not 5 B—Q4? (or 5 B—B6?), P—N6 ch; 6 K—B1, P—N7 ch; 7 B × P, K—Q6!=

6 P—Q3! K—B6

The other feasible defense is 6 ... K—B7!? but it also loses after 7 B—B6! P—K7; 8 B—R4 ch, K—K6; 9 B—K1, P—N6 ch; 10 K—B3, P—N7; 11 B—Q2 ch+.

7 B—Q4!

If 7 K—Q1? K—B7!; 8 B—Q4, P—N6; 9 B—B6! K—B6! with a "positional draw".

7 ...	K—K7!	9 B—B1! wins	
8 B—N2!	K—B6!		

A "positional draw" mostly occurs when an exceptional position requires a repetition of moves to avoid loss of material, but may also maintain the draw in the face of superior forces.

Alg.: 1 ♗c1, ♔d3; 2 ♔b3, ♚e2; 3 ♔c2, ♚e1; 4 ♗b2, ♚e2; 5 ♗a1, e3; 6 d3, ♚f3; 7 ♗d4, ♚e2; 8 ♗b2, ♚f3; 9 ♗c1+.

DIAGRAM 207

O. FRINK

(Amended)

THE CHESS AMATEUR

1928

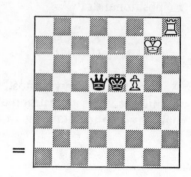

=

The draw is more exceptional than appears on the surface. In most such cases, improved technique leads to a win for the queen versus rook and pawn (compare also diagram 8). For instance:
1 R—R5?, Q—N7 ch; 2 K—R6, K—B3+; or 2 K—B7, Q—N5+. Or 1 P—B6? Q—N7 ch; 2 K—B7, Q—QN2 ch; 3 K—N6, Q—K5 ch; 4 K—B7, Q—B5 ch; 5 K—N6, Q—N5 ch; 6 K—B7, Q—K3 ch; and 7... Q×P ch+.

1 R—KB8! Q—N7 ch

If 1 ... K—B5; 2 R—B7, K—N4; 3 R—B8, Q—K4ch; 4 K—R7, Q—K2 ch; 5 K—N8, K—R3; 6 R—B6 ch! Q×R(=).

2 K—R7	Q—N4	5 R—B7!	K—Q3
3 K—R8	Q—R3 ch	6 R—KN7!	
4 K—N8	K—Q4		

The pivotal waiting moves.

6 ...	Q—R5	9 R—B6 ch	K—Q4!
7 R—KB7!	Q—Q1 ch	10 R—B7	draw
8 K—N7	Q—K1		

White achieves this result by having the pawn stay put. Frink's original presentation was with Black's king on Q5 instead of

288

K4. This allowed the ordinary book draw 1 R—Q8, Q×R; 2 P—B6 and 3 P—B7.

In 1956, A. Chéron eliminated this minor blemish by shifting the king as shown in the diagram, at the same time correcting a faulty assessment of J. Berger's.

Alg.: 1 ♖f8, ♛g2†; 2 ♔h7, ♛g5; 3 ♔h8, ♛h6†; 4 ♔g8, ♔d5; 5 ♖f7, ♔d6; 6 ♖g7, ♛h4; 7 ♖h7, ♛d8†; 8 ♔g7, ♛e8; 9 ♖f6†, ♔d5; 10 ♖f7=.

DIAGRAM 207 (A)

B. GURETZKY-CORNITZ§ *(1864)*
amended by
O. FRINK

THE CHESS AMATEUR

1928

=

A Theoretical Analysis. With the rook apparently tied to the king's bishop's file to protect the pawn, the position was considered won for Black after 1 R—B8, Q—N4 ch; 2 K—R7, K—K2.

Frink shattered the illusion, demonstrating the draw after

1 R—KN7!	Q—R5	4 R—B6 ch	K—K4
2 R—KB7	Q—Q1 ch	5 R—B7	draw
3 K—N7	Q—K1		

Alg.: 1 ♖g7, ♛h4; 2 ♖f7, ♛d8†; 3 ♔g7, ♛e8; 4 ♖f6†, ♔e5; 5 ♖f7=.

DIAGRAM 208

O. FRINK

THE CHESS AMATEUR

1927

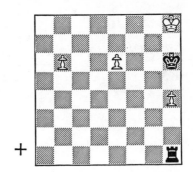

+

A pleasing exhibition of one "do" and three "don'ts".
(A) 1 P—K7? R—K8; 2 P—N7, R × P; 3 P—N8(Q), R—K1 ch;
4 Q × R,⊜.
(B) 1 P—N7? R—QN8; 2 P—K7, R × P; 3 P—K8(Q), R—R2 ch;
4 K—N8, R—R1 ch; 5 K × R,=.
(C) 1 K—N8? R—N8 ch; 2 K—B7, R—B8 ch; 3 K—K8,
R—QN8⊜.

Hence, a very subtle waiting move which not only breaks up the
stalemates but also stops the drawing move K—N3.

   1 P—R5! R—K8

1 ... R—KB8 (or ... Q8, or ... QN8); 2 P—K7, winning.

   2 P—N7 R—QN8   3 P—K7 wins

Orrin Frink's composing career was brief—predominantly confined to a span between 1923 and 1928—when the endgame
column of the *Chess Amateur* was conducted by the famous
T. R. Dawson—but very productive. Besides being an expert
player, he was head of the department of mathematics at Penn
State University.

Alg.: 1 h5, ♖e1; 2 b7, ♖b1; 3 e7+.

DIAGRAM 209

A. EFRON

SCHACH-ECHO

1958

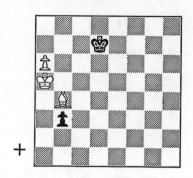

+

A Lilliputian masterpiece of domination by the New Englander Andrew Efron—and unique.

1 P—R7!

If 1 B—B3, K—B1; 2 B—K5, P—N7; 3 B×P, K—N1 =.
Again, the bishop of the wrong color, allowing Black to draw,

| 1 ... | P—N7 | 3 Q—N7 ch K—K3 |
| 2 P—R8(Q) | P—N8(Q) | |

If 3 ... K—Q1; 4 B—K7 ch wins the queen "by discovery".
Upon 3 ... K—K1 comes mate—obviously.

4 Q—K7 ch K—Q4

The other diagonal is forbidden ground now and later, because of 4 ... K—B4? 5 Q—R7 ch, winning the queen. The conclusion is easy but sweet.

| 5 Q—Q6 ch K—B5 | 7 Q—B3 ch K—B7 |
| 6 Q—B5 ch K—N6 | 8 Q—R3 mate |

Alg.: 1 a7! b2; 2 a8(♕), b1(♕); 3 ♕b7†, ♚e6; 4 ♕e7†, ♚d5; 5 ♕d6†, ♚c4; 6 ♕c5†, ♚b3; 7 ♕c3†, ♚a2; 8 ♕a3 #.

DIAGRAM 210

A. EFRON

SCHACH-ECHO

1957

+

A difficult formula because such heavy material is rather cumbersome to handle adroitly.

If 1 K—B5, K— R5; 2 Q—Q1 ch, K—R6 = (but not 2 ...
R—N6; 3 Q—Q4 ch, and 4 Q—R1 ch+).

  1 K—B4! R—R2

If 1 ... K—R5; 2 Q—Q1 ch, and mate in a few moves.

  2 K—B5 R—R3

If 2 ... R—N2; 3 Q—R8 ch+.

  3 Q—Q2 ch and mate next move

Alg.: 1 ♔c4, ♖a7; 2 ♔c5, ♖a6; 3 ♕d2†+.

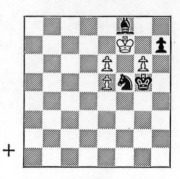

DIAGRAM 211

A. EFRON

L'ITALIA SCACCHISTICA

1963

4th Hon. Mention

+

An impossible win—by isolated and doubled pawns against two pieces—comes to look very smooth and easy!

  1 P×P B—N2   2 P—K7 B×P!

If 2 ... N×P; 3 K×B, N—N3; 4 P—K6+.

  3 P—K8(Q) N—Q3 ch   5 K×B wins
  4 K—K6   N×Q

1 K×B loses to ... K×P; 2 P—K7, N—N2.

Alg.: 1 g:h7, ♗g7; 2 e7, ♗:e5; 3 e8(♕), ♘d6†; 4 ♔e6, ♘:e8; 5 ♔:e5+.

A. EFRON

L'ITALIA SCACCHISTICA

1963

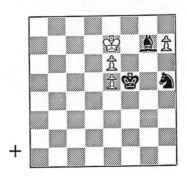

DIAGRAM 212

+

Another fanciful miniature.

1 K—B7 B—R1!	3 K—N8 K—K3
2 P—K7 N—N2	

If 3 ... K×P; 4 K×B, K—B3; 5 K—N8 wins; and if 4 ...
N—K1; 5 K—N8, N—B3 ch; 6 K—B7 wins.

4 K × B K—B2	6 P—K8(Q) ch K×Q
5 P—K6 ch N × P	7 K—N8 wins

Alg.: 1 ♔f7, ♝h8; 2 e7, ♞g7; 3 ♔g8, ♚e6; 4 ♔:h8, ♚f7; 5 e6†, ♞:e6;
6 e8(♛)†, ♚:e8; 7 ♔g8+.

DIAGRAM 213

F. W. ANDREW
1925

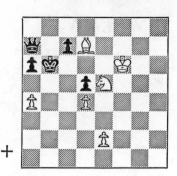

+

An elementary yet superb sampler of domination. We follow I. Chernev's* poetic characterization of "the dread power of *Zugzwang*—against which even a queen is helpless".

    1 P—R5 ch K—N2

"Naturally, he does not take the pawn, as the knight fork would win his queen."

    2 N—B6 Q—R1   3 K—N7!

"A strange position! Black's queen must move, and in doing so give up its life!"

* I. Chernev: *The Fireside Book of Chess* (1949).

Alg.: 1 a5†, ♔b7; 2 ♘c6, ♛a8; 3 ♔g7+.

DIAGRAM 214

T. McDERMOTT

CANADIAN CHESS CHAT

SEPTEMBER, 1967

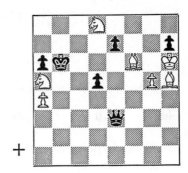

A somewhat heavy-handed forcing overture by an American "Santa Barbarian" of California—resulting in a neat star-flight design, presented in strict isolation.

1 N—B4 ch P×N   3 P—R5 ch! K—N4!
2 B—Q4 ch Q×B

The only square accessible without immediate disaster. Any other escape allows a losing fork.

4 B—K8 ch K—B4   6 N×Q K×N
5 N—K6 ch K—Q4   7 K×P

with a clear win.

Alg.: 1 ♘c4, d:c4; 2 ♗d4†, ♕:d4; 3 a5†, ♚b5; 4 ♗e8†, ♚c5; 5 ♘e6†, ♚d5; 6 ♘:d4, ♚:d4; 7 ♚:h7+.

Insights into the Composer's Workshop

Triumphs and Disappointments

The compilations shown next are what the artist may consider the endproduct of an imaginative idea, hammered into consolidated shape after many fruitless tries, a timely stroke of luck, a lot of applied knowledge and technique and plenty of hard work—all propelled by innate ambition, the "hobbyist's" enthusiasm, and the enjoyment of beauty achieved.

Many attempts are dismissed as useless or unworkable; or as having been done before. But at last the task is accomplished and the finished marvel unveiled. For decades it glitters—and then one day, unexpectedly, someone detects a serious flaw and the opus must regretfully be discarded. Sometimes it can be repaired, as was the case in diagram 73, which is rectified in diagram 74 or in the following pair of diagrams 215 and 216.

For almost sixty years, the exquisite domination created by a French nobleman and renowed composer stood unimpaired. In 1961 it was "busted", but then happily restored and the idea retained. Very often the detection of a flaw and its correction may even lead to further enrichment by additional sidelines. In such instances of successful rescue by constructive critics, the original study and the composer's name are augmented by the addition of the "repairer's" name. The research described in the adjoining diagrams provides a case in point of demolishing and subsequent progressive rebuilding.

The Making of an Endgame Study—Input and Output

The composer's happiest moment arrives when after smooth—but mostly rough—progress from an initial idea, through trial by error, experimentation and improvement, he witnesses the emergence of a polished model.

A glimpse of that process is allowed by the preliminary settings that lead to the construction of diagram 217 as illustrated in its sub-diagrams A and B.

Another legitimate—inspired and inspiring—challenge is to perfect or substantially amend the first form of an exceptional point that deserves further development. It may originate from an attractive turn observed during an actual game or read into it by an alert artistic mind; it may be a refinement over a setting of one's own—or a colleague's—(a subject already touched upon in the chapter on "originals"), but possibly on a more thoroughly constructive level. Serving the specific purpose of a didactic effect upon the reader, such an attempt is made in the sub-diagrams A and B following the impressive bombshell of Kujoth's in diagram 218.

DIAGRAM 215

COUNT J. DE VILLENEUVE-ESCLAPON§

L'ÉCHIQUIER FRANÇAIS

1909

+

A famous and often quoted position which excelled in its short, pointed and domineering key moves.

   1 B—B3! R—R4   2 B—N4!

The white bishop, directly or by ultimate pins, controls all the squares which the rook might try to enter in order to prevent White's pawn from queening—an admirable model of control of maximum space, with minimal means, known as "domination". If 1 ... R—QB8; 2 B—Q2 ch obviously wins the rook. "*Obviously*"? Fifty-one years later it came to light that the solution contained an optical illusion and that the inherent Réti triangular march of the king to catch the distant pawn had been there all along and persistently overlooked as a case of mass chess-blindness that caused a blockage of further thought. *Id est*:

   After 1 B—B3, R—QB8; 2 B—Q2 ch, K—K4; 3 B×R, K—Q3 Black's king captures the supposedly winning pawn.

   Fortunately, the setting is capable of remedy as demonstrated in the next diagram 216.

Alg.: 1 ♗c3, ♖h5; 2♗b4+, or 1 ... ♖c1; 2 ♗d2†, ♚e4; 3 ♗:c1, ♚d6 (=).

DIAGRAM 216

J. VILLENEUVE-ESCLAPON, W. KORN and N. GUTTMAN

CHESS REVIEW

1962

+

The restoration of diagram 215 proceeded by firstly placing a black pawn on Black's Q3 so as to block the king's march à la Réti, e.g.: 1 B—B3, R—QB8; 2 B—Q2 ch, K—K4; 3 B×R and now 3 ... K—K3 is Black's only defense. But it suffices because of 4 K—N8, P—Q4; 5 B—B4, K—K2 and Black draws.

So, next White's king is placed on KN8 instead of KR8, thus picking up a needed move with 4 K—B8, P—Q4; 5 B—B4, P—Q5; 6 K—K8, P—Q6; 7 P—B7 and White wins.

Publication, however, brought in (much later) another *erratum* pointed out by the noted problemist Newman Guttman, namely 1 B—B3, R—R4; 2 B—N4, R—N4 ch! 3 K—R8, R—N7! and 4 ... R—QB7, stopping the white pawn. Therefore, Black's pawn on KR3 was moved to KN3, thus eliminating this particular drawback.

The main solution remains the same minus the previously discovered flaws.

(A) 1 B—B3, R—QB8; 2 B—Q2 wins as shown above.

(B) 1 B—B3, R—R4; 2 B—N4, R—R7 (or R—QN4); 3 B×P ch, wins.

J. E. PECKOVER

HOUSTON CHRONICLE
Tourney

1965

Special Prize, best U.S. Entry

DIAGRAM 216 (A)

+

In contemporary style, skillfully prefaced, interwoven with an interplay of tries, the same aspect as used in the Villeneuve-Esclapon is paraphrased here, sixty years later.

  1 P—B5

If 1 P—B7? B×P; 2 B×B, K—Q5; 3 B—Q5, K—B4; 4 B—Q8, R—R1 ch; 5 K—K7, R—R5=.

  1 ... B—R4

(A) 1 ... B×P; 2 B×B ch, K—Q6; 3 P—B7, K—B5; 4 B—Q6+.
(B) 1 ... B—R2; 2 K—N7, K—Q5; 3 P—B7+.
(C) 1 ... B—Q1; 2 P—B7+.

  2 P—B7

2 K—N7? K—Q5; 3 K—B6, B—N5; or 3 P—B7, B×P; 4 B×B, K×P=.

  2 ... B×P

If 2 ... K—Q5; 3 P—B8(Q), R—R1 ch; 4 K—K7! R×Q; 5 B×R, B—N5; 6 P—B6+, but 4 K—B7? would only draw.

302

ʒ B×B   R—R2!   5 P—B6   R—KR2
4 B—Q6   R×B

If 5 ... R—R7; 6 B—B5 ch, K—K5; 7 P—B7, R—KR7; 8 K—N7+.

6 K—N8   R—R5   8 P—B7 wins
7 B—B5 ch K—any

The rook is cut off from all preventive lines of access.

Alg.: 1 c5, ♗a5; 2 c7, ♗:c7; 3 ♗:c7, ♖h7; 4 ♗d6, ♖:b7; 5 c6,♖h7; 6 ♔g8, ♖h4; 7 ♗c5†, ♔∞; 8 c7+.

DIAGRAM 217

W. KORN

CHESS

1943*

=

Crisp and no waste!

1 P—K7!	K—Q2	4 R—Q2 ch	Q×R
2 N—B5 ch	N×N	5 P—K8(Q) ch	K×Q
3 R×P	P—Q8(Q)	stalemate	

If 1 N—Q6 ch? K—B2! (1 ... K—Q1?; 2 P—K7 ch, K×P; 3 N—B5 ch, and 4 N—K3=); 2 P—K7, P—Q8(Q) wins for Black.

The lonely White pawn sacrifices itself on move five, to ensure the final stalemate. In chess such a performer is known as a "desperado". His other role here is that of a decoy, enticing Black's king to enter square Q2(d7) where the king is exposed to a crucial knight check. A desperado is also used to cause as much havoc as possible before its own doom.

---

* Diagrams 217, 217A and 217B are taken from an article by W. Korn, "More about Endgame Technique" in *Chess*, England, September 1943.

Alg.: 1 e7, ♔d7; 2 ♘c5†, ♘:c5; 3 ♖:b2, d1(♕); 4 ♖d2†, ♕:d2; 5 e8(♕)†, ♔:e8⊜.

DIAGRAM 217 (A)

W. KORN

CHESS

1943

Black moves, White draws.

This diagram serves as the matrix, sometimes called "thematic aggregation", that gave cause to the ultimate construction of the preceding diagram 217. Such an "aggregation", conceived in the mind or occurring in actual play, may become the springboard for an artistic concentrate. The execution in the matrix is simple and straightforward, the resulting stalemate is "pure":

1 ... N—B4 ch; 2 K—R3, P—Q7; 3 R—K2, P—Q8(Q); 4 R—Q2 ch, Q × R stalemate. But the motif as shown is too primitive for a study—and the demand "Black moves, White draws" is disallowed in the *Codex*—the international codification of rules for composing. Therefore, further exploration is called for and the next frame tries a further advance.

DIAGRAM 217 (B)

W. KORN

CHESS

1943

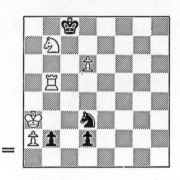

=

Thematic extension.

This sketch already contains some lively play, namely:

1 P—Q7 ch, K×P; 2 N—B5 ch, N×N; 3 R×P, P—Q8(Q);
4 R—Q2 ch, Q×R stalemate. In comparison with the foregoing aggregation, this diagram includes another white pawn on
QR2. Without it, Black would win by (1 P—Q7 ch, K×P; 2
N—B5 ch), K—B3!; 3 N×N, P—Q8(Q); 4 N×P, Q—R8 ch,
whereas with it White draws after 4 N×P, Q—Q3 ch; 5 R—N4.
Simultaneously, the added pawn also allows an added try
1 P—Q7 ch, K×P; 2 R—Q5 ch, K—B3; 3 R×N, P—N8(Q);
4 R×P, Q×N, and, contrary to appearances, White cannot
draw against the queen with his rook's pawn on the original
square—he loses. However, again comparing with diagram
217(A), the final stalemate in the above diagram is no longer
"pure" because the square QR2 is inaccessible to the white king
for two reasons. It is covered by Black's queen and also blocked
by a white pawn; further, the pawn is superfluous for the final
stalemate and therefore, in this concluding line, is "unecono-
mical". Diagram 217 not only contains a try (1 N—Q6 ch?),
and a pure and economical ("model") stalemate, but also starts
with a "quiet" move, 1 P—K7. While starting with a forcing
check is not necessarily a defect, a quiet move is preferable, if it
can be technically achieved. Thus, diagram 217 is a rightful
version of the desired goal.

DIAGRAM 218

R. KUJOTH

CHESS LIFE & REVIEW

JULY, 1972

**4th Prize
3rd USCF Tourney, 1972–3**

Black's deadly threat 1 ... Q—N7 mate, or ... Q—N8 mate, forces drastic action, converting the imminent mate into an enforceable asset:

1 R×P ch! N×R

Prompt defeat follows on ... K—N3; 2 Q—B7 ch+.

2 N—B7 ch K—N3   4 Q—N8!! Q×Q
3 N—R8 ch Q×N

Blow by blow, a diabolical bombshell of a self-stalemate that can hardly be rivalled.

The solution to the study as published the following month, carried the editor's commentary "usually Black chases White's king into stalemate—this different approach is more paradoxical."

Whether paradoxical, or novel, the device as invented in diagram 218 need not remain singular and inspires other approaches.

  * R. Kujoth of Wisconsin gained global fame with some smashing quickies, e.g. one against Fashingbauer, Milwaukee 1950: 1 P—K4, P—QB4; 2 P—QN4, P×P; 3 P—QR3, N—QB3; 4 P×P, N—B3; 5 P—N5, N—QN1; 6 P—K5, Q—B2; 7 P—Q4 (7 P×N, Q—K4 ch!), N—Q4; 8 P—QB4, N—N3; 9 P—B5, N—Q4; 10 P—N6!, Black resigns as he must lose a piece (10 ... Q—Q1; 11 R×P, R×R; 12 P×R, Q—R4 ch; 13 N—B3! N×N; 14 P×N(Q), N×Q; 15 B—Q2, Q—Q1; 16 K×N+).

Alg.: 1 ♖:a7, ♘:a7; 2 ♘c7†, ♔b6; 3 ♘a8†, ♕:a8; 4 ♕b8, ♕:b8⊜.

THE MAKING OF AN ENDGAME STUDY inherently means methodical dissection of potential facets, analysis of all angles and postures of presentation on the board, and synthesis into an optimally effective form.

Kujoth's precept in diagram 218 is unusual because of the abruptness with which Black's queen is entrapped by a sacrificial offering, and forced to administer a stalemate in escaping, or else invite a loss. The thunder of this combinational stroke still reverberates. But the phases of this particular stalemate pattern may be capable of more flexibility with the execution susceptible to subtler positional treatment. The inquisitive composer will systematically pursue the different faces of the design. Progressively, they may develop as in the thematic schemata shown in diagrams 218(A) and (B).

DIAGRAM 218 (A)

W. KORN

EXPERIMENTAL SCHEMA

No. 1

1973

(A) 1 . . . K—N4; 2 Q—N8 ch, Q × Q (=).

(B) 1 . . . K—N6 (or B6, or Q6); 2 Q—N3 ch, Q × Q (=).

(C) 1 . . . K—Q4; 2 Q—B3 ch, K—K3; 3 Q—N3 ch +
    (if 2 . . . K—Q3 (or K4); 3 Q—N3 ch, Q × Q (=)).

Suddenly, the scope of the theme has been widened. A horizontal capture in variation (A), and a vertical one in variation (B) leading to stalemate; and a diagonal loss of queen in variation (C).

(In such drawings, the idea is often shown with Black's defensive answers first, and White defeating them. An introduction is constructed subsequently.)

Alg.: (A) 1 . . . ♔b5; 2 ♕b8†, ♕:b8(=).(B) 1 . . . ♔b3 (c3, d3); 2♕ g3†, ♕:g3,(=).(C) 1 . . . ♔d5; 2 ♕f3†, ♔e6; 3 ♕b3†+.

DIAGRAM 218 (B)

W. KORN

EXPERIMENTAL SCHEMA
No. 2

1973

A change of venue in several respects.

A black bishop substitutes for one of Black's stalemating pawns, somewhat restricting the range of White's queen and strengthening the defense. Moreover, it inserts a combination with another theme, that of a loss or draw against a rook's pawn and wrong bishop.

1 Q×Q ch? K×Q; 2 K×P, B—B1; 3 K—N2, K—N5; 4 K—B2, K×P; 5 K—K2, K—N6; 6 K—Q2, K—N7+ is an abortive attempt. Hence:

 1 Q—Q8 ch Q—B2

If 1 ... K—N2; 2 K×P, B—K3; 3 K—N3 (or 3 P—N6), draws, but not 3 Q×P, Q—KB7 ch and Black wins.

 2 Q—N8 ch! Q×Q stalemate

Ineffective is now 2 ... Q—N2 ch; 3 Q×Q ch, K×Q; 4 K×P, B—K3; 5 K—N3, B—N6; 6 K—B4, B×P; 7 K—K3 and White reaches the QP corner comfortably as Black's king is further removed from the scene than in the initial false lead with 1 Q×Q ch?

This combination of two *sujets* already strongly resembles

a legitimate study but it waters down the original intention of fully implementing all possible mutations of the archetypal stalemate theme. Therefore the task will boil down to the eventual climaxes in diagrams 219 and 220.

Alg.: 1 ♕d8†, ♕c7; 2 ♕b8†, ♕:b8 (=).

DIAGRAM 219

W. KORN

ORIGINAL

1973

Twin $=$

"After a Theme by R. Kujoth"

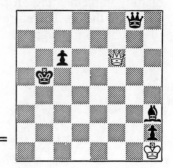

Position I

Black threatens a bifurcated mate—by ... Q—N7 or ... Q—N8. If 1 Q—K5 ch, Q—Q4 ch wins. The text is White's only and quite natural course.

   1 Q—N2 ch K—B4

If Black sidesteps on to the rook's file by 1 ... K—R3, or ... R4, or ... R5, then 2 Q—R2 ch, Q × Q is stalemate, with the queen protecting the rook's pawn horizontally. If 1 ... K—B5; 2 Q—R2 wins the queen. Black's next move is forced for the same reasons.

   2 Q—R3 ch K—Q5!   3 Q—N2 ch K—K6

3 ... K—Q6; 4 Q—R3 ch, K—K5; 5 Q—N4 ch, K—K4; 6 Q—B3 ch, K—B4; 7 Q × B ch and 8 K × P draws.
3 ... K—K5; 4 Q—B2 ch, K—Q5; 5 Q—N2 ch, or 4 ... K—B5; 5 Q—B2 ch, or 4 ... K—K6; 5 Q—B3 ch leads to repetition of moves or to the same turns as in the main lines or the other sub-variations.

   4 Q—K5 ch K—Q7

With 4 ... K—B6, or 4 ... K—B7; 5 Q—N3 ch, K × Q! stalemate, another variable of a vertical stalemate is added,

312

supplied by Black's king. Otherwise, also after 4 ... K—Q6, 5 Q—N3 ch, the stalemate by Q×Q still persists.

5 Q—B4 ch	K—B7		8 Q—B2 ch	K—B8
6 Q—B2 ch	K—Q8		9 Q—K1 ch	K—N7
7 Q—B3 ch	K—Q7		10 Q—B2 ch	K—R6!!

The purpose of Black's king's march becomes apparent—after 11 Q—N3 ch, Black interposes ... Q—N6 instead of ... Q×Q? with the now typical stalemate!

    11 Q—R7 ch! K—N7!

If 11 ... K—N6; or 11 ... K—N5; 12 Q—N8 ch! Q×Q with a diagonal stalemate.

    12 Q—B2 ch K—R8!   13 Q—K1 ch! draw

If 13 Q—R7 ch? Q—R7! and Black will eventually win after some protracted staircase maneuvers. After 12 Q—N8 ch?, Q—N6! wins again by interposition, lifting the stalemate.

All three types of stalemate that can be extracted from the setting are present in this study, as well as the diagonal capture of the queen in the first sub-variation. Also note the subtle shift in the geography of the battlefield—the main attack comes "from the North", not "from the East".

Alg.: 1 ♕b2†, ♚c5; 2 ♕a3†, ♚d4; 3 ♕b2†, ♚e3; 4 ♕e5†, ♚d2; 5♕ f4†, ♚c2; 6 ♕f2†, ♚d1; 7 ♕f3†, ♚d2; 8 ♕f2†, ♚c1; 9 ♕e1†, ♚b2; 10 ♕f2†, ♚a3; 11 ♕a7†, ♚b2; 12 ♕f2†, ♚a1; 13 ♕e1†=.

DIAGRAM 219 (A)

W. KORN

ORIGINAL

1973

Twin =

"After a Theme by R. Kujoth"

Position II

Finally, another presentation, with a simpler and less sophisticated solution—but again shifting the direction of the attack which this time starts at the opposite wing, "from the West". After 1 Q—K7 ch, K—N3; 2 Q—N4 ch, K—B2; 3 Q—R5 ch, K—N1, or 2 Q—Q3 ch, K—N2; 3 Q—K7 ch, K—B1, the king reaches shelter and Black wins. White's initiative is forcing and forced.

    1 Q×RP ch! K—Q3!

The familiar blueprint again, after (a) 1 ... K—N4 (or N5); 2 Q—N8 ch, Q×Q⊜, or (b) 1 ... K—B5 (or Q4); 2 Q—R2 ch and 3 Q×Q+.

    2 Q—R3 ch K—Q2

Once more, if 2 ... K—B2 (or K4), or 2 ... P—B4!? 3 Q—N3 ch, Q×Q⊜, and if 2 ... K—K3; 3 Q—N3 ch and 4 Q×Q+.

    3 Q×B ch Q—K3   4 Q—R7 ch!!

Avoiding the trap 4 Q×Q ch, K×Q, or 4 K×P, Q×Q ch, or 4 Q×P, Q—K8 ch!, forcing the exchange of queens with victory for Black.

4 ... K—Q3   5 Q×P ch K—B4

5 ... Q—K4; 6 Q—R6 ch, K—B4; 7 Q—B1 ch draws.

6 Q—KB2 ch! K—N4   7 K—N2 drawn

Alg.: 1 ♕:a7†, ♚d6; 2 ♕a3†, ♚d7; 3 ♕:h3†, ♕e6; 4 ♕h7†, ♚d6; 5 ♕:h2†, ♚c5; 6 ♕f2†, ♚b5; 7 ♚g2=.

W. KORN

ORIGINAL

1973

DIAGRAM 220

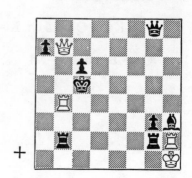

+

Having progressed, by a sort of linear programming, from the "tic-tac-toe" grip to a kind of penultimate synopsis, two chores remain. One, to search for further possible input of ideas or a different scenario by reshuffling the material, and one such mutation is indicated in diagram 221.

But the ultimate aim at this point is to go beyond a mere mechanistic formula as distilled in diagram 219(A) and, by retroanalytical experiment, establish an artful model, with the practical play-off resulting in the thematic conclusion. Such an end-product might shape up as in the diagram above. It adds some combinational ingredients.

> 1 R/4×R!!

The saving move, and by the skin of the teeth. Wrong is 1 R/2×R?, R×R/5 with an easy win for Black. But disaster follows either:

(A) 1 R×B!? R—R7 ch (1 ... R×R is also good); 2 R×R, R×R ch; 3 K—N1, R—R2; 4 Q—R6, Q—Q4; 5 Q—R5 ch, K—Q3; 6 Q—Q8 ch, R—Q2; 7 Q—N8 ch, K—K2; or 7 Q—B6 ch, K—B2+. Or

(B) 1 Q—K7 ch!? K—Q4; 2 Q—K4 ch, K—Q3; 3 R—Q4 ch, K—B4+; or 3 R×B!? R×R!+.

> 1 ... R×R ch

The alternative 1 ... R×R/N7 is a take-off for deadly acrobatics, e.g.

(A) 2 R×R? Q—Q4 ch; 3 K—N1, Q—Q8 mate.

(B) 2 Q×RP ch? K—Q3; 3 Q—R6 (3 Q—Q4 ch? Q—Q4 ch; 4 Q×Q ch, K (or P)×Q; 5 R×R, B—B8; 6 K—N1, P—N7+), K—B2; 4 Q—R5 ch (4 Q—R7 ch, R—N2; 5 Q—R5 ch, K—N1; 6 Q—K5 ch, K—B1+), R—N3; 5 Q—R7 ch, R—R2; 6 Q—R5 ch, K—N1; 7 Q—K5 ch, K—B1+.

(C) 2 Q—K7 ch?! K—B5!!; 3 Q—K4 ch, K—N6!? (or 3 ... K—B6; 4 Q×P ch, Q—B5; 5 Q×Q ch, K×Q; 6 R×R, B—B8; 7 R—QR2!=); 4 Q—K3 ch!! (but not 4 Q—Q3 ch, K—R7; 5 Q—R6 ch, K—N8; 6 Q—Q3 ch, K—R8! and Black wins), K—R7; 5 Q×P ch, K—N8; 6 Q—N1 ch with a perpetual check.

1 ... P×R!? 2 R—B2 ch allows White at least a draw, and after 2 ... R×R; 3 Q×BP, K×Q another and novel type of stalemate pattern materializes.

2 R×R P×R   3 Q×RP ch

with the same continuation as from diagram 219(A).

Alg.: 1 ♖:b2, ♖:h2†; 2 ♖:h2, g:h2; etc., as in diagram 219(A).

DIAGRAM 221

W. KORN

ORIGINAL

1973

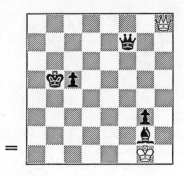

=

Experimental Modification.

The previous matrix is being varied by reversing the position of Black's bishop and knight's pawn, with a similar stalemate effect of a different kind.

1 Q—N2 ch with the following mutations:

(A) 1 ... K—B5; 2 Q—R2 ch and 3 Q×Q+.
(B) 1 ... K—R3 (or R4, or R5); 2 Q—R2 ch, Q×Q (=)
(C) 1 ... K—B3; 2 Q×B ch and 3 Q×P =.

The "backswing" 1 Q—N8 ch!? discloses another submerged line of intersection after, for instance, 1 ... K—R5? 2 Q—R8 ch, K—N6 (2 ... B×Q(=)); 3 Q—Q5 ch (or 3 Q—N7 ch), Q×Q or B×Q, stalemate.

   Starting from this, or any modification, the inquisitive student of composing will research further facets and variations that create an unequivocally correct matrix and try to find an introduction just as diagram 220 added one to diagram 219(A); then evolve a main play and wind up with a thematic finale.

DIAGRAM 222

R. ULREICH

CHESS REVIEW

1967

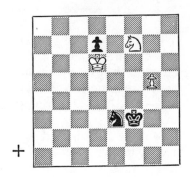

+

This study by a neophyte and its sophisticated epilogue in diagram 223 form an instructive tandem and an object for comparison and choice according to taste.

   1 N—R6 N—B5 ch

1 P—N6? N—B4 ch draws easily and so does 1 K—K5? N—N5 ch; 2 K—B5, N—K6 ch; 3 K—K5 (3 K—B6, N—Q4 ch; 4 K—K5, N—B5 =), N—N5 ch with a perpetual check.

   2 K—Q5

If 2 K × P, K—B5; 3 P—N6, N—K4 ch =.

   2 ... K—B5

2 ... N—N3 ch, or 2 ... N—K6 ch; 3 K—K5, N—B5 ch; 4 K—B6 winning, but 3 K—B5? permits a draw after either 2 ... N—N3 ch; 3 K—B5, N—B1; 4 P—N6, P—Q3 ch; 5 K—Q5, N—K2 ch; or 2 ... N—K6 ch; 3 K—B5, N—N7; 4 P—N6, N—B5; 5 P—N7, N—K3 ch.

   3 P—N6 N—Q3   4 K × N

4 P—N7? N—K1; 5 P—N8(Q), N—B3 ch =.

4 ... K—N4	6 N—B5 wins
5 P—N7 K—B3	

When the study was published by the endgame editor*, he added this comment: "The crux of the position lies in the mistaken attempt to win by promotion: 6 P—N8(Q), Stalemate! or underpromotion: 6 P—N8(N) ch? K—N2; 7 K—K5, P—Q4; 8 K—Q4, K—R2, arriving at what often is a theoretical win: two knights against an immobilized pawn, except that here the king is the immobilized piece!

As conceived, however, the subject has less competitive value as the idea is relegated to a defensive aberration, with White winning through a simple and pedestrian 6 N—B5.

If the idea could be worked out in an active line, with colors reversed, showing White thus to draw, it would have merit; is the task attainable?"

The answer was not long in coming, as witness diagram 223.

---

* W. Korn of *Chess Review.*

Alg.: 1 ♞h6, ♞f5†; 2 ♚d5, ♚f4; 3 g6, ♞d6; 4 ♚:d6, ♚g5; 5 g7, ♚f6; 6 ♞f5+.

DIAGRAM 223

H. M. LOMMER[§]

THÈMES 64

1970

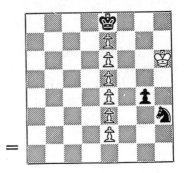

=

Utilizing the technique of a pawn column originally designed by Fred Lazard in 1924 in conjunction with a different theme, grandmaster of composition Harold M. Lommer took up the challenge issued in the comments to diagram 222. He hammered out a modern configuration that reverses the inverted solutions in Ulreich's concept—just what the editor had ordered.

1 K—R5 P—N6		3 K—B3 P—N8(N) ch!	
2 K—N4 P—N7			

If 3 ... P—N8 (B); 4 K—N2 wins a piece and draws, and 3 ... P—N8 (Q or R) stalemates. White's escape "west" is obstructed by his own pawn barrier which acts as an artificial edge of the board. Charming!

4 K—N2 K×P		5 K—R2 (or B1)!	

Not 5 K—N3, N—N4!! 6 K—N2 (or N4), N/8—R6 and Black will capture all pawns but the one on White's K2, achieving the theoretically (and practically) won ending of two knights versus pawn.

5 ...	K×P	8 K—N2	K×P
6 K—N2	K×P	9 K—B1!! drawn	
7 K—B1 (or R2)	K×P		

Not 9 K—R2? K—B7; 10 P—K4, N—N4; 11 P—K5, N/8—B6 ch; 12 K—R1, N—K5 and 13 ... N—N6 mate. The knights are tied to each other's protection. But if 9 ... K—B5?; 10 P—K4, K—N5; 11 P—K5, N—B6 ch; 12 K—R1! N—B7 ch; 13 K—N2, N—K5; 14 P—K6, N—B3; 15 P—K7, N—K8 with a draw as the pawn is too advanced to allow for the theoretical win of two knights versus pawn.

The acme of perfection and introspection, with Ulreich having supplied the impetus.

Alg.: 1 ♚h5, g3; 2 ♚g4, g2; 3 ♚f3, g1(♘)†; 4 ♚g2, ♚:e7; 5 ♚h2, ♚:e6; 6 ♚g2, ♚:e5; 7 ♚h2, ♚:e4; 8 ♚g2, ♚:e3; 9 ♚f1=.

DIAGRAM 224

W. KORN

BRITISH CHESS MAGAZINE

1954

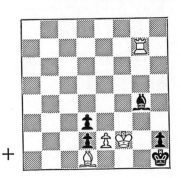

+

A simple stalemate-avoidance of a different genre.
If 1 R×B?, P×P; 2 B×P, P—Q8(Q); 3 B—B3 ch, Q×B ch;
4 K×Q⊜.

   1 R—Q7 P×P

If 1 ... B×P; 2 R×P! or 1 ... B×R; 2 P—K4, B—N5;
3 B×B and mate in two.

   2 B×P B×B   3 R×P and wins

Not a *sonata*, yet a modest and unassuming *sonatina*.

Alg.: 1 ♖d7, d:e2; 2 ♗:e2, ♗:e2; 3 ♖:d2+.

C. B. JONES

CHESS LIFE & REVIEW

1971

DIAGRAM 225

(3rd Commend. 2nd USCF Tourney 1970–1)

$=$

The tourney judges*: "Each side has a knight, but Black's two unobstructed extra pawns should normally win.

The manner in which White's knight gets into action and controls the distant pawn is very adroit."

1 P—R6! P×P		2 N—N6! K—Q3

If 2 P—B6, K—Q3+. If 2 N—B7? K—Q4; 3 N—Q8 (3 P—B6, K—K3; 4 N—K5, P—Q3+), K—K4 (3 ... P—N5; 4 P—B6, K—Q3; 5 K—N2, P—N6; 6 N—N7 ch=); 4 N—N7, P—N5; 5 N—B5, K×P+.

3 N—B4	K—K4	8 N—B1	K—B5
4 K—N2	K×P	9 K×N	P—N7
5 N—Q5!	K—K4	10 N—Q3 ch	K—any
6 N—B3	P—N5	11 N×P	draw
7 N—R2	P—N6		

If White starts with 1 N—N6? Black wins by 1 ... P—R3!

---

* R. Brieger and W. Korn.

Alg.: 1 h6, g:h6; 2 ♘g6, ♚d6; 3 ♘f4, ♚e5; 4 ♚g2, ♚:f5; 5 ♘d5, ♚e5; 6 ♘c3, b4; 7 ♘a2, b3; 8 ♘c1, ♚f4; 9 ♚:h1, b2; 10 ♘d3†, ♚∞; 11 ♘:b2=.

DIAGRAM 226

C. B. JONES

NEW STATESMAN

1971–2

=

4th Hon. Mention, Study Tourney

Two black pawns on the way to queen, while the two white pawns are easily stopped by Black's king. White faces an almost impossible burden.

The judges'* comment: "The main play centers around an unexpected 'reciprocal Zugzwang' after 5 N×NP, as Black would win if he did not have the move".

1 P—R7	P—R7 ch	3 N—B5 ch K×P
2 K—R1	K—N2	

3 ... K—R1; 4 N×NP, K×P; 5 N—K2 ends in a draw.

4 P—N6 ch!!

This position is one of a mutual bind. Noteworthy is Black's win after 4 N×P, K—N3; 5 N—K2, K×P; 6 N—B3, K—B5; 7 N—Q5 ch, K—B6; 8 N—B3, P—K7+.

4 ... K×P!

If 4 ... K—N1; 5 N×NP, K—N2 (or 5 ... K—B1; 6 N—K2, K—N2; 7 N—B4, K—R3; 8 N—K2, K×P; 9 N—N3 =); 6 N—B5 ch, K×P; 7 N×P and White draws, keeping Black's pawns under unbroken surveillance.

* D. Hooper, A. J. Roycroft and H. Staudte.

5 N×NP!

5 N×KP, K—N4, etc., will, however, win for Black with this particular pawn formation.

5 ... K—B2

Black is under siege. If 5 ... K—N4; 6 N×P ch, K—B5; 7 N—B3, K—B6; 8 N—N5 =. If 5 ... K—R3 (or K—N2); 6 N—B5 ch, K any; 7 N×P with the same outcome as in the main line. The judges remarked that Black was in Zugzwang but in the absence of a clearer compulsion one may simply say that Black had no other, better, move.

6 N×P! P—K7

The stage is set for one of the pawns to be taken so as to sacrifice the knight for the other king's pawn, with a stalemate to follow. If 6 N—K2, K—K3+.

| 7 N—N5 ch K—N3 | 9 N—K1! K—B4 |
| 8 N—B3   K—B3 | 10 P—R5 |

10 N—Q3? K—K5; 11 N—K1, K—K6; 12 P—R5, P×P; 13 N—Q3, P—R5+.

| 10 ...   P×P | 12 N—B1! draw |
| 11 N—Q3 P—R5 | |

If 12 ... P—K8 (Q or R) stalemate.

Alg.: 1 h7, a2†; 2 ♔a1, ♔g7; 3 ♘f5†, ♔:h7; 4 g6†, ♔:g6; 5 ♘:g3, ♔f7; 6 ♘:e4, e2; 7 ♘g5†, ♔g6; 8 ♘f3, ♔f6; 9 ♘e1, ♔f5; 10 a5, b:a5; 11 ♘d3, a4; 12 ♘c1(=),or =.

The Canadian Chess Clan

Our Canadian chess neighbors have maintained a proud and independent group in every respect—sending their own successful teams to the Chess Olympics, and running their own chess magazines of high quality. *Canadian Chess Chat* featured a valuable column on endgame study, for many years edited by Harry Rombach.

Canadian studies have met with international recognition, draw on their own on local resourcefulness and can derive inspiration from total Anglo-American tradition.

Jonathan Berry of Vancouver (diagram 232) made his debut in the American *Chess Life & Review* while the American T. McDermott appeared first in *Canadian Chess Chat* (diagram 214).

DIAGRAM 227

A. H. BRANTON and H. ROMBACH§

CANADIAN CHESS CHAT

AUGUST, 1966

=

A joint USA–Canadian production with one partner providing the tune and the other the orchestration. With quite equal forces, the demand "White to draw" would sound tautological but for the devastating 1 ... N—B4 ch, winning the exchange and game.

    1 N—Q1!

1 R—N2?, N—B4 ch; 2 K—N5! (2 K—R5, P—N6+), N×P; 3 R—N3, N—B8!; 4 R×P, R×N; 5 R×P, R—B3+.

    1 ... R—N8

If 1 ... R—Q7; 2 R—N1 =. The text keeps White in a bind— at least for the time being!

    2 R—N1

defends the knight and avoids the deadly fork.

    2 ...   N—B4 ch   4 K—R5 dis. ch! N—N2 ch
    3 K×P   R×N

If 4 R×R, N×P ch+.

5 K—R6! R×R stalemate

If 5 ... R—Q4; 6 R×N ch, K—B1; 7 R—R7, K—N1 =.

Alg.: 1 ♘d1, ♖b1; 2 ♖g1, ♘f5†; 3 ♔:g4, ♖:d1; 4 ♔h5†, ♘g7†; 5 ♔h6, ♖:g1⊜.

DIAGRAM 228

A. H. BRANTON
and H. ROMBACH§

CANADIAN CHESS CHAT

JUNE, 1967

=

Another cooperative venture, with rich play and some splendid tries.

1 N—N1!

Not 1 R/4×P, R—K8 ch; 2 K—N2, N—K6 ch+. Nor 1 R—Q1, R×N; 2 R×P, R—R8!+; or 1 K—N2, R×N; 2 R—Q1, P—N8(Q)! wins; and not 2 ... R—R8?; 3 R—QN1!! R×R; 4 R×N ch, stalemate!

1 ...	R—K8 ch	3 R—Q1 R—R8!
2 K—N2 R×N		

Avoiding the same trap 3 ... R×R; 4 R×N ch stalemate.

4 R—QN1

If 4 R×R, P×R (B)!; or 4 R—K1, P—N8(Q); 5 R×Q, R—R7 ch, winning for Black.

4 ... K—N4!

White also escapes after 4 ... R—R7!; 5 R—B3! or 5 R—K4! but not 5 R×BP, N—K6 ch; 6 K—B3, P—N7; 7 R—QN5, R—R8; 8 R/5×NP, P—N8(Q); 9 R×Q, R×R; 10 K×N, K—N6+.

5 R×P ch K—B5   6 R—B4 ch K—K4

6 ... K—K6 deprives the knight of his attacking square.

7 R×P N—K6 ch   9 R—N5 ch K—any
8 K×P N×R   10 R×P   drawn

The blocking maneuvers on White's QN1 square are engrossing.

Alg.: 1 ♘b1, ♖e1†; 2 ♔g2, ♖:b1; 3 ♖d1, ♖a1; 4 ♖b1, ♔g5; 5 ♖:c5†, ♔f4; 6 ♖c4†, ♔e5; 7 ♖:b2, ♘e3†; 8 ♔:g3, ♘:c4; 9 ♖b5†, ♔∞; 10 ♖:h5=.

DIAGRAM 229

H. ROMBACH[§]

CANADIAN CHESS CHAT

1962

+

Trying the obvious with a player's instinct does not work; for instance 1 P—R7, R—K5 ch; 2 K × B, R—Q5 ch; 3 K—K7, R—K5 ch; 4 K—B7, R—B5 ch; 5 K—N6, R—B1!; 6 B—K6, R—KR1!=

1 P—R8(Q) ch	K × Q	3 K × B	R—Q5 ch
2 P—R7	R—K5 ch	4 K—B7!	

It is the play on the other wing that will block the rook, plus . . .

4 ...	R—B5 ch	6 K—R6!	R—N1
5 K—N6	R—N5 ch	7 B—B3 ch wins	

A positional compression, worthy of exhibition anywhere.

Alg.: 1 a8(♕)†, ♔:a8; 2 h7, ♖e4†; 3 ♔:d7, ♖d4†; 4 ♔c7, ♖c4†; 5 ♔b6, ♖b4†; 6 ♔a6, ♖b8; 7 ♗f3†+.

DIAGRAM 230

H. ROMBACH[§]

(In Cooperation with Hillel Aloni)

(Israel) SHAKHMAT

1966

Ring Tourney, 1st Hon. Mention*

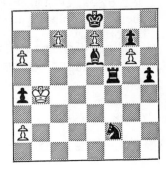

The queen's quadrangular rhythm is entrancing, so is the variety of the stalemate figures emerging after an elegant introduction.

   1 P—R7 N—Q6 ch   2 K—R3!

2 K×P, N—N7 ch; 3 K—any, R—R4+.

   2 ...   R—R4   4 P—R8(Q)   R—QB4!
   3 P—B8(Q) ch B×Q

4 ... R×Q results in a "pure" stalemate. But, threatening mate, Black tried for even bigger booty. A piquant round of hide-and-seek follows.

   5 Q—R5! K×P

Black maintains the thematic tension and reciprocally threatens mate. 5... R×Q still stalemates.

If 5 Q×P ch, B—Q2; 6 Q—Q4, R—R4 ch; 7 K—N3, N—B4 ch and 8 ... N—K3+. If 5 K×P, K×P; 6 Q—K4 ch, N—K4; 7 Q—R4 ch, K—Q3; 8 Q×P, B—Q2 ch; 9 K—N3, B—K3 ch; 10 K—R4, N—B3!!; 11 Q—R2 ch, K—Q2 wins.

   6 Q—R7 ch B—Q2!   7 Q—B7!!

   * Judge: Milu Milescu.

Now the queen intends to become a perpetual sacrificial offering herself, by ... Q—Q6 ch–KB8 ch–QN8 ch, etc., as her capture by the king establishes stalemate.

The ordinary 6 ... K—B3!?; 7 Q—B7 ch, K—N4; 8 Q—K7 ch, K—B4; 9 Q—B7 ch also draws for White but only if he avoids the sting of venom in 8 Q×P? B—B4! with a win for Black.

7 ... R—QN4

Postponing the sacrificial perpetual by one more, and last, move.

8 Q—B5 ch!!

The last nail. If 8 ... K—any; 9 Q×R, B×Q, again with a "pure" stalemate, just as after the immediate 8 ... R×Q.

But with 8 ... N×Q! Black creates yet another facet of the stalemate. Even though not pure (White's square QN3 is controlled by two pieces, Black's pawn and rook), the final picture is different.

Alg.: 1 a7, ♘d3†; 2 ♔a3, ♖a5; 3 c8(♕)†, ♗:c8; 4 a8(♕), ♖c5; 5 ♕a5, ♔:e7; 6 ♕a7†, ♗d7; 7 ♕c7, ♖b5; 8 ♕c5†=.

DIAGRAM 231

H. ROMBACH[§]

SCHAKEND

1971

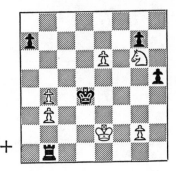

+

3rd Prize, Kon. Ned. Schaakbond

Another construction wherein the obvious is not the best. If 1 P—K7?, R—N7 ch; 2 K—B1, R—N8 ch; 3 K—B2, R—N7 ch; 4 K—B3 (4 K—N1, R—K7=), R×P ch; and 5 ... R—K6=.

 1 N—K5! R×P   **2 K—Q2**

An important stall. If 2 N—B3 ch, K—K5; 3 P—K7, R—K6 ch; and 4 ... K—B5; winning for Black.

2 ...	R—K6	5 P—N3 ch!	R×P
3 N—B3 ch	K—K5	6 P—K7	R—K6
4 N—K1!!	K—B5	7 N—N2 ch wins	

Alg.: 1 ♘e5, ♖:b3; 2 ♔d2, ♖e3; 3 ♘f3†, ♔e4; 4 ♘e1, ♔f4; 5 g3†, ♖:g3; 6 e7, ♖e3; 7 ♘g2†+.

DIAGRAM 232

J. BERRY§

CHESS LIFE & REVIEW

1969

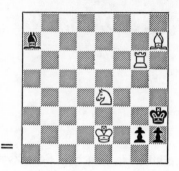

**3rd Commendation, 1st U.S.C.F.
Tourney, 1968–9**   =

The young composer's first—and a galaxy of fireworks it is.

   1 R—N3 ch K—R5   2 B—B5 P—N8(N) ch

White threatened mate. If 2 ... P—R8(Q); 3 R—N4 ch, K—R6 (3 ... K—R4; 4 N—B6 ch and 5 R—N6‡); 4 N—N5 ch, K—R7; 5 N—B3 ch, K—R6; 6 R—N5‡.

   3 K—Q3!

Intending 4 R—N4 ch, K—R6; 5 R×N+.

   3 ...   P—R8(Q)   5 N—N5 ch
   4 R—N4 ch K—R6

After 5 R×N dis. ch, K—R7; 6 R×Q, K×R the ensuing ending of knight and bishop versus bishop remains a draw.

   5 ... K—R7   6 R—R4 ch N—R6

If White's move had been 3 K—Q1, or 3 K—K1, with White's king on the first rank it would now be discovered check and a win for Black.

7 R×N ch K—N8   9 R×Q K×R
8 N—B3 ch K—N7   10 B—R3!!

Black's bishop is helpless in the face of 11 K—K2, 12 K—B1; and 13 B—N2‡.

Compare the last moves in this and the next diagram.

Alg.: 1 ♖g3†, ♔h4; 2 ♗f5, g1(♘)†; 3 ♔d3, h1(♕); 4 ♖g4†, ♔h3;
5 ♘g5†, ♔h2; 6 ♖h4†, ♘h3; 7 ♖:h3†, ♔g1; 8 ♘f3†, ♔g2;
9 ♖:h1, ♔:h1; 10 ♗h3+.

DIAGRAM 233

I. A. HOROWITZ
and I. KASHDAN

THE CHESS AMATEUR

1926

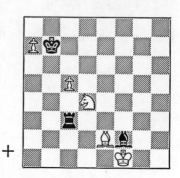

+

"This ending is exceptionally difficult for such an apparently simple position." (T. R. Dawson, Editor)

    1 P—B6 ch R×P

Black loses after the seemingly natural reply 1 ... K×P; 2 N—N5 ch, K—N3; 3 N×R, B—Q5 (attacking the N); 4 P—B7! K×P; 5 N—N5 ch, or 3 ... B—K6; 4 P—B7, B—Q5 ch; or 3 ... B—N6; 4 B—B3, winning for White. Black also loses after 1 ... K—R1; 2 K×B, R—B4 (2 ... K×P; 3 N—N5 ch); 3 N—N5.

    2 P—R8(Q) ch K×Q   4 B—R6!
    3 N×R   B—any

Black's king is immobilized, but his bishop can roam; this allows White's king to march to QB8, with B—N7 mate.

If 3 ... K—N2; 4 N—R5 ch, K—N3; 5 N—B4 ch, K—any; 6 K × B wins.

Alg.: 1 c6†, ♖:c6; 2 a8(♕)†, ♔:a8; 3 ♘:c6, ♗ ∞; 4 ♗a6+.

R. BRIEGER

ČESKOSLOVENSKÝ ŠACH

1972

DIAGRAM 234

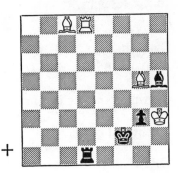

Amended by W. Korn

1974

+

White forces an under-promotion and wins by a positional squeeze.

1 R—B8 ch	B—B6	3 B—N4 ch
2 R×B ch	K×R	

A frequently occurring pattern of a direct attack on one piece (in this instance, Black's king) along with an indirect attack on another piece on the same line at the back of the first one; when the first one moves away, the second one falls. In practice, this is known as a "skewer" or "X-ray attack".

3 ...	K—B7	5 B—R4 ch K—B8
4 B×R	P—N7	

The battle lines are drawn. If 5 ... K—N8?; 6 B—K2, K—R8; 7 B—B3, K—N8; 8 B—Q5, wins (but 8 B×P? stalemates). The following tempo play is subtly forcing.

    6 B—QN3!! P—N8(N) ch!

Else Black is mated by 7 B—B4.

    7 K—N3!   K—K7

If 7 ... N—K7 ch; 8 K—R2, N— any; 9 B—B4 ch, N—K7;
10 K—R3 wins.

8 B—K6!	K—Q6	11 B—N5 ch	K—Q8
9 K—B2	N—K7	12 B—N4	
10 B—B5 ch	K—Q7		

Crowning the tactical maneuvering by a "pin" that cannot be broken. The "pin"—the reverse of a "skewer"—wins the knight and game.

In the diagram as originally published, White's rook was on KR8 (h8). O. Frink pointed out a cook by 1 R×B, R—R8 ch; 2 K—N4, R×R; 3 K×R, and 3 ... P—N7 does not draw as presumed but loses after 4 B—R4 ch, K—K6!; 5 B—Q8!!—A very concealed resource.

Alg.: 1 ♖f8†, ♗f3; 2 ♖:f3†, ♔:f3; 3 ♗g4†, ♔f2; 4 ♗:d1, g2; 5 ♗h4†, ♔f1; 6 ♗b3, g1(♘)†; 7 ♔g3, ♔e2; 8 ♗e6, ♔d3; 9 ♔f2, ♘e2; 10 ♗f5†, ♔d2; 11 ♗g5†, ♔d1; 12 ♗g4+.

DIAGRAM 235

R. BRIEGER

TIDSKRIFT FÖR SCHACK

1972 (Award publ. October 1973)

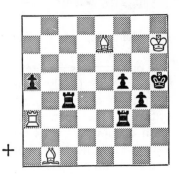

4th Prize, 1972 Study Tourney

$+$

Sparkling diagonal threats and line clearances. Black's rook's pawn prevents 1 R—R6, P—N6; 2 R—R6 ch, K—N5; 3 R—R4 mate.

    1 B—R2 R/6—B5!

If 1 ... R×R; 2 B×R (threatening 3 B—B7 mate. Black must create an escape square), 2 ... P—N6; 3 B—K2 wins.

    2 B×R

Of no avail is the waiting move 2 K—N7 because of 2 ... R/B5—K5; 3 B×R, R×B ch with a draw.

    2 ... R×B   3 R—R1! R—B6!

3 ... P—N6; 4 R—R1 ch, K—N5; 5 R—R4 ch wins the rook and game.

    4 R×P!!

A demoniacal vice in such a primeval landscape.

    If 4 ... P—N6; 5 R—R4!! and there is no rescue from mate in three at the most.

    Now the rook's pawn is annihilated with an active threat.

4 ...	R—KB6	6 R—R6 ch	K—N5
5 R—R6	P—N6	7 R—R4	mate

A model mate, both pure and economical.

A pure mate is a mate in which every square next to Black's king is guarded only once. To heighten the artistic effect, the "guarding" of the squares adjoining Black's king is supplanted by three of Black's men, self-blocking their king's escape.

An economical mate is one in which all of White's forces (except king and pawns) are playing a meaningful role—in this case the rook and bishop.

If both demands are met, the mate is called a "model mate".

Alg.: 1 ♗a2, ♖ff4; 2 ♗:c4, ♖:c4; 3 ♖a1, ♖c3; 4 ♖:a5, ♖f3; 5 ♖a6, g3; 6 ♖h6†, ♔g4; 7 ♖h4 ‡.

DIAGRAM 236

P. BENKO
and B. JONES

CHESS LIFE & REVIEW

DECEMBER, 1972

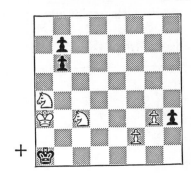

$+$

Another tandem wherein study-composer Jones supplied the ingenious and inspired basic idea, but did not succeed in eliminating a stronger defense pointed out after close scrutiny by the magazine's endgame columnist Benko, to whom the study had been sent for publication. But Benko's technical know-how, plus his own creative fancy, succeeded in igniting the original spark into a magnificent illumination.*

1 N—N5!!

"A real key move which is surprising, for it allows the black king to escape from the mating net and takes the knight further away from Black's queening pawn (Benko)."
   The try 1 N—K2, P—R7; 2 N/4—B3, P—N4; 3 N—Q4, loses because of 3 ... P—N5 ch; 4 K×P, K—N7! winning.

1 ... K—N8!

The main line that was envisaged in Jones's original setting shines through in the alternative 1 ... P—R7; 2 N/4—B3, P—R8(Q); 3 N—Q4, Q—B8 ch; 4 K—N3, Q—N7 ch; 5 K—B4, P—N4 ch; 6 K—Q3, Q×P; 7 N—N3 ch, K—N7; 8 N—Q1 ch+.

* In the *CL & R* column, editor Benko also reproduced the original imperfect matrix under the initials "B. J." and submitted his own successful correction to the endgame study tourney of Magyar Sakkszövetség of 1972 where it secured a first prize.

2 N/4—B3 ch K—B7!   3 N—Q4! ch K—Q6!

White wins easily after 3 ... K×N; 4 N—K2 ch! K—B5!; 5 P—N4, P—R7; 6 N—N3, K—B6; 7 K—R4, K—B5; 8 P—N5, P—N4 ch; 9 K—R5, queening with a check.

SUB-DIAGRAM 236 (A)

In the diagram White plays:

4 N—Q1!

Black wins after:

(A) 4 P—B4, K×N/6; 5 N—K2 ch, K—Q6; and Black wins as White has no N—B4 ch. Or

(B) 4 P—B3, K×N/6; 5 N—K2 ch, K—Q7!; 6 N—N1, P—R7 and now 7 N—B3 is blocked out. And a draw results from

(C) 4 N—B3, K×N; 5 K—R4, K—B5; 6 P—N4, P—N4 ch; 7 K—R5, P—N3 ch!; 8 K—R6, P—N5; 9 P—N5, K—Q4; 10 P—N6, K—K3; 11 N—N5 ch, K—B3; 12 N×P, P—N6; 13 N—B4, P—N7; 14 N—Q5 ch, K×P; 15 N—B3, K—B5 =.

4 ...   P—R7   5 P—B4   K×N

If 5 ... P—R8(N)!; 6 P—B5!+.

6 N—B2   K—B6

If 6 ... K—K6; 7 N—N4 ch!+.

7 P—B5   P—N4   9 K—R2! K—B7
8 P—B6   P—N5 ch   10 P—B7 P—N6 ch

11	K—R3	P—N7	13 Q—KB5 ch wins
12	P—B8(Q)	P—N8(Q)	

(namely by 13 ... K—B8; 14 Q—KB4 ch, K—B7; 15 Q—K4 ch!, K—B8; 16 Q—K3 ch, K—B7; 17 Q—Q3 ch! and mate next move).

Benko appends a memorable postscript: "I hope I have succeeded in raising the intensity of creative mood among would-be composers so that they will be able to compose artistic endgames for the pleasure of all chess lovers."

Alg.: 1 ♘b5, ♚b1; 2 ♘ac3†, ♚c2; 3 ♘d4†, ♚d3; 4 ♘d1, h2; 5 f4, ♚:d4; 6 ♘f2, ♚c3; 7 f5, b5; 8 f6, b4†; 9 ♚a2, ♚c2; 10 f7, b3†; 11 ♚a3, b2; 12 f8(♕), b1(♕); 13 ♕f5†, ♚c1; 14 ♕f4†, ♚c2; 15 ♕e4†, etc.+.

DIAGRAM 237

M. MAJOR
and W. KORN*

1954

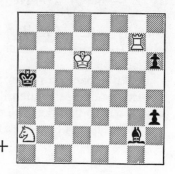

Twin   +

Position I

The topography of these twins conceals a variety of tries and hidden defenses.

1 K—B5 K—R5   2 K—B4

2 N—B1 fails for 2 ... K—R6; 3 R—R7 ch, K—N7; 4 N—Q3 ch, K—N8!

2 ... B—B8 ch

2 ... K—R6; 3 N—B1, K—N7; 4 N—Q3 ch, K—B7; 5 N—B2 K—Q7; 6 R—N3!+.

3 K—B3 B—N7?!

3 ... P—R7; 4 R—N4 ch, K—R6; 5 K—R4, K×N; 6 R×Pch!+

4 R—N4 ch K—R6   5 N—N4 K—R5

If 5 ... P—R7; 6 R×B, P—R8(Q); 7 R—R2‡. Or 5 ... P—R4; 6 N—B2 ch, K—R7; 7 R—R4 ch and mate next move.

6 N—Q3 dis. ch K—any   7 N—B2 wins

---

* From 1953 to 1960, W. Korn conducted the endgame column "All's well that ends well" in *Chess Life*, edited by Montgomery Major. The original *sujet* was published by M. Major in the *British Chess Magazine*, 1953, with White's king on Q4, but it had two solutions and thus was cooked; the columnist subsequently amended the idea.

Alg.: 1 ♔c5, ♚a4; 2 ♔c4, ♝f1†, 3 ♔c3, ♝g2; 4 ♖g4†, ♚a3; 5 ♘b4, ♚a4; 6 ♘d3†, ∞; 7 ♘f2+.

DIAGRAM 237 (A)

M. MAJOR and W. KORN

Twin +

Position II

1 K—B4 B—B8 ch!

1 ... P—R7; 2 K—B5, K—R5; 3 N—B1, K—R6; 4 R×B, P—R8(Q); 5 R—R2‡.

2 K—B5 K—R5   4 N—B1! K—R6
3 R—N1 B—N7

Again 4 ... P—R7; 5 R×B, P—R8(Q); 6 R—R2‡.

5 K—B4   K—N7   7 K—Q4   B—R1
6 N—Q3 ch K—B7

White plans 8 N—K1 ch, and 9 N×B. If 7 ... K—Q7; 8 N—B4 wins.

8 R—B1 ch K—N6

If 8 ... K—Q7; 9 R—QR1, B—B6; 10 R—R2 ch, K—Q8; 11 K—K3+.

9 N—B2   K—N7   11 R—KR3 wins
10 R—B3   P—R7

Alg.: 1 ♔c4, ♗f1†; 2 ♔c5, ♔a4; 3 ♖g1, ♗g2; 4 ♘c1, ♔a3; 5 ♔c4, ♔b2; 6 ♘d3†, ♔c2; 7 ♔d4, ♗a8; 8 ♖c1†, ♔b3; 9 ♘f2, ♔b2; 10 ♖c3, h2; 11 ♖h3†+.

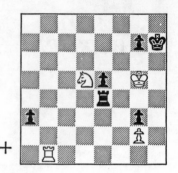

DIAGRAM 238

G. KOLTANOWSKI

SAN FRANCISCO CHRONICLE

1926

Dedicated to Grandmaster P. Keres

+

An unbroken chain of compulsion spells finis.

　　1 N—K7　P—N3

The threat was 2 R—R1 mate.

2 R—N7	P—R7	6 R—N7 ch	K—B1
3 N×P dis. ch	K—N1	7 N—K6 ch	K—K1
4 K—B6	R—B5 ch	8 R—K7　mate	
5 N×R	P—R8 (Q)		

Alg.: 1 ♘e7, g6; 2 ♖b7, a2; 3 ♘:g6†, ♔g8; 4 ♔f6, ♖f4†; 5 ♘:f4, a1(♕); 6 ♖g7†, ♔f8; 7 ♘e6†, ♔e8; 8 ♖e7‡.

348

DIAGRAM 239

W. KORN

*THE EVENING NEWS OF
LONDON*

MARCH 11, 1940

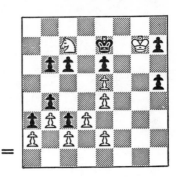

=

Several distinct phases stand out strategically and multi-thematically.

1 N—N5! P×N

As a start, White creates a pawn barrier but also confronts Black with the problem of either taking the knight, or not taking it but marching on with 1 ... P—R5!?; 2 N—Q4, P—R6; 3 N—B3? P—B4!; 4 K×P (what else?), P—N4; 5 K—any, P—B5 with a breakthrough.

But White does better: 3 N—B5 ch!! K—Q2 (3 ... P×N; 4 P×P, P—R7; 5 P—B6 ch with at least a draw); 4 K—B7, P—R7; 5 N—N3, P—B4; 6 P—Q4, P—B5; 7 P—Q5, again with a draw in hand.

If 1 ... P—B4; 2 N—Q6! P—R5; 3 N—B5 ch and White wins easily.

The next phase is the extended triangulation as seen in earlier diagrams 103 and 104:

2 K—R6! P—R5   4 K—B4 P—R7
3 K—N5 P—R6

Black's pawn is beyond reach and White switches to another strategic saving clause—to shut himself into a stalemate situation.

5 K—K3 P—R8(Q)   7 P—K3
6 K—Q4 Q—KB8

SUB-DIAGRAM 239 (A)

Black to move

If 7 ... Q—B3; 8 P×Q ch, K×P; 9 P—K5 ch, K—B4; 10 P—K4 ch, K—B5 with a similar stalemate as now on the board.

White appears to be impenetrably walled in and immobilized, notwithstanding Black's material plus of queen and passed pawn. But Black can command a move that shatters the deception and allows one more try

    7 ... Q—B4?!   8 P×Q P×P

The third phase requires deft temporizing, mindful of the lesson learned from diagram 105, but neither side able to force a decision.

Before anything else, White must break the hammerlock he is in and open a trail to Black's passed pawn. The by-play is forced yet subtle.

    9 P—K4 P—B5!   10 P—K6! P—R4!

Now the role of the forlorn-looking rook's pawn is also revealed. It originally prevented the "minor dual" (1 N—N5, P×N) 2 K—N6 as an unclean alternative to 2 K—R6. In addition, it comes to life at this moment as a second line of attack that White has to defend against.

If 10 ... K×P; 11 P—K5! K—B4 (11 ... P—B6; 12 K—K3, =; or 11 ... P—R4; 12 K—K4, +); 12 K—Q5=.

If 9 ... K—K3; 10 P×P, K×P; 11 K—Q5 wins.

11 P—K5!	P—R5!	15 K—B2!	K—K3!
12 K—K4	P—R6!	16 K—B3!	K—Q4
13 K—B3!	K×P	17 K—B2!	
14 P—Q4	K—Q4		

Draw! The corresponding tempo plays cancel each other out. The QP is taboo as its capture allows the KP to queen quickly.

An ingredient that deserves attention in this or any fanciful set-up is its "legality", or legal position, if it can indeed arise from the initial position on the board at the start of a game, by a regular sequence, however tortuous and obstructed the route.

Diagram 239 indicates that six black pawn captures and three white pawn captures must have occurred to reach the given pawn structure. With seven white and seven black pieces each off the board, the position—and the study—appear to be "legal".

The reconstruction of possible courses of play to arrive at a given diagram, has in many cases been a painstaking subject of competition and is similar to "retro-", or "retrograde" analysis.

The alternate seesaw and pawn formation at move 15, strongly reminds one of "communicating vessels".

For ultimate resolution, play may continue 17... K×P; 18 P—K6, P—R7; 19 K—N2, K—K6; 20 P—K7, P—B6 ch;21 K×P, K—Q7; 22 P—K8(Q), K×P, and now either

(A) 23 Q×P, K—N7; 24 Q×P/4, P—B7; 25 Q—Q2, K—N8; 26 Q—Q3=.
(B) 23 Q—K1, K—N7; 23 K—N3! P—B7; 25 Q—Q2, K—N8; 26 Q—Q3, K—N7; 27 Q—Q2, K—N8; 28 K×P, P—B8(Q); 29 Q×Q ch, K×Q; 30 K—K3, K—N7; 31 K—Q3, K×P; 32 K—B2! =.

A fitting conclusion, stripped right down to essentials.

Alg.: 1 ♘b5, c:b5; 2 ♔h6, h4; 3 ♔g5, h3; 4 ♔f4, h2; 5 ♔e3, h1(♕); 6 ♔d4, ♕f1; 7 e3, ♕f5; 8 e:f5, e:f5; 9 e4, f4; 10 e6, h5; 11 e5, h4; 12 ♔e4, h3; 13 ♔f3, ♔:e6; 14 d4, ♔d5; 15 ♔f2, ♔e6=.

O. WEINBERGER

DIAGRAM 240

MAGYAR SAKKÉLET

1963

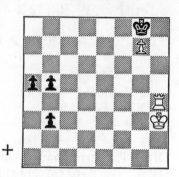

3rd Prize (awarded 1964)

+

Glancing back at the same composer's diagram 174, one notices a similar feature in the combined race of both kings towards the black pawns' squares of promotion. In 1960, Weinberger might have rushed to establish his "copyright" to diagram 174 while a broader picture may have been germinating which found fruition in 1963.

White loses the king's race after either

(A) 1 K—N4? P—N7; 2 R—R1, P—R5; 3 K—B5, K×P; or
(B) 1 R—R5? P—N5; 2 R×P, P—N7+.

1 R—R8 ch!! K×P	2 R—R5 P—N5

If 2 ... P—R5; 3 R×P, K—B3; 4 R—QN4, K—K4; 5 R×RP, K—Q4; 6 R—N4+.

The deep finesse of White's first move lies in the removal first of White's own pawn which was protecting Black from the crucial check at move 4.

3 R×P P—N7	5 R—N1 K—K4
4 R—N5 ch! K—B3	6 R—Q1!

6 R—QN1, K—Q5; 7 R×P, K—B6=.

6 ... K—K5	8 K—B1 P—N6
7 K—N2! K—K6	9 K—K1! wins

9 ... K—K5; 10 K—K2! K—K4; 11 R—QN1, K—Q5; 12 K—Q2+.

Alg.: 1 ♖h8†, ♔:g7; 2 ♖h5, b4; 3 ♖:a5, b2; 4 ♖g5†, ♔f6; 5 ♖g1, ♔e5; 6 ♖d1! ♔e4; 7 ♔g2, ♔e3; 8 ♔f1, b3; 9 ♔e1+.

Composition in Practical Play

A composer's intuition need not be compressed into mere abstractions divorced from the fighting scene. Many composers master practical play to a high degree. Their compositions may often be sublimations from positions arrived at during active competition.

In reverse, trained artistic insight may help a practicing expert detect and use the only winning strategy in a seemingly drawn ending, or finally rescue a game from an apparent loss. There was a foretaste of this ingredient in Loyd's diagram 22. The triad presented in diagrams 243–5 more explicitly shows the connection between artistic talent and virtuosity in action.

Isaac Kashdan—the co-composer of our diagrams 100 and 103—is the factual orchestrator of two gems, diagrams 243–4, born directly of grandmaster practice. With uncanny precision he selects the single, and singular, route to triumph. In diagram 245 Kashdan is at the receiving end of a similar but very hard struggle with Anthony Santasiere—another connoisseur of both art and combat in chess.

Thus, prime acquaintance with composition may be of great pragmatical value for achieving victory over the board.

DIAGRAM 241

P. MORPHY—
J. THOMPSON

NEW YORK, 1859

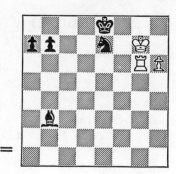

Off hand game (at odds)   =

Morphy had little occasion to prove his excellence in the endgame —his opponents rarely got so far.

1 R—K6!!?

The only move to save an otherwise lost game.

If 1 P—R7, N×R; 2 K×N, B—B7 ch wins. White's text move prevents 1 ... N—B4 ch and 2 ... N×P winning. The rook pins the knight—at the rook's own peril?

1 ... B×R?!

Black swallows the forced bait instead of salvaging the draw by 1 ... B—B7; 2 K—B6, K—B1; 3 R×N, K—N1; 4 R×P, P—R4; 5 R—QB7, B—Q6; 6 P—R7 ch, K—R1, etc.
Now White seems to win.

2 P—R7!?

If 2 ... N—B4 ch; 3 K—B6 or 2 ... N—N3; 3 K×N, B—B2 ch; 4 K—B6+, but White is unable to win after 2 ... N—B3, 3 P—R8(Q) ch, K—B2 (Frink). A case of queen-fright.

Alg.: 1 ♖e6, ♗:e6; 2 h7+.

DIAGRAM 242

H. N. PILLSBURY— I. GUNSBERG

HASTINGS TOURNAMENT

1895

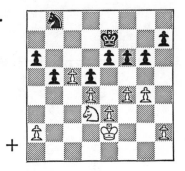

+

One of the most beautiful endgame studies forged in the heat of over-the-board battle.

Black had just played 26 ... N/2—N1, to stabilize his position with 27 ... N—B3 and activate his queen-side pawns. Precisely at this moment, the dynamics of chess come into play at their best.

27 P—B5!!

Literally, a smashing conception. The direct threat is 28 P×KP, K×P; 29 N—B4 ch, winning the QP and game, 27 ... NP×P; 28 P×P, P×P; 29 N—B4 leads to the same conclusion, and 27 ... KP×P; 28 P×P, P—N4; 29 N—N4 leads to the same sequence as in the actual game.

| 27 ... | P—N4 | 29 P—B6!! K—Q3 |
| 28 N—N4! | P—QR4 | |

If 29 ... P×N; 30 P—B7!

30 P×P N×P

Again, if 30 ... P×N; 31 P—K7, K×KP; 32 P—B7 and queens.

31 N×N	K×N	34 K—K3 P—N5
32 P—K4!!	P×P	35 K×P P—R5
33 P—Q5 ch!	K—Q3	36 K—Q4 P—R4

Black has a pawn majority on each wing, but none offsets White's center pawns. All variations are precision-tooled by White, e.g.

(A) 36 ... P—B4; 37 P×P, P—N6 (if 37 ... K—K2; 38 K—B5, P—N6; 39 P—Q6 ch, K—Q1; 40 P—B6, P×P; 41 P—B7+, and if 37 ... P—N5; 38 P—B6, P—R4; 39 P—B7, K—K2; 40 P—Q6 ch, K—B1; 41 P—Q7+); 38 P×P, P×P (or 38 ... P—R6; 39 K—B3, K—K2; 40 P—N4, P—N5; 41 P—N5+); 39 K—B3, K—K2; 40 K×P, P—N5; 41 K—B4, P—R4; 42 K—B5, P—R5; 43 P—Q6 ch, K—Q1; 44 P—B6 and wins.

(B) 36 ... K—K2; 37 K—B4, P—N6; 38 P×P, P×P (38 ... P—R6; 39 K—B3, P—B4; 40 P×P, P—R4; 41 P—N4, P—R7; 42 K—N2, P—R8(Q) ch; 43 K×Q, P—N5; 44 P—N5, P—R5; 45 P—N6, P—N6; 46 P×P, P×P; 47 P—Q6 ch, K×P; 48 P—N7, etc., queening with check); 39 K×P, P—B4; 40 P×P, P—N5; 41 K—B4, P—R4; 42 K—B5, P—R5; 43 P—Q6 ch, K—Q1; 44 P—B6, wins.

37 P×P	P—R6	39 P—R6	P—B5
38 K—B4	P—B4	40 P—R7	resigns

Alg.: 27 f5, g5; 28 ♘b4, a5; 29 c6, ♚d6; 30 f:e6, ♘:c6; 31 ♘:c6, ♚:c6; 32 e4, d:e4; 33 d5†, ♚d6; 34 ♔e3, b4; 35 ♔:e4, a4; 36 ♚d4, h5; 37 g:h5, a3; 38 ♔c4, f5; 39 h6, f4; 40 h7+.

DIAGRAM 243

I. KASHDAN (USA)— S. FLOHR (CSR)

HAMBURG OLYMPICS

1930

+

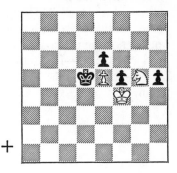

One must have done one's homework well in advance to be able to take a purposeful direction in the midst of a fierce Olympic contest. The diagrammed set-up was reached after the 64th move. White proceeded:

65 N—B3!	K—B5	66 K—N5

Delusive is a "quick" win by 66 N—R4, K—Q4; 67 N×P? P×N; 68 K×P, P—R5; 69 P—K6, K—Q3 (69 ... P—R6?; 70 P—K7, P—R7; 71 P—K8(Q), P—R8(Q); 72 Q—R8 ch+); 70 K—B6 and both players queen, with a resulting draw.

66 ...	K—Q4	68 N—R4
67 K—B6	P—B5	

"The text initiates an accurately calculated maneuver that ends a remarkable theoretical win" (Földeák: *Schacholympiaden*).

68 ...	K—K5	73 P—K7	P—R7
69 K×P	P—B6	74 P—K8(Q)	K—N7
70 N×P	K×N	75 K—N4	P—R8(Q)
71 K—B5!	P—R5	76 Q—K2 ch	K—N8
72 P—K6	P—R6	77 K—N3!	

and mate follows.

In 1930, when this game was played, Salo Flohr was of world championship caliber, aspiring to challenge Alekhin.

However, this novelette proves a point about the limitations of a "studylike ending" as compared to a true composition.

Leaving aside the criterion of novelty and substance, the game ending of diagram 243 would be disqualified as an artistic endgame study of even an elementary type, because of the other option not mentioned by Földeák:

68 N—N5, P—R5; 69 N×P, P—B6; 70 N—B4 ch, K—K5; 71 N—R3, K—K6; 72 N—N5, simply queening the king's pawn.

Alg.: 65 ♘f3, ♚c4; 66 ♔g5, ♚d5; 67 ♔f6, f4; 68 ♘h4, ♚e4; 69 ♔:e6, f3; 70 ♘:f3, ♚:f3; 71 ♔f5! h4; 72 e6, h3; 73 e7, h2; 74 e8(♕), ♚g2; 75 ♔g4, h1(♕); 76 ♕e2†, ♚g1; 77 ♔g3+.

DIAGRAM 244

A. PINKUS—
I. KASHDAN

MANHATTAN CHESS CLUB
CHAMPIONSHIP

NEW YORK, 1929

Black to move, won
In the diagram, the colors are reversed*

+

The game was adjourned in the given position. The spectators considered it drawn. Kashdan discovered a narrow path leading to a forced win. Truly a study, with Kashdan playing White.

63 K—N6 K—B5	65 K—Q8!
64 K—B7 P—N5	

This must be played before B—Q6. If at once 65 B—Q6, P—R6; 66 P—Q5, K—Q5! 67 K—Q8, P—R7 and White's bishop cannot win the queen as it will in the main play that follows.

65 ... B—B2	66 B—Q6! P—N6!

If 66 ... P—R6; 67 P—Q5! K—Q5!; 68 P—Q8(Q), B×Q; 69 K×B, P—R7; 70 B—B8+.

67 B—R3 K×P

If 67 ... K—B6; 68 P—Q5, P—N7; 69 B×P ch, K×B; 70 P—Q6, P—R6; 71 P—Q7, P—R7; 72 P—K8(Q)+.

68 P—K8(Q) B×Q	70 P—R5 P×P
69 K×B K—B6	

If 70 ... P—N7; 71 B×P ch, K×B; 72 P—R6!+

* The composers' "Codex" prescribes that study presentations must always start with White to move, and the diagram simulates that precept.

71	P—N6	P—N7	77 Q—Q4 ch	K—N6
72	B×P ch	K×B	78 K—Q7	P—R5
73	P—N7	P—R6	79 K—B6	P—R6
74	P—N8(Q)	P—R7	80 K—N5	P—R7
75	Q—N2 ch	K—N6	81 Q—R1! wins	
76	Q—Q5 ch	K—N7		

After 81 ... P—R8(Q); 82 Q×Q, K—N7; 83 Q—N2 ch, K—N8;
84 K—N4, P—R8(Q); 85 K—N3 the chess map is identical with
the finale in the preceding diagram 243!

Alg.: 63 ♔b6, ♚c4; 64 ♚c7, b4; 65 ♚d8, ♗f7; 66 ♗d6, b3; 67 ♗a3,
♚:d4; 68 e8(♕), ♗:e8; 69 ♚:e8, ♚c3; 70 h5, g:h5; 71 g6, b2;
72 ♗:b2†, ♚:b2; 73 g7, a3; 74 g8(♕), a2; 75 ♕g2†, ♚b3; 76
♕d5†, ♚b2; 77 ♕d4†, ♚b3; 78 ♚d7, h4; 79 ♚f6, h3; 80 ♚b5,
h2; 81 ♕a1, h1(♕); 82 ♕:h1, ♚b2; 83 ♕g2†, ♚b1; 84 ♚b4,
a1(♕); 85 ♚b3+.

DIAGRAM 245

A. SANTASIERE-
I. KASHDAN

U.S. OPEN CHAMPIONSHIP

BOSTON, 1938

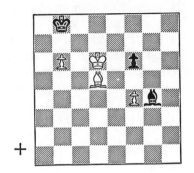

+

Black seems to be as favorably placed for defense as can be, his king blocking the passed pawn; if the QNP were further back, it would take Black a long time to capture it and White might win easily. In the diagram, a win looks unattainable, but the course of the game—and supporting analysis—shows how to bring it about.*

1 K—K7 P—B4	3 K—K5
2 K—B6 B—R6	

If 3 K—N5, K—B1; 4 B—K6 ch, K—N2!; 5 B×P, B—N7; 6 B—Q3, B—R6; 7 B—K2, K×P; 8 B—N4, B—B8; 9 P—B5, K—B4; 10 P—B6, B—B5; 11 K—N6, K—Q3; 12 K—N7, K—K4; 13 B—R5, K—B5, and Black draws by maintaining what is known as the "vertical opposition".

3 ... K—B1?

A questionable move, not because Black could save the game otherwise, but because he could have tried the more tenacious 3 ... B—N5; and if White answers 4 B—K6? K—N2; 5 B×P, B—K7; 6 B—K6, K×P; 7 P—B5, K—B4; 8 P—B6, B—R4! draws. White still has 4 B—N2, K—B1; 5 K—B6, K—N1;

---

* With a few minor corrections added by the author, the position is quoted from M. Euwe and D. Hooper, *A Guide to Chess Endings* (1959).

6 K—N5, K—B1; 7 B—K4! capturing the bishop's pawn with the gain of an important tempo. Black's 7 ... P×B obviously loses as proven by an easy count. Therefore, 7 ... K—N1; 8 B×P, B—B6!; 9 B—R7, K—N2; 10 P—B5, K×P; 11 P—B6, B—Q4; 12 K—N6, K—B4; 13 K—N7, K—Q3; 14 B—N8 wins as Black cannot catch up.

4 B—K6 ch K—N2	6 B—K6 K×P!
5 B×P B—B8	

In the actual game, Kashdan chose 6 ... B—Q6?; 7 K—Q4, resigns.

7 P—B5 K—B2	9 B—B7 B—Q6
8 P—B6 K—Q1	

Or 9 ... K—Q2; 10 K—B5, K—Q3; 11 K—N6, B—N4; 12 K—N7, K—K4; 13 B—N8 and Black falls short of one move.

10 K—B4 K—Q2	13 K—N7 B—N4
11 K—N5 K—Q3	14 B—N3 B—K1
12 K—R6 K—K4	15 B—B2 wins

What makes the win so exceptional, and difficult to discern, in an innocuously drawish position, is the unfavorable location of Black's bishop. If in this diagram the bishop were posted elsewhere, e.g. on square Q6(d3), Black could secure a draw after precarious but accurate maneuvering**.

** As shown by J. Awerbach, op. cit., example No. 263 (1972).

Alg.: 1 ♔e7, f5; 2 ♔f6, ♗h3; 3 ♔e5, ♚c8; 4 ♗e6†, ♚b7; 5 ♗:f5, ♗f1; 6 ♗e6, ♚:b6; 7 f5, ♚c7; 8 f6, ♚d8; 9 ♗f7, ♗d3; 10 ♔f4, ♚d7; 11 ♔g5, ♚d6; 12 ♔h6, ♚e5; 13 ♔g7, ♗b5; 14 ♗b3, ♗e8; 15 ♗c2+.

DIAGRAM 245 (A)

R. FINE

From: R. Fine,

BASIC CHESS ENDINGS

1941

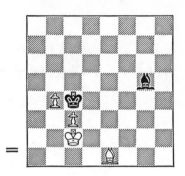

=

Another exceptional example of White unable to win with two passed pawns and bishops of equal color. A classical case of a blockade. Black's king securely blocks the BP, maintaining control over the other pawn.

White's attempts at breaking or circumventing the blockade prove futile.

1 K—N2

1 K—Q1, K—Q6!; 2 P—N5, B—Q1!; 3 any, K—B5 =.

1 ...	B—B5	3 K—R4 B—Q1!
2 K—R3	B—N4	

Denying White the vital square QR5 (a5).

4 B—B2	K×P	7 K—B6 K—B5
5 K—N5	K—N6	8 P—N5 B—R4
6 B—B5	K—B6	9 B—N6 B—K8

White gets nowhere. If 4 P—N5, B—N3 =.

Alg.: 1 ♔b2, ♗f4; 2 ♔a3, ♗g5; 3 ♔a4, ♗d8; 4 ♗f2, ♔:c3; 5 ♔b5, ♔b3; 6 ♗c5, ♔c3; 7 ♔c6, ♔c4; 8 b5, ♗a5; 9 ♗b6, ♗e1=.

DIAGRAM 246

J. R. CAPABLANCA— MONA N. KARFF

MARSHALL CHESS CLUB

NEW YORK, 1941

(Position in diagram with colors reversed)

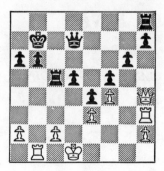

White (Capablanca) conducted his game in a colorless and diffident manner. Capturing a pawn the wrong way on his 24th move, he allowed Black (Miss Karff) to bring off a surprise finish in two moves.

The mechanism of the win has typical—and beautiful—overtones of a composition, containing themes of overloading and deflection.

1 Q—B6!

Threatening to mate or win a rook, Black's next move expects to safeguard the situation, the pawn plus and the win.

1 ... Q—Q1!   2 R × RP ch!!

Tableau: Not even Capablanca lost to a U.S. Women's Champion merely out of chivalry.

Alg.: 1 ♛f6, ♛d8; 2 ♜:h7†+.

DIAGRAM 247

W. KORN—
A. PHILPOTT

WEST LONDON C.C.—
FINCHLEY C.C.

FEBRUARY 1940

"Clock" Tournament, London

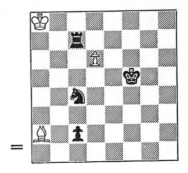

=

After some trial and error of actual play, the diagrammed position arose on board one, with Black's pawn ready to queen without hindrance. White's game looked lost despite a previous, desperate, journey by White's king in support of another one of his pawns.

1 P × R N—N3 ch

In the logical—but as it turns out, mistaken—belief that Black has a clear win.

With hindsight, Black might try the other choice of 1 ... N—Q3! Amazingly, this fails, because of 2 B—N1!! P × B(Q or R); 3 P—B8(Q) ch, N × Q; stalemate. Or 2 ... P × B(B); K—N8 =.

2 K—N7 P—B8(Q)   3 K × N Q—N7 ch

A position of king and bishop's pawn on the 7th versus queen is a well-known draw, as the king, retreating into the corner, is stalemated if the queen captures the pawn. But White has a bishop to spare which upsets the stalemate. Hence, White keeps offering the bishop as a lure—or protection!

If 3 ... Q—K6 ch; 4 K—N7, Q—K2; 5 B—Q5, K—K4; 6 K—N8, Q—Q3; 7 K—N7=.

4 B—N3! Q—Q5 ch   5 K—B6 Q—QB6 ch

If 5 ... Q—B3 ch; 6 B—K6 ch, draw.

  6 B—B4 Q—B3 ch   7 B—K6 ch draw

The ending was originally reproduced in the *British Chess Magazine*, August 1940.

Alg.: 1 d:c7, ♘b6†; 2 ♔b7, c1(♕); 3 ♔:b6, ♕b2†; 4 ♗b3, ♕d4†; 5 ♔c6, ♕c3†; 6 ♗c4, ♕f6†; 7 ♗e6†=.

DIAGRAM 248

S. LOYD—
C. F. GOLMAYO

PARIS CHESS CONGRESS

1867

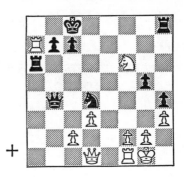

Not quite an endgame study, but a conclusion belonging to the province of "brilliancies". However, the exceptional personality of the winner, the interplay of two exquisite strategic themes and mating patterns, and the intuition displayed in seeing through and beyond the technical knock-out 1 R×R, P×R; 2 N—K4 with a strategically won game, indelibly impress an artistic imprint on the reader's mind.

    1 R—R8 ch!!

Clairvoyant give-away of a whole rook.

1 ...	R×R	4 N—N6 dis. ch K—N1
2 Q—N4 ch K—N1		5 Q—B8 ch!?
3 N—Q7 ch K—B1		

Did White wrongly see a black pawn still standing on Black's QR2, with the continuation 5 ... R×Q; 6 N—Q7 ch and smothered mate—Philidor's Legacy?

5 ...	R×Q	7 R—R1 ch Q—R4
6 N—Q7 ch K—R2		8 R×Q mate

That's what Loyd saw. Wondrous.

Alg.: 1 ♖a8†, ♖:a8; 2 ♕g4†, ♔b8; 3 ♘d7†, ♔c8; 4 ♘b6†, ♔b8; 5 ♕c8†, ♖:c8; 6 ♘d7†, ♔a7; 7 ♖a1†, ♕a5; 8 ♖:a5#.

DIAGRAM 249

S. RESHEVSKY—
B. IVKOV

INTERNTL. TOURNAMENT
PALMA DE MALLORCA

1970

+

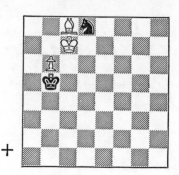

A compact miniature of telescopic proportion.

Every ordinary mortal would agree to a draw. The pawn cannot advance without being captured, securing the draw for Black. The knight on the other hand must not be taken, as the pawn would fall. Black's king can shuttle to and from the squares B4, N4, R4, and even the square R3 is available if the bishop moves away.

    1 B—R3!! K—B4   2 B—Q7!!

Black is helpless against either loss of knight or the pawn marching. If 1 ... K—R3; 2 B—B1 ch, K—R4; 3 B—B4!, cutting off both the knight's checking square, and the black king's square N4. If 1 ... K—R4; 2 B—N4, K—N4; 3 B—K2 ch, K—B4; 4 B—B4!! N—B3; 5 P—N7, Black must again relinquish all guards.

  A tightly knit ending with three variations, conceived by a venerable grandmaster.

Alg.: 1 ♗h3, ♔c5; 2 ♗d7+.

DIAGRAM 249 (A)

AUTHOR UNKNOWN

THE CHESS PLAYER'S CHRONICLE

1856

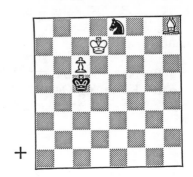

+

Composition-wise, this early model preceded the actual occurrence in master practice as depicted in diagram 249.

Including grandmasters, the reader of much chess literature may often absorb such forerunners into his chess synapses. Often the master's inherent insight may intuitively discover across the board a solution laboriously contrived by a composer. Whichever way this comes and goes, the above profile is the quite incidental prototype for Reshevsky's conduct, and with the position shifted by one file to the right, it covers an even richer range of probabilities.

With Black to move, e.g. 1 ... K—N4; or 1 ... K—Q4; White's 2 B—Q4 achieves an airtight blockade and victory. Thus, the win revolves around a tempo play to be invoked by White. Useless is 1 B—Q4 ch, K—Q4; or 1 B—K5, K—N3; 2 B—Q4 ch, K—N4, with White becoming the victim of a (reciprocal) squeeze.

1 B—B3! K—N3!   2 B—R5 ch!

Clearly, 2 ... K×B; 3 K×N wins for White, but the text is designed to transfer the bishop to Q8 for reasons seen later.

1 ... K—N4; or 1 ... K—Q4 would have been answered with 2 B—Q4, winning.

2 ...   K—N4   4 B—R4 K—N4
3 B—Q8 K—B4

369

Not 4 ... K—Q4; 5 B—K7, or 4 ... K—N3; 5 B—B2 ch, K—N4; 6 B—Q4, again with *Zugzwang*.

But White's next move creates a deadly stranglehold just the same:

5 B—N5!	K—B4	7 B—Q4!	N—Q3
6 B—K3 ch	K—Q4	8 P—B7	wins

Alg.: 1 ♗c3, ♔b6; 2 ♗a5†, ♔b5; 3 ♗d8, ♔c5; 4 ♗h4, ♔b5; 5 ♗g5, ♔c5; 6 ♗e3†, ♔d5; 7 ♗d4, ♘d6; 8 c7+.

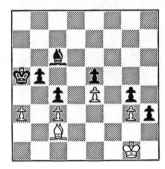

DIAGRAM 250

A. B. BISGUIER—
R. J. FISCHER

U.S. CHAMPIONSHIP

1966–67

11th Round   Black won

Sometimes the biology of an endgame study might be equated to a masterfully executed game ending. This is the original version won by the defender.

The diagram shows a seemingly blocked position where Black's king cannot penetrate anywhere so as to utilize his pawn plus. The sacrificial key move proves truly dynamic.

　　1 ... B×P!!

To be two pawns up, but minus a bishop!

　　2 B×B K—R5　　　　　　　3 B—B5

White tries to activate his own knight's pawn.

　　3 ... K—N6!!

If 3 ... K×P; 4 B×P, P—N5; 5 P×P, P—B6; 6 B—Q1+.

　　4 B×P P—K5　　　　　　　5 B×P

Releasing the king from watching Black's RP. But it is too late.

　　5 ... K×BP　　　　　　　6 P—N4 K—Q7!!

A last finesse gaining all-important time for the right pawn to queen.

If 6 ... P—K6; 7 B—B1!—preventing Black's BP from queening with a tempo-saving check in subvariation (A) 7... K—Q7; 8 P—N5 and now (A) 8 ... P—B6; 9 P—N6, P—B7; 10 P—N7, P—B8(Q); 11 P—N8 (Q), P—K7; 12 Q—R2 ch=. Or (B) 8 ... P—K7; 9 B×P, K×B; 10 P—N6, P—B6; 11 P—N7, P—B7; 12 P—N8(Q), P—B8(Q) ch; 13 K—N2, Q×P; 14 Q—K8 ch and 15 Q×P=.

7 B—N2 P—K6	8 B—B3 P—B6

and Black won.

Alg.: 1 ..., ♗:e4; 2 ♗:e4, ♔a4; 3 ♗f5, ♔b3; 4 ♗:g4, e4; 5 ♗:h3, ♔:c3; 6 g4, ♔d2; 7 ♗g2, e3; 8 ♗f3, c3+.

Prognostic Epilogue

This volume has attempted to recall the historical eminence that American chess art at one time enjoyed in the chess world at large, and to summarize past and present achievements.

In this century, domestic promotion of this particular branch remained deplorably low. A scrutiny of the first appearance of the diagrams composed during this period discloses that they were mostly published abroad.

In the first half of the 1900s, this aesthetic domain of chess was pre-empted partly by the western Europeans (Chéron, Halberstadt, Lazard, Lommer, Mattison, Réti, Rinck, the powerful Czech school of composers, *et al.*) and partly by the Russian triumvirate of Kubbel, the brothers Platov, and Troitsky. After World War II, the Soviet Union secured dominance by lavish subvention of its chess talent which took to chess as a welcome outlet for pent-up ambition. The U.S.S.R. recognized that a total perspective of chess activity and attention to all facets was essential for qualitative success and that, equally so, chess provided an impressive tool for advancing a cultural image of intellectual and professional prowess. Yet, throughout this momentary phase of dominance, a continued undercurrent of creativity maintained its healthy hold also in the Anglo-American sphere, with a hopeful promise to break new ground.

In our lands, superficial opinion polls might "prove" that only a small percentage of students of chess are interested in composition, but that otherwise combinations, "quickies", brilliant traps and wins in the openings are the vogue. It might be the media themselves who, deceiving themselves, deprive the American chess public of a magnificent sector of involvement.

Chess composition does not strive for mass popularity; rather, it produces individualistic addicts to the sheer beauty of depth, to strict discipline of thought, to consequential concentration and other fascinations that transcend merely combinative

373

factors. In a competitive world that threatens to engulf useful recreation, along with everything else, chess composition stands for leisure at its relaxed and singular best. The enjoyment of chess art, for composer, solver and reader alike, maintains stability unencumbered by limitations of age, or the physical pressures and timetables of tournament play. There are two sides to the universe of chess and both should be expanding and knowledgeably assisted also in the Western hemisphere.

Concluding on an optimistic note, the author sincerely looks forward to a future edition which will also absorb the achievements of the recultivation and expansion of American chess art.

Bibliography

J. Awerbach (Editor), *et al.*, *Lehrbuch der Endspiele* (Vols. I–IV), Berlin 1958

J. Awerbach, *Lehrbuch der Schachendspiele* (Vols. I–II), Berlin 1972

J. Berger, *Theorie und Praxis der Endspiele*, Berlin-Leipzig 1922

P. R. v. Bilguer, *Lehrbuch des Schachspiels* (8th edition), Berlin-Leipzig 1922

F. S. Bondarenko, *Galeria Shakhmatnykh Etyudistov*, Moscow 1968

R. Brieger, *Imagination in the Endgame*, Dallas 1973

O. A. Brownson Jr., *Chess Problems*, Dubuque 1876

I. Chernev, *The Fireside Book of Chess*, New York 1949

A. Chéron, *Les Échecs Artistiques*, Lausanne 1950, and *Lehr- und Handbuch der Endspiele* (Vols. I–IV), Berlin 1960–70

E. B. Cook, W. R. Henry and C. A. Gilberg (and J. C. Romeyn) *American Chess-nuts*, New York–Kingston 1868

F. Dedrle, *Studie*, Prague 1925

M. Euwe and D. Hooper, *A Guide to Chess Endings*, London 1959

P. Farago, *Idei Noi in Sahul Artistic*, Rumania 1956

R. Fine, *Basic Chess Endings*, Philadelphia 1941

J. Halpern, *Chess Symposium* (Vols. I–II) 1904–5

D. Hooper, *A Pocket Guide to Chess Endgames*, London 1970

B. Horwitz and J. Kling, *Chess Studies and End-Games*, London 1884

G. Kasparian, *2500 Finales*, Buenos Aires 1963

—*Shakhmatnye Etyudy* (*Dominatsia*), Erevan 1972

H. Keidanz, *The Chess Compositions of E. B. Cook of Hoboken*, New York 1927

P. Keres, *Praktische Endspiele*, Hamburg 1973

J. Kling and B. Horwitz, *Chess Studies*, London 1851

W. Korn, "All's Well that Ends Well", *Chess Life* 1951–60

—"The Finishing Touch", *Chess Review*, 1960–69

M. Lamarre, *Fins de Partie*, Paris 1924

H. M. Lommer, *1357 End-game Studies*, London 1975

L. PORTISCH AND B. SÁRKÖZY, 600 *Végjáték*, Budapest 1973

V. RANGELOV AND A. TANIELIAN, *Izbrani Zadachi i Etyudi*, Sofia 1970

A. J. ROYCROFT, *Test Tube Chess*, London 1972

A. RUEB, *De Schaakstudie* and *Bronnen van de Schaakstudie* (dbl. Vols. I–IV), Gouda 1948–55

H. STAUDTE, *Aus der Welt der Schachstudie*, Nauheim 1961

H. STAUDTE AND M. MILESCU, *Das 1 × 1 des Endspiels*, Berlin 1965

M. A. SUTHERLAND AND H. M. LOMMER, *1234 Modern End-Game Studies*, Dover Publications 1968

C. E. C. TATTERSALL, *A Thousand Endgames* (Vols. I–II), London 1910–11

P. WENMAN, *175 Chess Brilliancies*, London 1947

A. C. WHITE, *Sam Loyd and his Chess Problems*, Dover Publications 1962

B. F. WINKELMAN, *Modern Chess Endings*, Philadelphia 1933

O. WURZBURG, A. C. WHITE AND G. HUME, *The Golden Argosy*, Stroud 1929

Chess Columns, Journals and Periodicals and other separate sources as quoted in the text.

Register of Terms

Unless otherwise noted, numbers refer to diagrams.

Index of Composers and Diagrams

The numbers refer to diagrams

An (§) after the name denotes a non-American author

Almgren, 120, 121, 122, 123, 125, 173
Aloni §, 230
Andrew, 213

Barbier §, 15
Barrett, 41
Benko, 164, 165, 165A, 236, 236A
Berger §, 107A*
Berry (Canadian), 232
Bowly, 51
Branton, 54, ,162, 169, 170, 171, 172, 176, 177, 178, 179, 206, 227
        228
Brieger, 18, 133, 141, 154, 155, 159, 161, 189, 190, 234, 235
Bron §, 160
Buchwald, 167, 167A, 195, 196
Burger, 113

Chéron §, 26, 97, 207*
(*The*) *Chess Player's Chronicle*, 248A
Cook, 1, 2, 3, 4, 6, 7, 9, 10, 11, 12, 27, 29, 30, 61, 63, 66, 68,
        69, 83, 120A, 132, 137, 138, 192

Diesen, 49, 49A, 49B, 94
Dolan, 92

Efron, 199, 202, 209, 210, 211, 212
Evertz §, 82

Games and names of players (capital letters indicate the winner)

An * after the diagram indicates a mention within the text of the respective diagram.